A
LITTLE PIECE
OF

ENGLAND

A
LITTLE PIECE
OF
ENGLAND

Andrew Gurr

JB
JOHN BLAKE

Published by John Blake Publishing Limited,
3 Bramber Court, 2 Bramber Road, London W14 9PB

First published in hardback 2001

ISBN 1 903402 379

British Library Cataloguing-in-Publication Data: A catalogue record for this
book is available from the British Library.

Printed in Great Britain by Creative Print and Design (Wales),
Ebbw Vale, Gwent

1 3 5 7 9 10 8 6 4 2

Papers used by John Blake Publishing Limited are natural, recyclable
products made from wood grown in sustainable forests. The manufacturing
processes conform to the environmental regulations of the country of origin.

TABLE OF CONTENTS

To
Jean
The Love of my Life

Introduction

The war gave the Falklands significance. The distant colony had become a largely forgotten and practically unwanted backwater before General Galtieri decided to take the risk of invasion. Before that intrusion successive British governments had flirted with the idea of Argentina somehow taking them over. If that had happened, the rest of the world would surely have turned away from any Islander protests. But the ambition of an unelected Argentine general changed the course of history.

The vast majority of the British nation applauded the victory. Heroes had been made, the aggressor put back in his box, and the name of the Falklands branded into the memories of all that were born before 1975. A significance far outweighing reality was born. Two thousand people suddenly had rights and effective political power that had been denied their predecessors for one hundred and fifty years. Lord Shackleton revived his report – which was now accepted as wise and practical, whereas it had been shelved only five years before. Cash began to pour into the Islands. New ideas, or more likely old ideas that now had a listening audience, emerged. Farming and land ownership required a fundamental restructuring, a policed fishing zone was at last taken seriously, the infrastructure needed bringing up to date. Even a Chief Executive was required.

All that was back in the early Eighties. In 1994, it changed my life...

Chapter 1

I gazed out of the window at the sunset over the darkening South Atlantic. An orange sun was dipping below the horizon, and a layer of cloud picked out the variations in colour with a changing beauty that demanded attention even from the bug-eyed. The brief stop for refuelling in the heat of Ascension Island lay ahead. Most of the passengers on the RAF Tristar appeared to be sleeping with a success that had always eluded me on aircraft. To travel sixteen thousand miles with one's wife for an interview had been an unusual experience. But then everything about this situation was unusual. Two and a half months before I had been contentedly settled in my job and the Falkland Islands was just a place at the extremity of the civilized world in which we had thumped the Argentines some twelve years before.

One day in late February, I had been sitting in the lounge with the *Sunday Times* on the coffee table, its sheer fatness defying the first unfolding. I peeled apart the sections and settled down to my after-lunch reading. I opened the Appointments Section. Why should a gainfully employed manager find this such compulsive reading? Was I confirming job security, or merely idly curious? It can be useful to check one's market positioning and occasionally the more interesting possibility of being able to deduce that some business acquaintance is about to be replaced presents itself. If so, a quick phone call to the threatened executive to outline the assumed threat always helps to pass the time. Whatever the motive, it can be reassuring on a Sunday afternoon just to absorb the fact that so many opportunities exist. My eyes darted across the page. The adverts were supposed to catch the eye, but what concerned me was the fact that I seemed to be behind the pace on acronyms.

> *C.R.U.M. MANAGER REQUIRED – Fabulous package/Unbelievable benefits*
> *At least 15 years' world-class C.R.U.M. achievement essential, you must demonstrate incredible innovative ability, yet be prepared never to use it as you accept modern slavery in this turgid company, going nowhere fast...*

I was struggling with the 'C' when something caught my attention. There at the top of a double-column box was an unknown crest that had a sheep and a sailing ship on it. The position advertised was that of Chief Executive of the Falkland Islands Government who, apparently, would '... probably be married'. It went on, 'The task is demanding, requiring energy, innovation, political sensitivity, considerable powers of leadership, resilience and the ability to work well under pressure.' But so what? All adverts say that kind of thing.

The Falklands were famous. The images and triumphs of 1982 were embedded in the national psyche and would remain there for a generation or more — but I had no idea that a chief executive was involved. It was rather quaint to imagine that one could apply for such a position. I reasoned that it must be an internal Foreign Office appointment, or there would be an Islander lined up for it. It was likely they had to advertise merely to salve consciences by proving that competition exists when it was actually absent. Or possibly the tentacles of the European Union had stretched to the South Atlantic, and therefore all opportunities must be advertised so that everyone, everywhere could apply for everything. In any case, companies, charities and even football clubs have chief executives, but not countries; and if they did, they certainly would not advertise them in the *Sunday Times*!

I expect it had been one of those frustrating weeks at work; maybe my biorhythm had reached its most restless phase, or the unusual nature of the advert played on my mind. Whatever the vibration, my wife Jean reflected it with surprising vigour when I shared my musings, by resoundingly advising, 'Go for it.'

I sent for the details of the position and they were both tantalizing and comprehensive. It appeared that the successful candidate would run a civil service, which in turn ran a mini civilization. There were companies to chair, committees to sit on, a multiplicity of services to provide, and to add to the package, the holder of the job was referred to as 'Honourable'. I had never imagined that anyone would ever address me as 'Honourable', and I unwittingly welcomed the vanity of the thought, but only for an instant. There were many acronyms to grasp, and they would prefer someone with both private and public sector management behind them. I could make a case for having that. However, they also required experience of launching oil exploration — I had acquired an 'A' level in geology thirty-one years ago, but that might not be enough. Not only would the successful candidate 'probably' have a wife, there was a strong emphasis on that very wife being 'dedicated and supportive'. Fortunately, I had secured the necessary wife some twenty-seven years previously, after a bruising struggle, and she had subsequently proved beyond all reasonable doubt the nature of her dedication and support. A requirement entirely new to me had also been slipped in: 'A developed sense of humour would be an asset.' Could I demonstrate the necessary state of development in this area?

I remembered a friend had once applied for a position where a sense of humour was stated as being desirable in the advert. He had decided that the logical approach would be to retell some of his favourite jokes in his letter of application. The fact that he had failed to get an interview may have been a commentary on his apparent levity, or possibly on the quality of the jokes themselves. I felt it wise to leave the jokes until much later in the process.

If you have read hundreds of other people's CVs you will know how difficult it is to hit the right balance. There are those who have had training in how to prepare a CV, and they usually apply boring rules and formats that are fairly evident to the scanner. Some end up being unwittingly pompous and others are downright scruffy. The last thing the consultant wants to feel as they sieve the CVs is that they are wasting time reading something that comes from a production line. Thus, the offering must be tailored and succinct. Above all, it must relate to actual achievements rather than responsibilities. Preparing one is not the work of an instant; nevertheless I brought mine up to date and stuck it in the post.

There was no kicking of heels in impatience; I relegated any idea of being Falklands bound from the 'highly unlikely' category to 'impossible'. Then, one morning, my PA announced that a Mr Sampson was on the phone from the Falkland Islands. That name had been in the advert; this was the incumbent, the one who would be leaving. The name had stuck because I remembered pondering the supportive nature of Delilah and whether his sense of humour had not been quite up to scratch. He spent several minutes waxing enthusiastically about the Islands, the job, the tax status of the colony, the travel, the house and the view from his office window. I looked out of mine – a grey car park near Warrington on a drab March day, with the sound of the M6 droning outside the window. He fondly described his as being over a picturesque harbour to distant mountains with the union flag flying proudly in the balmy breeze, the only sound being the occasional cry of a logger duck or giant petrel.

'Will I be interviewed?' I asked.

'Yes of course, the whole thing has been passed over to a consultant who will be in touch.'

'Why are you leaving?' This seemed like a key question in the circumstances.

'It's the end of my contract and I want to leave in August.'

Jean and I discussed it. It seemed a long shot, we had only moved house a few months before, and the children were not really 'off our hands' yet. There must be hordes of far better-qualified applicants, so there was no need to get serious. But the Chief Executive getting in touch did seem a bit unusual. If I were going to be interviewed I would need to find out far more about the place. I researched what I could, but the information was woefully inadequate. In any case, I was both settled and happy where I was.

The recruitment consultant began to earn his corn. He seemed a cheery fellow on the phone and he invited me to have a chat with him in London.

He was equally cheery in person and seemed to be terribly impressed by the cobbled-together CV. He confided that there had been two hundred and fifty applicants but that only a few had been invited to take the test, and that he would really appreciate it if I could take it too.

'What sort of test?' I enquired, assuming the relaxed manner of one who is being pushed rather forcibly into a corner.

'Psychometric.'

'When?' I asked, anticipating a few late night cramming sessions before the big day.

'Now.'

'How long will it take?'

'No more than three and a half hours.'

The corner was pretty narrow and there was no room for manoeuvre. In any case, I could hardly drive back north having given up on a simple test. I agreed to the cerebral exercises that normally constitute this kind of thing with an enthusiasm that was as hollow as it must have appeared.

Psychometrics can be entertaining. So you think you are numerate? Answer this:

Place the next two numbers in this sequence: 1, 2, 3, 5, 7, 11, ..., ...

At first the 11 seems to be wrong – surely it should be 9? Then the 2 is wrong. But no, the answer is 13 and 17. These are all numbers that are divisible only by themselves – obvious, isn't it? Well, it may be obvious reading a book, but sat at a school-type desk in the anteroom of a recruitment consultant, it seemed like the kind of question Einstein would spend several hours researching before composing one of many available solutions.

There were more sinister implications away from the numeracy subject and into what I suspected was the personality area:

Please rank the following statements in the order that describes you best:
a) I regard global warming as a threat to civilization
b) I generally run up flights of stairs
c) I believe that children should be seen and not heard

a) I enjoy a good party
b) I regard global warming as a threat to civilization
c) I am never late for an appointment

a) I believe that children should be seen and not heard
b) I enjoy a good party
c) I generally run up flights of stairs

Scurrying through this kind of forced-choice question is so time constrained that any thought of deciding what style of manager they want you to be, or what kind of chap you really are, is not possible. However, the three and a half hours hurried to its close and left my brain wondering whether I enjoy parties enough or whether my habit of running up stairs should be regarded as good or bad. The cheery consultant indicated that marking the test would take some time – apparently a massive computer was required – and that I would need to return for another session the following week.

This time it was in Birmingham. Being a top consultant he had more than one office, and Birmingham itself presented yet another test. The City of Birmingham may be one that can be driven through by the local inhabitants without the need for a satellite positioning system, but I have never seen it that way. In fact, years before, I had spent some time as a salesman in this area and purchased a large-scale map so that I could find my way around. As a geographer I have always felt that I relate to maps easily, but I could never fathom the complexities of Birmingham. The roads appeared to move overnight. It was as though the map publishers also awarded the road-building contracts and kept changing the roads in order to stimulate demand for a revised edition. I uncovered some evidence for this scheme when I stayed in a city centre hotel and found that a gang of men was in fact moving the road outside my window throughout the entire night.

But all that was years ago, and had stood me in good stead – this time I used the ring road to perfection and found the right exit. The consultant had sustained his cheeriness and appeared to be very impressed by the results of the test. I had imagined that the outcome of the meeting would be my exposure as a random box ticker, but no, I had been identified as having all sorts of desirable characteristics. Jean would be pleased to know that after all these years.

Furthermore, this same series of tests had identified the shortlist of five and I would be one of them. The next step would be a torture far more complex and exquisite than the afternoon of psychos. The consultant happily announced trial by dinner with wives at the Army & Navy Club, and all five candidates would be there at once.

We were a strangely assorted group. There was a retiring air vice marshall (retiring from the air force, not in disposition), a colonel, and a businessman, complete with suitably supportive wives, as the original advert had demanded, and the 'Islander' candidate. The consultant had led me to believe in the token nature of this Islander but he clearly knew far more about the Islands than any of the rest of us. The air vice marshall had been to the Falklands as part of his job, and the colonel was with the pace on military matters. I was beginning to feel that I lacked some of the detailed knowledge necessary.

The assessors were just as varied as the candidates. An ex-governor plus wife, an ex-military commander plus wife, the present Chief Executive plus wife, an ex-Island councillor (no wife at present), the cheery consultant whose wife was unable to come at the last minute, and the Falkland Islands

Representative in London, who was female anyway. The assessors took their job very seriously. They parted the candidates from their spouses and then they rotated around the table in between courses in order to obtain the maximum impact. I thought that if this had been France they would have had to carry their knives with them. They did take their napkins, though.

This kind of a meal creates an interesting atmosphere. The contents of the menu have long passed into oblivion, but I do recall the rather strained conversations in every direction. Sorting out the assessors from the candidates was bad enough, but being competitive, gracious, informed, conversational and interesting all at once while holding one's knife and fork properly and not belching was a good test of something. All the while, supportive wives were also being appraised. I noticed that Jean was having a particularly animated conversation with the ex-military commander's wife. The ex-governor seemed to be talking sense to me, but I had no idea as to how the evening was influencing any decision. I heard no belches, so presumably the impact had been neutral.

As we picked up our coats from the cloakroom, one of the candidates emerged with wife alongside. 'You wouldn't catch me working for this crowd,' he proffered. I had no way of knowing whether this was an advanced form of gamesmanship or whether the view was genuinely held. It had been an unusual evening, but then so many things about the Falklands were already turning out to be unusual. That sense of humour was clearly an essential requirement.

Situated in the basement of Falkland House in London were two claustrophobic rooms with the kind of air-conditioning system that only had two settings; Antarctic or clammy. On the day after the Army & Navy Club dinner, serious interviewing began with a panel in each of the rooms. Fresh glitterati joined the appraisers of the night before: a man from the Foreign Office, a previous Chief Executive, an engineer and so forth. Panel interviews are something of a lottery. Each interviewer seems to have a pet theme or question and there is no time to strike up any rapport or discussion. At the first one, Mr Sampson gave the impression of having stored up this googly:

'What would you do if you are Acting Governor and some St Helenans at Mount Pleasant Airport wanted to vote in a by-election?'

He seemed so pleased with the apparent complexity of the question that I realized a can of worms lay open in front of me. I remembered that Mount Pleasant was the military base, but that wasn't much help.

'Why should it be a problem?' I asked, desperately seeking more information.

'They are entitled to a vote because of residence of over five years, but have never exercised that right. The Islanders don't want them to, as they fear a dilution of control through the democratic process.'

'I would consult with all my advisers,' I stumbled, feeling that this sounded sufficiently like a civil servant.

'All right, you consult and find that the views are evenly balanced,' he countered.

'I would search for precedent,' I suggested, feeling more like Sir Humphrey by the second.

'There isn't one,' he said with more than a hint of triumph in his voice.

'Are they legally entitled to vote?' I asked.

'Yes.'

'Then I'd let them vote,' I concluded, feeling that I had asserted a sound principle.

There was a total lack of response. In the years that followed I have never had any inkling of the value of that question or the answer, but the interview ploughed on.

'What has been your greatest achievement?'

'Persuading my wife to marry me.'

I thought this might be considered a canny juxtaposition of the required supportiveness aligned with humour, but no reaction was forthcoming.

'What do you feel the Islands need most at this time?' This was a good question, a bone with some meat on it. I took the risk of spouting some conclusions reached on the basis of inadequate knowledge (well, who doesn't occasionally?). I pontificated about the apparent reactive nature of the Islands over many years, and the fact that now could be the time to become proactive, to plan, to improve the image from one that was historically based to one that had a promising future. The po-faces of my interviewers showed a faint twinge of agreement with that one.

The second panel met in the smaller of the two rooms and had a slightly more jovial atmosphere. The predictable 'We'll let you know' aftertaste lingered on our mental palates on the train journey home.

Before long the cheery one was back in touch, indicating that Jean and I were invited to the Falklands for final interview. Two other couples were also being asked to come at different times; what dates suited us? Things were beginning to get serious. A few interviews can be quite challenging. A bevy of psychometric tests may appeal to an innate desire to prove oneself. A free dinner at the Army & Navy Club and learning about the Falklands from those who had been there had been worthwhile in its own right. However, the Falklands were a long way, at least a week needing to be taken as holiday, and I could hardly take this next step without talking to my Chairman about it. I was also concerned that there was no hint of clarity as to who would actually make the decision between the candidates. It appeared that everyone who wanted to meet us would be able to do so, and that they, along with others who had never met us, would then chatter among themselves and with His Excellency the Governor, until a consensus emerged. This technique had not been on the syllabus at business school, but we were to learn that it could be a pretty effective way of getting things done in a small community.

I shared the improbable news with my chairman. It isn't every day that one's chief executive indicates that he has been invited to attend a final selection for the running of a government eight thousand miles away. The chairman had always impressed me with his visionary sense of adventure, and his swashbuckling style gave me hope that he would empathize. In the event, he was marvellous, 'Not wishing to stand in my way' and taking a positive interest in the unique nature of the situation.

It then transpired that one of the three couples lining up to compete had dropped out – 'Due to promotion to brigadier', apparently. I had no idea then what a brigadier was but it sounded like a reasonable thing to become if one was in the army. The contest had come down to the last two – us and the other couple visiting the Islands two weeks before us.

We arrived at Brize Norton at around 2100 hours for the RAF Tristar flight via Ascension Island to Mount Pleasant Air Force base in the Falklands (known as MPA to acronym buffs and normal people alike). This was the only jet link with the Islands, and we had received appropriately gruff written instructions warning us of the many hazards involved.

I am particularly fond of bags. I don't know why, but I find suitcases, briefcases, computer cases, satchels and rucksacks absolutely fascinating. I can spend hours in luggage shops just enjoying myself. Freud might have had something to say about that. I also have the same problem with a number of other consumer items, compact discs being the most apparent to my family and friends. One colleague, with whom I strolled the streets of Prague, believed that I suffered from a rare form of compulsive phobia, being unable to walk past such attractions. Prague did seem to me to have a plethora of CD shops, all selling top-class products at giveaway prices, but it may have been no more than a passing twinge. However, my bag interest meant that I happened to know that the size of bag that may be carried in the cabin on any normal airliner is clearly specified by someone or other and as long as your carry-on bag is that particular size, you can carry it on. Jet-set executives actually buy them for that purpose. Simple, isn't it? Not for the Royal Air Force – they have entirely different measurements to judge bags by, and they enforce them with a rigour that would do an officious fraulein with whom I once had an argument in Hanover Airport proud.

The obvious danger of yellow fever had not been our first thought when preparing to depart, but we had to undergo inoculation in case the flight diverted to West Africa. Apparently there isn't any yellow fever in West Africa as a result of this precaution, but this logic was beyond me. It was also made crystal clear that even though an innocent civilian might pay well over £2,000 for the privilege of travelling on this classless flight, the RAF do not guarantee to actually transport anyone anywhere within a specific time frame. It seemed to be a risk-laden Pandora's box of a flying experience.

Bleriot would have felt the whole prospect far too challenging. On top of all this, there is an overwhelming sense of civilians being treated in a military manner by people in uniform trying their level best to behave in a civilian manner.

On entering the terminal, I felt I had arrived in Sparta (I assume, not having had a classical education, that it had been somewhat Spartan there). The check-in zone was devoid of both colour and comfort. In this utilitarian atmosphere we were allocated seats, given boarding cards and directed to what was referred to as a 'departure lounge'. The bleak furnishings and the 1950s ambience were influenced by the gradual increase in occupants. It felt as though we had stumbled into an anteroom behind the popular end at Elland Road. This must be where all the Leeds United fans in the heart of the south congregate. All around were youths with short hair, looking fit and aggressive. However this could not be Elland Road – the youths were all impeccably behaved. Not for the last time a feeling of 'What are we doing here?' came over us. That feeling remained for most of the next five days. Well, more like the next five years, really.

There was a large-screen TV in the lounge. The fact that it was a colour set was somehow out of place in 1956. It was showing a *Blackadder* video, as was a similar set on Ascension Island, on the way there, and on the way back. For some reason Blackadder is a cult figure with the military. It may have something to do with the zany, unreal, highly characterized structure within which military types live.

The Tristar lifted into the Oxfordshire darkness and after a short time a box containing some food was served. On a bad day in the gulag, Ivan Denisovich might have liked it. Sleep was at best fitful, and we arrived at Ascension some seven hours later, having crossed the equator and witnessed a tropical dawn.

Ascension was hot and humid. All the passengers were escorted from the aircraft into a caged compound while the winged giant refuelled surrounded by firemen clad in aluminium foil as though they were ready for roasting. In that heat they probably were. The cage was surprisingly pleasant to sit in, the odd palm tree waved nearby and a warming breeze reminded us that this was the tropics and caused yet more self-pinching to see if it was real. A TV blared from inside. Blackadder was still in his First World War trench and I think Baldrick was roasting a pigeon, without the benefit of foil.

The runway at Ascension is very long, with the ability to take a landing space shuttle in the event of a diversion. If you can find the island on a map you will appreciate the strategic significance of the place that became so relevant in 1982. It is in essence a volcanic aircraft carrier in the middle of the Atlantic. The dark grey ash that once spewed from the volcano is the major feature of a barren landscape, which is enlivened by occasional patches of vegetation. Giant turtles migrate from Brazil annually and move into the local beach accommodation, digging holes to lay eggs. The Tristar passengers bound for the Falklands only get to see such sights if the aircraft is delayed. The odds on a door not closing properly are fairly short and if you travel the route several times a year, tropical sightseeing becomes a near certainty. There was never a native population, so all the present inhabitants are on contract to someone or other. The whole social structure has a built-in transience. The place has an air of unreality, encouraged by the temperature change and the inadequate sleep en route experienced by virtually all visitors. The airport is appropriately named 'Wideawake', after a local bird.

We shuffled back into the Tristar and restarted, winging southwards on the last leg of our journey. Only ocean was underneath us. Mile after mile, hour after hour, the day stretched on with the westward component of our journey. The view from the window was hypnotic, that vast dark blue expanse of the South Atlantic, lonely and deserted. No other aircraft spewed vapour trails around us, no ships made wake beneath us, there was just sea. There were more spare seats on this leg of the journey, as we had actually left some of the Leeds fan look-alikes at Ascension, maybe incarcerated in the cage by order of the FA, pending the return leg. The vacant seats were necessary as the lack of diversion capability in Argentina meant that we had to have enough fuel to be able to approach Mount Pleasant Airport, fail to land, and fly back to Montevideo. Nothing below, enemy coast over two hundred miles to the west, and to the east South Africa, but thousands of miles away. This was beginning to feel like the end of the line. Even Paragon Station in Hull could not compare with the feeling of having left civilization behind.

All good stupors come to an end, and we prepared to descend and get our first view of the Falklands. There was some cloud, a glimpse or two of a beige and barren landscape and then we were down, the first view of Mount Pleasant indicating that it had a great deal of catching up to do if it was going to live up to its name. The sight of military personnel standing on a bank of earth as we taxied past, holding up scores, was as we discovered later, intended to provide a helpful professional appraisal of our pilot's landing skill. The RAF, playing domestic airline games, made the customary announcement about not standing up until the plane has been motionless for at least half an hour. Not wishing to change the habits of a lifetime's travelling, I naturally stood up as we stopped. Jean yanked me back into my seat. Nobody else had moved – they may have looked like Leeds fans, but golly, they didn't behave like them.

The door of the aircraft was opened and it was at once clear that the weather outside was cool and windy. However, the real surprise was the air that struck us as we descended to the tarmac. It was so refreshing, so breathable, and so unremittingly pleasant. This was more than just a reaction to the artificial atmosphere of the last eighteen hours. It was as though the involuntary act of breathing had suddenly become physically satisfying in a new way. We squeezed into an arrivals area that made Kirmington, South Humberside airport seem like Schipol, and to our amazement and amusement a chap in uniform began to lecture us all on the dangers of land mines. What a welcome! The non-Leeds fans did not hurl the expected abuse or chant alternative advice; they simply listened attentively. The speaker warmed to his theme, producing examples of mines of varying shapes and sizes, indicating that parts of us, in any combination or totality, could be blown to bits in an instant. He then added the surprising instruction that we were not to tamper with them, insisting that we must report any finding of such things to the headmaster, the prison warder, the nanny or somebody in uniform.

The carousel squeaked around its loop and I learnt for the umpteenth time the hard lesson that a watched carousel never produces your bag. Young men were heaving huge rucksacks from the moving belt for what seemed like hours before our very civilian-looking luggage emerged from the secret recesses of baggage handling, defying the fundamental rules of physics by moving more slowly than any of the other bags. The queue through customs and immigration speeded up as we reached the point of contact. I had been told that Peter King, who was both the government secretary and the deputy to the Chief Executive, was to meet us. We must have been as recognizable as away supporters in the Kop end, and thus we were spotted by Robert King, Peter's brother, who happened to be the chief customs officer, and were whisked through. Peter was the very essence of friendship and help, and we were soon comfortably seated in a long-wheelbase Land Rover.

'How far is it to Stanley?' I asked, having discovered in London that to say 'Port Stanley' is considered very gauche these days.

'About thirty-five miles.'

The journey was punctuated by the two of us asking Peter the questions that every first visitor asks when being driven along the MPA road. The questions are (in any order):

Why is the road in such a poor state and why doesn't the government do something about it?

Does the grass get greener than this?

How often do people get maimed in the minefields?

Do sheep get maimed in the minefields?

What on earth are those large birds?

How did the stone runs get here?

Why is there so much junk at regular intervals?

Are there any trees, anywhere?

When do we see penguins?

Do civilians and military get on well together?

Is it true there is a huge oilfield here?

The answers to these questions are self-evident to the inhabitants of the Islands. The state of the road has been caused by government trying to do something about it. The grass is at its absolute greenest right now. Neither people nor sheep get maimed by mines; people don't venture into the minefields and sheep appear to be too light to set them off. The birds are, in fact, upland geese, of which there are thousands all over the place. Nobody knows how the stone runs were formed, least of all geologists. The junk is the result of a government initiative in selling off fifty-acre plots for development along this road – it hasn't been a great success. Trees are few and far between. The penguins that are readily accessible from Stanley migrate in the winter and so this is the wrong time of year to see them. The civilians and the military coexist happily and, no, there is no proof as yet of a huge oilfield.

Peter answered patiently and as we approached Stanley the names of hills were pointed out. They all had an evocative sound: Tumbledown, Longdon, Two Sisters, Sapper, Harriet – a reminder of the freedom so recently and forcibly confirmed. We crested a rise in the road and there in front was Stanley, the whole town spread across a northward-facing slope, with a grid-iron street pattern and a fascinating view across a natural harbour almost totally enclosed except for a narrow outlet to the sea, known unsurprisingly as 'The Narrows'. The size was about what we had expected but the variety of housing styles caught the eye. Most were single storey. There were Scandinavian-looking wooden houses, houses clad in UPVC, houses finished in white-painted galvanized tin, more traditional homes with brightly coloured roofs – in fact, one roof was painted as a Union Jack – but nowhere could we see bricks, tiles or stone. We were left to freshen up at our hotel for a few minutes (it was by now mid-Tuesday afternoon) and then we began an incredible process of multiple exposure that was to last until the Saturday morning.

Tea with His Excellency the Governor at Government House was the first test. We were driven the three hundred yards by Mr Sampson, who muttered darkly about the visit of the competitors two weeks before. We were retracing their steps now in the interests of fairness.

David Tatham CMG and his wife Val were immaculate hosts, sympathetic, informative, urbane and full of restrained friendliness. The atmosphere within Government House was relaxed lush colonial, which contrasted with the fact that we felt on trial. The carpets were thick, the curtains well made, the furniture had a quality feel to it, and the staff carried out their duties silently and efficiently. A fire burned obediently in a grey stone fireplace. We were astonished that it was peat. It was emitting a heat not much less than that of a coal fire and glowed with a quiet liveliness that was immediately attractive. The view from the house looked directly over a well-kept lawn to the harbour and the shallow bare hills beyond. From the lounge this vista was pleasantly obscured by a splendid conservatory running the length of this part of the house. It was very, very British. So much so, that in spite of the ordeal of our journey we felt far nearer to the UK than we did to the South American continent only three hundred miles to the west.

The round of meetings, meals and discussions that crammed the three days is now blurred in the memory and tempered by later and fuller discoveries. However, there were three major impressions that emerged strongly.

Firstly, the people were very warm and friendly. We had been warned about the internal wrangling and Machiavellian contortions of small island communities. If it was present it certainly did not manifest itself at the time.

Secondly, the scenery was a revelation. The Tuesday afternoon and Wednesday were very dull, so was early Thursday morning, but on that morning we flew out in one of the Falkland Island Government Air Service (FIGAS) Britten Norman Islander planes to meet the councillors for Camp (all countryside outside of Stanley). Morgan Goss was our pilot and I sat next to him in the nine-seater twin-engined aircraft as we climbed through the low cloud above Stanley Airport and headed west. Over the intercom Morgan predicted that the weather would improve, and he was right. The cloud began to lift. I glimpsed majestic hills with the sun playing on them as it flashed and smudged its way through the rising cloud. The atmosphere seemed sharp and the quality of the air perfect. Even though the non-green nature of the whitegrass below created the (accurate) impression of a barren and unproductive place, the quality of the light generated a depth and variety of colour that was breathtaking. We landed on a peninsula at San Carlos, where the barren hills swept down to a sheltered inlet. Councillor Richard Stephens arrived to ferry us in his working Land Rover. This vehicle reflected his chosen existence as a sheep farmer. Jean, in her suitably impressive help-husband-get-the-job attire, clambered into the back where there was no room for one's legs and the aroma gave the impression that a dead, or very ill, sheep had just fallen out of the opposite door. Richard headed for a downward slope that no car I had ever driven could have negotiated and we held our breath. Our genial host simply kept firing questions as we gulped but easily survived our very first bounce across open country.

The third impression was that everyone is related to somebody. Of course, that was true back in the UK, but there we didn't often meet the relatives in the afternoon of those we had been talking to in the morning. In the Falklands it was commonplace and in many ways unnerving.

Visitors who wish to see the sights of Stanley are often given a structured tour around government departments. Sometimes they get it whether they wish it or not. We had managed to see a fair slug of Camp as well, and many people whose names we couldn't remember had enthusiastically greeted us. By our last evening our minds were in a whirl. Jean was being shown around Sulivan House, the Chief Executive's residence, and we were to dine there that evening. I was locked in a contractual discussion with Mr Sampson and it is fair to say that we didn't really see eye to eye on one or two salient points. I still had no real idea as to who would be making the decision on the job, but the meeting I had with the incumbent was so uninspiring that I felt it influenced our first meal in Sulivan House which, in turn, would not have featured in a book of great dinner conversations.

So here we were, back on the already familiar Tristar, heading northwards, the adrenalin seeping from our systems as we pondered the future. Nothing was clear, no offer was on the table, the competitors might get it, or the whole thing might be re-advertised. Our consolation was that it had been a wonderful experience and that the sun setting over the vast South Atlantic would rise again on us as we arrived back to the beginnings of an English summer.

A letter arrived by fax, representing the kind of offer that Mr Sampson had begun to discuss. But the pleasure in getting such an offer was muted by the deficiencies within it. Much as I believed that the challenge presented was worthwhile and exciting, it was a career risk of significant proportions and I was determined not to be short changed simply because I wanted to tackle it. I had the desirable option of staying where I was, and that is what I decided to do. I therefore replied to His Excellency in that vein, although I still had no idea who was pulling what strings back in Stanley. Then I received another fax with a rather better offer and a deadline for decision. Jean and I pondered, discussed, thought of all the angles, did the sums and still found the whole issue marginal. However, shortly thereafter the telephone rang – it was Charles Keenleyside, one of the Stanley councillors and as likeable a chap as you could wish to meet.

'What is going on?' he asked. I had thought he would have known exactly what was happening, but clearly he was in the dark. I explained about the first letter and my refusal, the subsequent second letter and our present state of indecision. Charles then proceeded to say some very helpful things about the unanimity of the councillors (I now realize how rare that state of affairs must have been) and, without pleading, was very persuasive. His call tipped the balance. We decided that our future lay with the people of the Falklands for the next few years, and I replied in the affirmative, undertaking to start around the beginning of September if I could persuade my employers to release me early.

Chapter 2

Making the decision had been difficult, but in June 1994 we were learning that living with the consequences also presented problems. The prospect of unpicking our lifetime adhesion to the UK and settling eight thousand miles away made the Falklands feel more foreign by the day.

My employers, who I am sure would admit to having been a motley crew, were superb. Their motliness was not of their doing. Training and Enterprise Councils (TECs) were structured to create just such a mixture for a very good reason. The government of the day wanted local movers and shakers running the TECs, so they created their boards from ten private-sector bosses and five public/charity-sector decision-makers. The idea was that this unusual agglomeration would provide the best management skills available in the area, thus ensuring efficient use of public-sector funding. However, as the cash was mainly channelled through the existing training schemes and needed increasing through such devices as matching and leverage, it was hard to sustain a focus on enterprise and growth. Our board, in North and Mid-Cheshire, along with all eighty-one other TEC boards, felt that there was too much training emphasis and not nearly enough cash for enterprise. They were a thoughtful and experienced group who could appreciate the lure of the Falklands job and they were magnanimous in releasing me early, so that I had time available to prepare for the task ahead.

The relationship between the UK and the Falklands is a complex one. In the colonial era, which lasted longer than most would admit, it was fairly simple. Everyone knew who the bosses were. One's station in life was clear. The absentee landlords, who had exploited the Islands for wool revenue that they had consistently repatriated to the UK, were roundly criticized for their cynical profiteering by Lord Shackleton in his reports. But times were moving on and by the mid-Nineties it reminded me more of the rapport between an emergent adolescent child and caring parents; the parents not quite understanding the stubborn nature of the child, and the child being suspicious of the parents. Yet the ties were close and I was to learn, in the short time before our departure, just how many commercial and cultural links exist and how strong they are.

I had meetings with the Foreign Office (from the Minister downwards), some wool agents in Bradford, the British Geological Survey in Edinburgh, David Taylor (the first Chief Executive after the war), General Malcolm Hunt and his wife Margaret (an ex-Military Commander and veteran of the war), General Sir Peter De la Billiere (another ex-Military Commander), the managing director of the Falkland Islands Company, the Falkland Islands Association, the staff in the Falkland Islands Government Office in London, Professor John Beddington of Imperial College (the Islands' fisheries consultant), UKFIT (the UK Falkland Islands Trust), Falkland Conservation, the Falkland Islands government's auditor in Aberdeen, various oil interests in Aberdeen, a shipping company in Hull, the relevant bankers, Cable & Wireless Ltd., and many others who either had useful information for the greenhorn, or were curious to meet the survivor of what was unofficially acknowledged to have been a selection process even more convoluted than this, or any other, sentence. They all spoke fluently and enthusiastically about their involvement and the challenges ahead, and their help was a real boost.

One name stands above all others in the recent history of the Islands – that of Sir Rex Hunt, who was chairman of the Falkland Islands Association. The powerful image of this lion-hearted yet modest and diminutive man standing up to the bullying occupiers of Stanley is one that history has already recorded. Sir Rex was particularly helpful. His approach to issues was practical and sympathetic, but also contained a valuable blend of cynical realism. The public weight of his name and his deep knowledge of the Islands enabled him to hold in a workable balance issues that might otherwise have created tension.

The packing began. This was not so much a process, more a disparate and chaotic activity driven only by the awareness that it simply had to be done. I hated it. We slogged our way through the separation from all those aspects of daily life that are taken for granted and, after weighing the pros and cons, we decided to let our house fully furnished. However, there was one major problem that did not have a satisfactory solution. It did not arise from our parents or even the children, but the dog.

Dogs have a way of making themselves indispensable, and ours was no exception. Branston had been a full member of the family from the moment I had brought him home as a hesitant soft bundle in a cardboard box from Lavenham in Suffolk some thirteen years before. He was a black-and-tan standard-sized dachshund. A sleek, cylindrical chap with dumpy legs that could propel him with the speed of a greyhound when he wished and yet as he lay in front of the fire you could hold the whole of his furry front limb in the palm of your hand.

He had been omnipresent in our lives, hanging around with as much apparent purpose as a teenager on a street corner. He had an exclusive relationship with Jean and was always to be found within feet of her. (The words 'limpet', 'leech' and 'parasite' spring to mind.) On an average evening I would return from work, having slogged away all day satisfying the unreasonable demands of the many, having travelled for aeons along crowded roads thick with lunatics and having skipped lunch to keep the 'in tray' at bay. All this was being done simply to earn crusts for the family. Opening the front door, I would be confronted by a barking sausage who would come and nudge me, his healthy ever-wet nose leaving an indelible light grey mark on my trousers when the glistening evaporated. He would then return to his Jean-watching fixation before I had a chance to respond to his totally inadequate greeting.

At Christmas and his birthday he would have his own presents: choc drops, rubber bones, chews, balloons and a squeaky toy. He would savage the squeaky toy until the squeaking stopped; one lasted ten seconds, but they normally survived about twenty minutes. Although Jean believed that Branston could achieve almost anything, he was unable to blow up his own balloons – but in that sphere, as in all others, his demands were met. He would attack these slowly bouncing globules with unwarranted ferocity and even though the maximum extension of his jaws would never enable him to get his teeth into the tightest curve, he would always succeed in reducing the balloon to burst limpness, then follow that up with a display of swaggering smugness.

In spite of his love of heat and lounging in front of fire and radiators, Branston was an outdoor dog. He regarded the garden as his domain and would chase his rubber ring into bushes with such abandon that we feared he might sever an artery. Any gardening activity took twice as long as originally estimated due to his insistence on playing with that wretched ring. He would roll a rubber ball under the garden gate and wait for innocent passers-by to return it. Some of them thought this was some kind of mistake – the poor doggie had evidently lost control of his ball and it had slipped beyond his reach. This was not so. Branston could spot a rambler at about three hundred yards. He would wait patiently and then roll the ball under the gate when they reached the twenty-yard mark. The good-natured soul, at peace with the bird song and lushness of the field opposite, would happily return the ball. To the pedestrian that should have been an end to the matter, but to Branston it was only the beginning of a game, even a relationship, that would last until nightfall if the deluded walker would let it. Occasionally we felt obliged to intervene, as a crowd would gather, ramblers who had entered into the spirit of the encounter and were taking turns to return the ball. This delighted Branston, but it put his audience in danger of missing the last train home.

Here was one much-loved dog, but the shipping lines serving the Falklands would not take him, as he was deemed to be too old. We acknowledged the truth of this, as age was not his only problem. He may have been healthy, but he was chronically neurotic. My dog-loving parents gamely offered to have him and we tried it out by leaving him with them for a weekend. I knew that it couldn't work when we picked him up and my mother asked, 'Does he always howl all night?' If Branston decided to do so, he could howl all night, and the next night, and the night after that. No theory of management seemed to work with him, X or Y, stick or carrot, smack or choc drops – they were all useless. Drugging him might have alleviated the problem, although when he got into that state with us we tended to put him in Jean's car in the garage, where he immediately went to sleep. In a human being these behavioural patterns would be socially unacceptable; in a dog they are often regarded as evidence of character or quaintness. Jean thought so, anyway.

The black day came. I was in London overnight, meeting Falklands-related folk, and Jean told me on the phone that she had had him put down. It was an inevitable and courageous act and to this day I do not believe that I could have done it. We were both devastated. This job in the Falklands may have promised to be wonderful but there was a high price to be paid for the experience.

There were other substantial colours in our lives that now had to be discarded. The illogical and quite unwarranted support that we had generously given to Oldham Athletic Football Club over the past six seasons was about to come to an end. We could no longer sit in the Lookers Stand for every home match, surrounded by the familiar faces of other season-ticket holders who had paid good money to watch their team losing a relegation battle all season. It had been great at the beginning – the atmosphere was so Lowryish and full of character. The smell of cigarettes, the pies, the chanting, the immense understanding of the crowd for the ongoing judgmental problems faced by referees – we loved it. Oldham had gained promotion to the very first Premier League with a truly exceptional team capable of beating anyone on their day, especially on their plastic pitch. But the pitch had to be replaced, the better players coveted more success than was likely at Oldham, and Joe Royle proved his mortality by buying players that were simply not the bargains of earlier years. A painful slide began, which we witnessed with increasing distress. The faces in the crowd around us – Saddam Hussein, Boris Yeltsin, Richard Branson, and other look-alikes – all took the situation stoically. At least we had the option of leaving for the South Atlantic. Our fellow sufferers were condemned to seasons of purgatory.

I also had to bid farewell to the Bramhall Over Forties' Cricket Team. This swashbuckling group of assorted brigands had never quite been capable of moulding themselves into a league-topping team, but what fun we had on Wednesday evenings! 'Going where?' they muttered, as some of them extracted last week's socks from their kit bags. Grunts and general disinterest followed. They knew in their heart of hearts that they wouldn't miss my cricketing prowess. One or two of them even had the decency to make sure I was acquainted with that fact. Such was their love of the game that they generally spent about half of their changing room conversation criticizing Cheadle Hulme for taking their matches too seriously and actually playing to win. Mind you, on the odd occasion when we did happen to win, the delight was genuine enough and the celebrations seemed pretty serious. The heavily understated comradeship would be something I sorely missed, and as for the smell of newly cut grass and the joy of holding that hard red ball as the batsman waited for my next best effort – I hardly dared think about the deprivation.

The inevitably lack-lustre farewell tour of family and friends brought to an end the frustrating inter-job period, and on 1 September 1994, we were left clutching bags at Brize Norton to enjoy once again the unique colourless check-in and the company of the non-Leeds fans.

The Tristar taxied eternally around every available piece of tarmac and then, just before midnight, we started our cathartic rush down the main runway and rose gently into the Oxfordshire night. The lights of the villages twinkled their goodbyes. Jean could picture the last moments of the beloved Branston. The bridges were burning behind us and we were on our way.

Chapter 3

The airborne hours passed and we entered the torpid state of suspended animation. There were books to read, naps to take and the sea and sky to commune with by way of a hypnotic stare, yet none of it helped to reduce the tedium. The steady rushing sound of engines and air conditioning, the relatively high altitude pressure and the uninspiring food created a state in which time was an endless loop, and even the sub-economy steerage seat assumed a numb comfort.

Eventually, and on time, we began our descent into Mount Pleasant. Misleading names can be a problem when one is not familiar with a place. Think of St Martin's in the Fields, Cheapside and the White City – none of them resemble their name in any respect. And what about Oldham Athletic? Just as athleticism has no relationship with the long thump up the middle and leaden-footed ball watching, so Mount Pleasant Airport has no real mountain and 'pleasant' is not the first adjective that would be used, even in an army-recruiting brochure, to describe it. This metal-and-plastic oasis in a whitegrass desert had been constructed in eighty memorable weeks after the war. It still showed the scars of having been conceived in such haste and delivered in logistical mayhem.

Peter King, who had driven us on our interview visit, ferried us along the gravel road. The scenery was dull and uninviting. It was early September – springtime – but there was a pallor about the countryside and a cool bite in the air. Peter delivered us to Sulivan House, left the Land Rover keys and walked to his home.

We sat in the echo-chamber kitchen, looking uneasily at each other and wondering what on earth we were doing. No food in the larder, no television in the lounge, no dog on the mat, just an invasive cat named Holly that was not especially pleased to see us. Branston would not have given this feline the benefit of any doubt and we tended to agree with his hypothetical posthumous conclusion.

We pulled ourselves together with the help of a thoughtfully concocted food parcel from the Attorney General's wife and began to look to the future.

After a few days our first impressions became an extension of our experience during the interview visit. Folk were most helpful; the job was totally fascinating. Working closely with His Excellency the Governor was efficient and productive. Hesitantly, we put down our temporary roots. We were as plants being re-potted. Routines that were going to serve for five years were starting to be established.

Although Sulivan House was 'fully furnished', for us the ambience improved dramatically as our own bits and pieces arrived in boxes and we were able to put our mark on the place. It gradually became home. We experienced what every expatriate does: that opening boxes that contain one's own beloved possessions is far more exciting than receiving a mammoth consignment of random gifts. It may be junk, but it was familiar junk.

Sulivan House was built in the 1930s and was finished on the outside with what Islanders call 'wriggly tin'. The tin was painted white and looked like horizontal wooden boarding. It whistled and creaked in the wind. There was a flagpole in the front garden that stimulated a daily ritual and a lean-to conservatory facing the main road along the northern frontage. By 'main road' I mean one on which a vehicle occasionally passed, but more often than not, one could lie down in the middle and have a snooze, should the inclination arise. We never actually tried that. On the other side of the road, a mere twenty yards from our front windows, was the waterfront.

To look out over water that faces the daily track of the sun was always one of the great pluses. Some weekend mornings, around the time of the shortest day, we could sit in bed, have coffee and watch the sun easing its way in to the sky over the hills across the harbour. It would begin by tingeing the high clouds with a deep red lining and then the colour would evolve towards orange as the light gathered momentum. Whenever we gazed at it, the view seemed to offer infinite variety, never being the same as at the last glance. We would find ourselves looking at the water as a child in a pram contemplates a mind-absorbing mobile. Mostly it was moving busily, but occasionally it was calm. When such stillness descended upon it, the glass-like surface reflected the light and exposed any seabird within half a mile. That reflection would capture the startling sky and add yet more variations as ripples and disturbances created flaws in the mirror. A logger duck halfway across the harbour would create a wake reminiscent of those familiar pictures of Sir Donald Campbell surging across Coniston in *Bluebird*, although the birds' progress was rather slower and more reliable. Occasionally, dolphins would scythe lazily through the surface of the water, curving back out of sight only to reappear some yards from where one had anticipated they would emerge. I took many photographs of featureless water because I made faulty assumptions about dolphins.

Under brilliant sun or full moon the tranquillity was captivating. It was made more so by the contrast with the normal turbulence. The prevailing westerly wind would create a surging movement of water from left to right as the surface allowed itself to be whipped along. When the wind strength climbed above fifty knots the spindrift would lash across between crests and we knew that going outside would be breathtaking. Wind in the Falklands is a serious matter, and can damage doors. Parking a Land Rover facing downwind means that opening the door requires skill, bulging biceps, and a well-developed sense of timing. Otherwise hinges complain as the door whips away from the grasping hand to thrash itself against the car body in a jarring motion. Less often the wind would blow from the east and the air became damp with a tendency towards mist and low cloud. When the weather came from the north, it would batter the house along its broad frontage and although we had new windows fitted after a couple of years, a good storm would call for a supply of towels to stop the carpets getting soaked. The southerly winds could bring Antarctic cold, but the climate of the Islands was far less cold than we had imagined. The clarity of the air and possibly the thinness of the ozone layer meant that even in the middle of winter, the undisturbed sun contained heat.

Dominating the view and bang opposite the house, only twenty yards offshore, the wreck of the *Jhelum* lay tilted yet dignified. She was a one-hundred-and-eighteen-foot-long barque, built in Liverpool in 1849 and reckoned to be the best surviving example of a class of ship that handled a large proportion of world trade for a short period. As a three-masted barque it must have cut an impressive sight. It rounded Cape Horn many times with a crew of eighteen or so. They lived on salted beef and often slept in damp hammocks. Now it rested, a jaunty skeleton, with huge grey timbers wrapping its hull. One hundred and thirty years after its final significant movement it managed to retain the lines of a graceful yet workmanlike creation.

On that last and fateful voyage in 1870, under the curiously named Captain Beaglehole, the *Jhelum* had been carrying guano to France. Guano was not a pleasant cargo; Beaglehole was not a particularly pleasant name. If the guano got wet, which it normally did, it began to exude ammonia, and would form hard 'cakes' that were capable of banging around in the hold and causing damage. In any event, after mooring in Stanley, there was considerable debate regarding the seaworthiness of the *Jhelum* and its ability to continue. So Captain Beaglehole thoughtfully sold the stinking cargo (the stock in the shops must have been even more limited than normal) and arranged for the ship to be beached right outside where our house was to be built some sixty years later. The *Jhelum* had plied the oceans and earned its keep for only twenty-one years. Now wind and tide were to assist in a much longer period of retirement and gradual decline.

The Maritime Museum of Liverpool has expended much effort on cataloguing the state of the vessel and arresting decay wherever possible, but its ultimate demise is certain. Its silent immobility is a ghostly reflection of its former creakingly active life. On some of those rare, still, moonlit nights, I would listen for the echoes of the seamen who lived and toiled inside the hulk; but they were long gone. The only activity I ever witnessed on the ship was that of the cormorants and giant petrels doing their level best to refill the hold with local guano.

The interior of Sulivan House was spacious and allowed us room to breathe. There were empty drawers to fill and uncluttered shelves to take the possessions we had shipped. The fact that the place had been the residence of the Colonial Secretary for many years before passing to the more trendily titled Chief Executive meant that it contained hints of a gracious past that would have been missing in the normal prefabricated expatriate home. It had an ambience, an inherited cosiness that was to make it a very acceptable alternative to our real home.

An unusual reminder of the war came when I was in the lounge one evening watching a video of a dramatization of the events of April 1982 called *An Ungentlemanly Act*. It starred Ian Richardson as Sir Rex Hunt. I suddenly realized that the drama unfolding on my screen had been filmed in the room I was sitting in! Mrs Hunt had moved out to Sulivan House on the night of the invasion. Several times after that I remembered the war when I looked out of a window and wondered what it must have been like to see Argentine troops in the garden and tanks patrolling Ross Road, driving on the right.

The hallway was graced with a huge map that hung on the wall and depicted the farms of the Falklands, as they were owned in 1883. Many of the names were familiar. A substantial proportion of the Islanders could trace their ancestry back well into the 19th century, a point that was not lost on them when talking to Argentines who almost always possessed shallower roots. Not that many of them did a lot of talking to Argentines.

Originally the house had been heated by peat, as had all other Island homes. Over the previous two decades oil had taken over but thankfully Sulivan had retained two open grates and that gave us a great deal of pleasure. Jean and I had been children in post-war England and we shared a love of an open fire. It was not merely to do with warmth and the thought of a dog on the mat; a fire was also focus, life, colour and movement. Here we had the ultimate – a local stone fireplace and an inexhaustible supply of peat. It was virtually a copy of the one we had admired in Government House during our interview visit. Peat was a revelation – what a wonderful fuel! We were both surprised at the gentleness and longevity of its burning, and the quality and evenness of its heat. It also had a glorious odour of... well, peat. It was an earthy, natural smell and after one had handled the peat, sniffing fingers brought the delicious odour of malt whisky. For me, whisky is rather like tobacco –

smelling it is more pleasurable than using it; but sniffing fingers is a nasty habit in a grown man.

The peat was cut by a local purveyor of the product, dumped outside our peat shed and then beautifully stacked inside. Before the advent of diesel and kerosene in the Falklands, most people had their own allotted peat banks. Those fit enough used to cut the stuff from the native earth and stack it to dry in 'riccles'. Some muscular traditionalists still do, but it is a hard way to earn a bit of energy from Mother Nature. The riccles were dismantled after a primary drying and the product carted to a personal peat shed. These still exist all over Stanley and generally consist of open lattice siding, which stops most of the rain getting in, but allows a free flow of air. Sulivan House had an old but magnificently proportioned peat shed.

On arrival we discovered our 'peat boy', Geordie. He was in his seventies and was particularly fastidious about the handling of peat and the preparation of the one fire that was his responsibility. It was probably the only remaining responsibility in Geordie's life. He was also on the 'black list'.

Alcoholism, of one form or another, seems to be a problem in most societies. The Falkland Islands has its share of alcoholics. However, in order to overcome the most self-destructive activities, the black list was created. This attempted not only to ban the individual from drinking alcohol for a period, but also banned people from supplying the person concerned. It could only work in a small society, and it only worked erratically in the Islands, but it was a helpful tool in the battle against individual oblivion. Geordie had been put on the list for his own good. He was cheerful enough about the whole thing. Who wouldn't be when the daily job lasted some two hours, but involved at the most ten minutes' work?

Geordie loved attending Sulivan House every day. He even came at weekends, when he received no pay for the visit. Mind you, he was always anxious to remind us of that fact. He would arrive around 8.30 a.m. and set to the task of eating his breakfast in the shed area next to our greenhouse. This would take quite a while. Then he would empty the ashpan from the fire of the previous evening, refill the peat buckets that were used to ferry the fuel to the fire and then set and light the fire. The buckets were worn out when we arrived, so I bought some new ones. Geordie complained bitterly that I hadn't acquired the right sort of bucket. Evidently, mine were not man enough for the job and wouldn't last five minutes. He wore a black beret (well, it looked black) and his clothes always had a slept-in appearance. He moved in a rather erratic manner, like a puppet controlled by a child. Some mornings, when the previous evening's breaking of the black list's grip was apparent on his breath and in his eyes, his movements would be even more discordant and occasionally he arrived with bandages swathed around his head, evidence of an 'accidental' fall.

The sweeping of the grate to clear the fine-grained but uniformly light grey ash, was done with a goose wing. The wing of an upland goose is a wonderful hearth brush; far superior to any product manufactured in brush shape in the sweatshops of far away Sheffield or Birmingham. Part way through his morning labours, Geordie would stop for 'smoko'. The Falklands has adopted this word as its own even though many say it originated in New Zealand. It described the morning break that farm hands had to have in the midst of their intensely physical work. It would include a cigarette and possibly a cup of tea and a cake. Latterly it has come to mean any old break in doing virtually anything and was a most useful invention, to be used sparingly by employers and frequently by employees.

Geordie smoked at every opportunity, mainly when he wasn't busy in the lip area drinking. He rolled his own, and the spindly, second-hand appearance of his cigarettes was a hallmark of the man. Just as it was with his ill-fitting clothes, his flaccid fag looked as though he had slept with it limp between mouth and pillow. He lived in the old folks' sheltered accommodation next to the hospital and he returned there after his two hours of marionetting and smoking at Sulivan. Occasionally he would trim the edges of the lawn with sheep shears – an activity about as efficient as crawling across Antarctica on hand and knees backwards. Also occasionally, he would tidy the peat shed; and he loved to chat.

He would, of course, chat to anyone within earshot and had a fund of fascinating stories from the Falklands of the past. On many occasions I found myself struggling to understand the sense of what he was saying. He had a casual way with the English tongue that matched his unkempt appearance, but I did a great deal of agreeing, which seemed to please him. For all I knew, he could have been asking for a swig of my whisky. He occasionally took one anyway, although he never knew that I knew. Sadly, he died in 1997. The maligned peat buckets had outlasted their detractor.

When Geordie stopped working for us, some months before his death, we decided that Jean could do the ten minutes or so of peat-related work per day. This was a successful bilateral decision as she took to the task with such a will and possessiveness that I was rarely allowed to make a fire or clear out the ashes. The peat shed was kept with a neatness that would have been the envy of any Japanese accountants interested in natural heat sources. The peat supplier once confided in me that it was the neatest peat shed in the whole of Stanley. I resisted the temptation to tell Jean for a while, as I felt that her humility could be affected by the news.

The peat, once delivered, was stacked so that it would dry over a period of time. Thus a rotational system was installed, ensuring that we consumed the oldest peat first. Emptying the ashpan was an interesting process, especially in a high wind. After the miraculous advent of wheelie bins, we were given two aluminium bins to hold ashes, as the remnants of a peat fire could contain residual heat for a long time. Jean, in fact, succeeded in proving this point by being the first person in Stanley to prove empirically that a plastic bin will melt when hot ashes are tipped inside it. The tray beneath the fire was rather larger than the opening in the aluminium bins; therefore, one had to contrive to pour feather-light ash from one exposed receptacle to another. In the normal wind one might as well have not bothered – the stuff went everywhere. The dust had a remarkably drying effect on one's hair. Expose your head for a fraction of a second to these pervasive hygroscopic particles and your hair just shrivels. Talk about dry and unmanageable! I suggested that just opening the back door and throwing the stuff out would be more efficient, as we would have achieved the same effect but spent less time.

Near to the peat shed was the greenhouse. This was an ancient lean-to structure that had seen far better days, but during our time in the Islands, the human resource to upgrade the thing was never available. Jean would potter away merrily in it for hours, growing things. A passing peer of the realm, the charming and resourceful Lord Strathcona, who was keen to demonstrate his engineering expertise, actually spent an afternoon fixing the roof-opening mechanism of this sagging edifice and confessed to having enjoyed the experience.

The peat fire was the focal pivot of my favourite room – the sitting room. There I had positioned the hi-fi and the television and it became the relaxation centre whenever time allowed. Although the leaving of family, friends and dog had been painful, there was yet another anguish. Back in the UK I had only recently acquired a remote-controlled mobile satellite dish of substantial dimension. There I could summon up some two hundred channels. Flicking through them had provided endless fun and wifely criticism. The option of replicating that pastime in the Falklands was simply not available.

When we first arrived on the Islands there had been only one television channel, BFBS – the British Forces Broadcasting Service. The programming was apparently determined by deciding which UK television programmes were most popular with the armed forces age group, and then buying them at a knock-down price to transmit in an amalgamated form to such places as Belize, Cyprus, Croatia and Germany. The outcome was a heavy emphasis on mindless soaps and violence. The fact that a live satellite link would have been exorbitantly expensive meant that the tapes had to be flown down, thus all the programmes were delayed by two weeks. This was of no consequence whatsoever when it came to soaps, although those travelling to and from the UK tended to find the sudden time warps confusing. Others said it made no difference as the plots were modular in nature and one could mix and match. However, it played havoc with Christmas. Carols from King's College were available on 7 January, and New Year's Eve programmes were relayed on the fourteenth. Things like the news and the weather forecast were missed out altogether, in case someone should get the wrong idea about what was really happening in the world. In December 1997 we acquired same-day TV as a new satellite made the option substantially cheaper, but prior to that the private sector was making headway in Stanley with CNN and some other choices imported from a South American footprint. When satellites can make footprints, then anything must be possible.

One day Des King, who had been the proprietor of the Upland Goose Hotel during the war and survived with honour, offered us some chickens, which he described as 'excellent layers'. He knew that we had enough space in the garden to accommodate the creatures and we asked the Public Works Department if they could come and build an appropriate shed. They provided a veritable wooden palace for these cautious cluckers and Des brought them round in sacks. There were originally four hens and a cockerel, although one of the hens subsequently had to be put down. We sought reinforcements to our ability to produce eggs by buying three maran hens from West Falkland.

These youngsters behaved as if they owned the place and were soon outlaying the East Falkland ones. Jean looked after them and things were progressing well until they all stopped laying at the beginning of the winter. We discovered that every other hen on the Islands seemed to go off laying at the same time. Finding eggs in Stanley became a real challenge, and we adopted the ritual remembered from post-war Britain of storing eggs in water glass, a syrupy preservative, when they were plentiful. Mind you, when it came to that time of year it could be difficult to get the water glass!

Peat, staff, chickens and views of ancient wrecks were all new. Yet we felt at home. Sulivan House was comfortable and inviting. We knew that we would be happy there.

Looking back on it, the settling in seemed to take hours rather than days. The whole orbit of work and socializing felt natural and seemed to fit. In no time at all I found myself instinctively using 'us' and 'we' in conversation, rather than 'you' and 'they'. For better or for worse, we had arrived.

Chapter 4

The daily journey to work was something that I must have undertaken over a thousand times over a five-year period and my first reaction to it was unalloyed pleasure. What a commute! The distance from Sulivan House to the quaintly named Secretariat is half a mile. On a calm day it is a very pleasant ten-minute walk. For our first week in the Islands, exhibiting all the freshness and enthusiasm of my honeymoon period, I walked it a few times. Then I found that my arms ached with the bulging case I carried. I also found that I needed the vehicle during the day, so I elected to drive. That was all very well – we were supplied with a vehicle – but it meant that Jean was immobile.

We decided that Jean's car, thoughtfully and riskily left in our son Paul's charge, should join us. So, after our first visit back to the UK, we delivered the ageing Golf to Gravesend for its seafaring adventure. Little did we realize what was in store. The vessel carrying it came through the mother of all storms (apparently the crew got worried when they saw the captain on his knees on the bridge, praying), and a forklift truck broke away from its moorings on the car deck. This bulky and jagged vehicle, having obtained its freedom, spent the stormy part of the voyage gaily crashing around among handily spaced vehicles. This was big boys' bagatelle; several cars were wrecked completely, and Jean's was very badly dented. Getting it fixed in Stanley seemed a real problem, but no, the resourcefulness of the local folk knew few bounds. Within a few weeks it was restored, the only remaining problem being the endless argument with an insurance company.

As you travel the London Underground to work, as you sit in an interminable motorway queue and as that bus fails to materialize, spare an envious thought for my two minutes' cruise to work along the harbour frontage of Ross Road at the statutory twenty-five miles per hour. Seldom would I find anything to hamper my progress. There were no traffic lights in the Islands and rarely any road works. When the Public Works Department decided to mend the road it was a cause of celebration, as the Stanley roads were notoriously weathered. So you think you've got potholes? Sometimes on the Falklands we got down beyond the wire reinforcing in the eroded concrete.

In spite of the occasional bump, it was bliss for a driver bearing the scars of many prolonged journeys to and from work in the UK. Very occasionally there would be a speed trap. The police had a radar device, and although it was rumoured that they found it distasteful to stop their relations, I was pretty sure that the scalp of the Chief Executive might constitute a success. My predecessor had direct experience of that fact when he was stopped on the Stanley by-pass. His comment in court, that he was merely charging his battery, was long remembered, and didn't serve to reduce the fine, or the merriment. The obvious place for the police to stake out was the Government House driveway, where they could be sure of hiding behind mature macrocarpa trees. I always kept a wary eye on that particular exit. Not that I was doing more than twenty-five miles per hour, you understand; I was more concerned with the calibration of their equipment.

The short journey provided a view that offered interest out of all proportion to the distance. I would reverse at speed, past the two peat ash bins and the gradually collapsing greenhouse, turn in the turning bay, and pull out on to the one-way street running along the eastern side of Sulivan House and separating us from Jhelum House. Jhelum House was smaller than Sulivan but similar in appearance. No more than twenty yards to Ross Road and the right turn. I would glance left. To the west, up the valley, lay the hills with names made famous from the war – Kent, Tumbledown, Longdon and the Two Sisters. Kent is evenly proportioned from this view, like a shallow pyramid, the radar facilities on the summit usually clearly visible, although they are at least ten miles away. Tumbledown looks like its name, rough and shapeless, whilst the Two Sisters are, not surprisingly, two in number and rise sharply into the coming weather.

As the prevailing air stream is from the west, it was common to look up the valley to see what was going to happen next. On a squally day in the winter, the approach of a snow shower was spectacular. A soft wall of greyness would whisper slowly down the valley and then seem to gather pace as it hurled white pellets in every direction. The hills to the west are the same grey quartzite with brownish grass that is characteristic of most of East Falkland. The gentle hills across the harbour are just a smaller version of the same geology.

I would always glance at the wreck of the *Jhelum*, sometimes spying cormorants perched on her, silhouetted against the rolling backdrop, then turn on to the main road running along the front. Ross Road, under the imaginative names of Ross Road East and Ross Road West, spans the harbour frontage. The first few hundred yards enables the early morning driver to settle to the immediate scene. The fact that the road is slightly elevated at this point, being about twenty feet above water level, meant that I could see across the bay to the Narrows, but not Stanley itself, as yet hidden by the brow of the rise. However, on a clear morning, and that was most mornings, I could see right across to the airport on Cape Pembroke Peninsula. The slanting wreck of the *Lady Elizabeth* was visible at the far end of the harbour. Being iron, its rusting hull created a colourful contrast to the greys and blues of most of the scene. A few hundred yards ahead, the memorial to the Battle of the Falklands stands prominently on a small headland. This particular edifice contains a great deal of detail, with bass reliefs of the battle, enumerating the ships that had a starring role in it.

The battle itself had been spectacular and a resounding victory for the British over the Germans. It took place on 8 December 1914 and was due to the fact that Winston Churchill, who was then in charge at the Admiralty, dispatched a squadron to the South Atlantic. The Germans had won the sea battle of Coronel (off the Chilean coast), and were dominating the region. The British had arrived in Stanley harbour and were taking on coal opposite Stanley when the German fleet was sighted making for the entrance to the harbour and not realizing that the British had arrived. All coaling was stopped in the hectic business of getting to sea for battle. The Germans were caught thoroughly off guard; they turned and ran, all their ships being sunk, including such famous names, to be repeated in the Second World War, as the *Scharnhorst* and the *Gneisnau*.

The First World War was not the only war that was brought to mind on this short stretch of road. There was a photograph from 1982 taken from this spot that is etched in my mind. It shows two immobile Argentine bodies lying in the gutter.

As I reached the crest of the shallow rise, there in front was a vista of Stanley. At the top of that knoll is one of the very best views in the Islands. It is worthy of a longer study than the transient glance that I could generally afford it. All the already described features of the harbour remain, but now the whole of the centre of the small town comes into view. To the right stands the dominating and reasonably impressive Government House, the home and office of His Excellency the Governor. Unfortunately, someone went and stuck a modern house in the front garden for the First Secretary to live in, so the view of the older house is obscured from this angle. Nevertheless, the whole thing looks solid – a suitable commentary on the firmness of British resolve.

More immediately to the right are thick gorse bushes. In November these are a riot of yellow, which is far more vibrant than one can imagine. It is as though a child had suddenly discovered the yellow in their paint box and had decided that the whole slope down to the road should benefit from that discovery. Gorse is a robust feature of the Falklands' spring and it smells strongly of coconut. Higher up and beyond Government House are the brightly coloured roofs of the Stanley houses;

the one painted as a Union Jack always catches the eye.

The Community School, which educates children aged eleven to sixteen, and anybody else who wants to learn, stands proudly against the southern skyline, elevated above the playing field, and is all the more impressive for its aspect.

Ahead is the straightness of Ross Road as it surges along the front passing most of the major buildings. In the distance the spire of the cathedral can be seen; nearer is the smaller spire of St Mary's, the Roman Catholic church, and opposite that, the utilitarian and unimaginative town hall. The government dockyard, which is seldom used as a dock at all these days, juts out into the harbour, and the small cream-coloured Gilbert House, where the eight councillors have their office, sits cosily at the landward end. In a fit of initiative, the then-director of public works, had decided to use fill material to enlarge the dockyard, and managed to achieve a significant amount of reclamation before the councillors spotted what was happening and brought it to a halt. On a still morning, Stanley reflects in the water as the logger ducks creak and the cormorants flap their wings energetically. The spires plunge downward in the blue mirror as a breath of wind distorts the scene.

Along the stretch of road in front of the Triangle (a wedge-shaped paddock to the east of Government House containing a helicopter landing pad) there is a length of the sea wall that is beloved by giant petrels. Any slight northerly component to a breeze and this wall, only about six feet high, provides uplift for these magnificent wizards of flight. Of all the wonderful bird life in the South Atlantic, there is none that plies the air as gracefully as the giant petrel. It swoops, it glides, and it allows its feathered wing tip to get within a micron of the surface of the water without touching it. It has a wonderful economy of movement. The poor old shags (cormorants) flap away vigorously just to get airborne, but the bigger and heavier petrels weave effortlessly through the air. They use the wind to advantage whenever they can and they thoroughly enjoy their in-built expertise. They have their own flight paths that are related to the micro airflows. One can deduce that easily, as when the wind is in a particular quarter, they will follow one another along the same route, albeit at a respectable distance, as though there is a giant petrel air-traffic controller somewhere.

The really weird sensation is to drive along to work and find that there is a giant petrel gliding along a parallel course, at your head height, about twelve feet from you and moving at precisely the same speed. So now you know that the giant petrel can glide at twenty-five miles per hour. However, they don't always observe the speed limit, as they have overtaken me from time to time. I could watch these creatures flying all day but the most amazing thing for me is the impassive expression on their faces. I suppose it isn't often that one can study the look on a bird's face in flight; they are usually flapping or flashing by too quickly. Not these grey-brown hang gliders. They slide through the air with such smoothness that one has ample time to study their visage. They show no emotion, their bills waver not, and they are disdainful, imperious and enormously gifted. They also love the sewer outfalls, a habit that rather spoils their attractiveness; the local name for them is 'stinker'.

If you were to opt for a brisk walk along this stretch of sea wall you would be in genuine danger of being hit on the head by a mussel. Such flying molluscs are not due to a previously unheard of mutation, but to the fact that sea gulls, showing incredible forethought, pick them out of the rocks and then fly over the wall, dropping them on to the concrete to smash them. The path and the road are often littered with fragments of mussel shells. The air is sometimes alive with feathery bombers and the patches of grass are often inhabited by rather satisfied-looking gulls. Occasionally the gulls mistakenly select small rocks for this treatment. Our worthy Attorney General had the windscreen of his car smashed in this unusual manner. Obviously the gull was taken to court and found guilty. The damages awarded were never paid.

In a small community everything is criticized by somebody and as the society is so small, that critic is generally heard, if not listened to, and carries a percentage weight out of all proportion to that which would be enjoyed in a larger, anonymous group. The helicopter pad caused quite a stir when it was installed. It had to be near the hospital for emergency cases. The rough seas and the sheer brutality of life on many Far Eastern fishing vessels provided opportunities for such unwanted use.

As soon as it became known that a pad was proposed it was criticized. It was thought by some to be a personal fad of the Governor's; it was held by others to be dangerous as it sloped and had undesirable wind characteristics. The playing field was thought to be a far better place for the pad. The Director of Education made it quite clear that, in her view, the school playing field was not ideal helicopter pad material. Location on the triangle might, it was said, disturb the Governor's own flock of sheep. However, the military wanted the pad and it was built. On occasions a Sea King would edge tentatively out of the sky towards the pad, creating more wind than even a petrel wanted, hovering noisily towards a gentle descent. The Falkland Islands government generally had a fire appliance alongside, with one of our chaps dressed in kitchen foil standing by. The scene was spectacular when glimpsed on the way to work.

The pad enjoyed happy use for a couple of years and then a new sweeping broom in the RAF decided that it really was too dangerous and banned his chaps from landing there. It had to be the playing field after all, and so the pad became a favourite site for seagulls to drop their mussels.

Sometimes there would be a flock of sheep being driven along the road to the abattoir, causing a rare traffic jam for a minute or two. Then there was the charming tradition of waving to other drivers. After a while it came automatically. Once the habit was formed it took a bit of breaking. It was during my first return holiday in the UK that I discovered the futility of waving to people on the M4.

The last few hundred yards of the journey took me past the old people's sheltered homes with their multi-coloured roofs, and the King Edward Memorial Hospital, with its own light blue roof, unintentionally, painted in the national colour of Argentina. In front of the Secretariat is the memorial to the brave men of 1982. It was designed thoughtfully. A replica of Britannia stands proudly atop the memorial itself. Around the horseshoe perimeter are the names of the heroes and their units. Many visitors lay wreaths there, and on 14 June every year the major remembrance takes place as the culmination of seventy-four days of retracing the pattern of the war. I turned right into Thatcher Drive and parked outside my office. Many Stanley roads are named after people or families who have played some part in the history of the Islands and the name of Margaret Thatcher will always carry respect in the Islands.

After a few days I got used to the two mighty cannons outside the office. I would struggle through the double doors, lurch up the narrow stairs and greet my PA, Maria, before settling into my office with its superb views across the harbour. Across the corridor was the Liberation Room, where the conditional surrender was signed in 1982. I realized during that first week that my impressions were correct; I was going to enjoy this job immensely.

In that enthusiastic dawn that goes with a new job, I suggested to some of my colleagues that working through lunch might be a good idea on certain days, and if they brought sandwiches we could get a great deal of work done during the lunch hour – well, hour and a quarter actually. They dutifully turned up with their packed lunches on a couple of occasions, but their demeanour told me that they lacked enthusiasm for the idea.

Then I discovered that a leisurely lunch at home is really part of the culture. As the community is so small there is no such thing as a 'school dinner'. Working mothers can get home and shove some calories into the little citizens-to-be. I gave up with good grace and discovered for myself the truth that has been lost to recent generations of UK dwellers – a sensible lunch at home and a bit of relaxation away from the workplace improves concentration in the afternoon.

Chapter 5

We climbed steadily through ten thousand feet. Captain Morgan Goss, in the pilot's seat beside me, was as impressed with the view as I was, and he has the chance to see it nearly every day. It was one of those wonderful occasions when everything conspires to create a perfect flight. The Pilatus Norman Islander plane of the Falkland Islands Government Air Service purred contentedly through the clear air as we approached the middle of Falkland Sound, the stretch of water separating the two main islands. It was late afternoon as we headed for Stanley. We were alone in the small aircraft and Morgan had decided to climb to eleven thousand feet in order to enjoy the view. 'It is unusually clear today,' he said over the headset above the drone of the engines. We agreed that he would be wholly justified in describing a wide circle so that we could view the full three-hundred-and-sixty-degree panorama. A gentle turn ensued and there it was: the entire Falklands, the size of Connecticut or Ulster, map-like below us.

It could never be mistaken for either of those other places, even from such height. It is bare. If ever a landscape could be described as naked, it was there below us. It is also primal, as though very little has happened since the dawn of time. There is no lushness to draw the eye, no soft green and no fluffiness of trees. Evidence of man's influence is scanty and there is no hint of a building. There is no linear road, no plume of smoke, no haze caused by multiple exhausts – just land and water. In some places the straightness of the coastline catches the eye; in others the pattern seems random and sunken, as though the sea has invaded the contours. We could see Cape Dolphin to the north, stretching like a finger towards the horizon, pointing at the vast emptiness of the South Atlantic. To the north-west the spinal hump of the Jason Islands was in view and on the western fringes appeared the thin shape of New Island. The rocky headlands around Cape Meredith at the south of West Falkland were identifiable and we picked out the relatively flat Sea Lion Island to the south of East Falkland.

The smooth red nose of the Islander slowly came back on our original north-easterly heading and the whole of the gently undulating plain of Lafonia stretched away to our right, as the hills around Stanley appeared clearly through the windscreen. Only the rather mystical and inaccessible Beauchene Island far to the south was out of our vision.

We began our long descent towards Stanley, Morgan cutting back the throttle gently. I watched the instrument that measures climb rate slip below the level mark. Details sprang out of the previously amorphous landscape. The initial impression of uninviting barrenness can be grossly misleading. If you were to visit the Islands for a day and the morning was one of those sunless, steely grey affairs when the white grass is at best insipid neutral beige and the water reflects the lack of colour in the sky, then justifiably you would pronounce the place to be well down the scenery league table. In fact, there have been visitors who have been far more insulting – Charles Darwin for one, in 1833. However, just wait for the afternoon. The weather can change with phenomenal speed and your early conclusion could prove to be totally unjustified.

Sunlight is very important to the appearance of the Falklands. The air is so clear that as soon as clouds depart, the sky assumes a deep blue that is reminiscent of either the tropics, or the rendition of a cheap colour film. The brilliance of that sky impacts upon everything else, the water in particular. The sun dances reflectively on sea, river and pond alike. The distance and clarity of the views demand inspection and study. It can be dazzling.

The general picture is one in which the pervasive whitegrass provides the matrix. This is not a grass that ever goes green. Rain and sun merely emphasize its frustratingly unverdant nature and prove the fact, once and for all, that the grass is not greener in the Falklands. On that initial mustard beige palette, the varying hues of grey quartzite appear as the rock surges and slashes through the surface of the peat. The most intriguing examples of this are the stone runs; nowhere else in the world do they occur in anything like this abundance. These look from a distance like rivulets of stone running down the hillside. On close inspection, they are undeniably static. They consist of sizeable chunks of rock, often pointing skywards at crazy angles, yet it is self-evident that at some stage they have been able to move freely. Here is a substantial geomorphological challenge: how on earth could they have been formed? Many geologists have suggested solutions. Erudite papers have been written on the subject, but to date none are wholly confident or convincing. The stone runs remain an enigma, but they create a distinctive pattern, as though a playful giant had scraped the hillsides with a large-toothed comb.

Sometimes a narrow valley is surprisingly green, the whitegrass having been eaten away, or never having been there to start with. Where there is such lushness, the sheep congregate. Normally the sound of a plane or helicopter causes them to run rather stupidly in the direction of flight, which only prolongs their disturbance. Lakes appear suddenly in the most unexpected places – hilltops, for instance. This merely adds another entry in the puzzle for landform specialists to catalogue. These lakes are generally fairly shallow, but come in all shapes and sizes. The rivers, where they achieve any size, cut through the landscape creating impressive little gorges as they snake along their sparkling courses to the ocean.

Across the barrenness, the fences stretch for miles, the straightness of their line clear evidence of man. It is astonishing how variable the grassland can look on two sides of one of these fences. I know full well that it is to do with different grazing regimes and I am always astonished that the presence of a few sheep on one side of a fence can change the colour and appearance of vast tracts of countryside. One seldom sees sheep munching near the fence to prove the process.

The sparse roads lie tape-like across the panorama. Tracks left by military BVs and struggling Land Rovers appear as dark brown wavy lines, sometimes converging and spreading again at a pass or field gate, gloriously stodgy, like the surface of a particularly moist Black Forest gateau. Settlements occur very rarely, but when they do they stand out. There is always a white house with a coloured roof. Beside it are outhouses, dog kennels, and the ubiquitous graveyard of old vehicles, waiting patiently as they rust for their long-promised reincarnation as employed spare parts.

Flying low over the jagged coast as the sun shafts its way through the blue water to the stone-white sand, all the hues of aquamarine and turquoise appear. Sometimes a body of stagnant water creates colours that for all their brilliance seem unnatural. One is reminded of chemical settling tanks. The thought is unworthy, but nature can play tricks on you in the Falklands.

From the air, Stanley is a stretched rectangle of streets and buildings. Far tidier from above than from below, it nestles cosily along the waterfront. I have always got a kick from flying over areas that I know on the ground. That may be the result of yesteryear's cartography lectures, or it could be the desire to see everything in perspective. Whatever the cause, I have long been capable of boring the rest of the family with photographs taken from aircraft. Unfortunately, clarity through a plane window is never of a high quality, and this kind of shot is far less arresting when one's offspring mutter mild protests staring at the projected slide, than it seems at the time. Nevertheless, there is something appealing about the breadth of vision possible from altitude. As far as Stanley is concerned, it can all be seen in one glance – the sixteen hundred or so people, the shops, those I work and rub shoulders with, the whole microcosm of existence that passes for civilization in this uttermost part of the earth. There is no settlement on this scale within four hundred miles. If you travel those miles and stumble across that humanity, it is markedly different and would seem alien to the denizens below.

Looking down on the land is fun, but the reciprocal act is equally appealing – just gazing up at the patterns in the sky. The entire world has sky to look at, but tourists and inhabitants comment on the fact that in the Islands the sky is not something to be taken for granted. So often it demands attention. For one thing, it is there to be seen, as there are no tall buildings, no trees and no towering mountains to obscure it, so the perspective is widened. For another, the lack of haze in the atmosphere lends distance to the view. Then there is the mobility as the wind fusses the clouds on their eastward journey, adapting their shapes in the process. The deep blue backdrop on a sunny day enhances the wispy patterns of cirrus and the bulging white candyfloss effect of fat cumulus. Very rarely does a vapour trail spoil the natural elements or lessen the brightness. If it does, it's one of ours! The sun uses the clouds to produce endless variations in colour and edging effects, changing almost too quickly. By the time one has dashed to get the camera, the shot on offer has changed.

This Falklands sky often creates a distinctly three-dimensional impression. At a distance, a shower falling from cloud looks as though an artist has smudged his watercolour. Storms provide threateningly black skies and at times the cloud will hug the rolling hills as though someone had packed cotton wool around the contours. Rainbows have a starkness and brilliance that looks unnatural and sunsets can challenge any in the world for sheer luminosity.

This clarity of the atmosphere has another benefit as darkness falls and the lack of towns and human-induced lighting merely adds to the stars' lustre. On a moonless night the Milky Way seems so brilliant as to be part of this world. It is a roof over our heads, a canopy that can almost be touched. The stars merge with each other into a dusty silver band across the heavens. Everywhere is variety and interest. No Plough, no Pole Star, but the Southern Cross, Orion and other vaguely familiar patterns present themselves.

On one of the many clear days, where the sky meets the sea, the horizon can be seen for what it is – a boundary rather than a misty nothingness. It is sharp and precise. If ever there were a straight line in nature, this is it, even though the sheer distance of the view must surely enable us to spot some curvature.

The most memorable scenery of all has to be that around the coastline. Whether the imposing irregular grey rocks or the virgin curve of white sand, it is this boundary where land meets sea that clutches at the memory and begs for visit after visit. Why did I find it so enticing? It may have been to do with the cleanliness and the unspoiled nature of everything. It certainly included the proliferation and tameness of the wildlife. I rather liked the fact that other human beings were few and far between. The most treasured rural retreats in the UK will always seem over-populated to me now. There is also a welcome lack of any non-natural noises. The impact on the senses is fantastic.

The spray splashing skyward from smashing against the rocks can be seen for miles. Whiter than white, it seems to hang on the air, enjoying the freedom of flight until it returns shimmering to the parent ocean. Getting close to this action is a natural response. To stroll along the broad, gentle beaches with time to spare is to indulge in a pleasure available to all too few. There is an overwhelming sensation of freedom. The multiple cares of modern existence pale in the awesome light of creation undisturbed by humanity. The predatory ruthlessness of nature is there all right, but the overall effect is more often one of serenity and balance. The breakers curl and foam, their regular sound resting the ears. Penguins watch the land from the clear water by popping their heads up above the surface and scanning the beach until satisfied. Then they emerge to shake themselves and put on their walking boots. The Falklands flightless steamer ducks (loggers) simply stooge around. Sometimes elephant seals lie like huge velvet cylinders, emitting noises and odours best forgotten.

Offshore, for the first few hundred yards, the presence of kelp is a major factor. It would be known as seaweed in the UK, but this stuff is prolific, heavy, and moves erotically in the swell. It smoothes any roughness of the sea and assumes a sinuous writhing motion. It sparkles in diamond flashes when it reflects the sunlight and can conjure up the impression of a skilled belly dancer. If that analogy doesn't work for you, don't blame me. It is also a home for myriads of sea creatures, some of them not even identifiable or classifiable, as was discovered when the government carried out its littoral baseline survey before drilling for oil began. Underwater it is a veritable forest, swaying in the movement of the sea and blocking the sunlight from the ocean floor.

One memorable day in January 1997, Jean and I walked from the small settlement on New Island, which is a privately owned island off the west of West Falkland, with just two spasmodically inhabited houses, to the northern end. We ran the gauntlet of attacking skuas and emerged into an area as magical as any I have ever experienced. The morning clouds burned away and a hot sun warmed us. There, within a half-mile stretch, we came across a breathtaking selection of the very best that the Falklands has to offer, both in terms of scenery and wildlife; and it was world class.

A substantial Gentoo penguin colony in the middle of a shallow amphitheatre was worthy of many hours' study. Further on in a small rocky bay, a pod of dolphins began to show off their leaping and splashing abilities only yards from us. They were Peale's dolphins, and occur only in the Falklands and adjacent South America. Their white underbellies were stark against the black of the rest of their supple bodies as they leapt elastically clear of the water, only to belly flop back with abandon. They calmed down and adopted their languid circular motion, where their fins emerged as arched bodies looped in and out of the water, cutting it like a knife. What a crowd-pleasing performance for just two people!

Beyond we encountered an enormous triple colony of rockhopper penguins, king cormorants and black browed albatrosses all nesting together in a truly multi-racial settlement. The albatrosses were flying in and out along predictable flight paths; the cormorants were doing the same but with far more effort. Watching the two rather different flying styles landing on a steep rock face littered with nests was rather like watching a Denis Norden programme of out-takes. Both birds employ the technique of sticking their feet out in front and losing air speed until they stall with the evident aim of crashing as near to their nest as possible. Not all of them seem to be able to spot their own nest from the air. There was constant slipping and sliding, falling over, and landing directly on top of friends and neighbours. Nevertheless they muddled through amid screeches and ribald comments to explain to their mates why they were late, and expound on the state of fishing: 'I swallowed one this big – honest.'

The rockhoppers sat on their nests or clambered patiently along vertigo-inducing pathways. We sat and watched, just them and us. There were two of us and thousands of them. It was their place; it felt like their place too. We were guests, uninvited but not unwelcome, simply irrelevant. The environment was crowded but we were miles from humanity. Sometimes it is hard to be non-intrusive, but we were as low key as we could be. Across the mirror sea, which looked tropical in colour and sheen, was the lush-looking Saddle Island, shaped as its name. The grass there looked artificially green, but then most of it was tussock grass.

Tussock grass is quite an experience. The first time we walked in it we felt as though we had stumbled across another world. Initially it just looked like big clumps of rather coarse grass. As we walked further we realized that it was growing well above our heads and we were walking on white sand in between the clumps. The randomness meant that there was no clear pathway through this jungle but one could stroll confident of reaching the destination. It was like a *Star Trek* set, it had an alien atmosphere. Great fronds of the stuff waved above us and cut out the whistling wind. It is uncannily silent deep in the tussock. On that occasion on Sea Lion Island the tussock was thin enough to be able to stroll through, but it isn't always so. Thick tussock can be impenetrable and one finds oneself staggering across the top of it, wondering what may be underneath and hoping that it isn't a sea lion. They sometimes creep into the tussock to rest and are not overjoyed at being disturbed. Tussock rarely exists more than half a mile from the sea. Grazing over the years has pitifully reduced it and what can be seen today is but a fragment of the original area. Of course, conservation measures have been taken, replanting has been organized, but it will be a long haul. However, where it remains in its original state, mainly on offshore islands, from a distance it looks like long, rich, green grass, and provides a wonderful contrast to the stark cliffs and the deep blue sea.

Our eyes lingered on the lushness then wandered back across the half mile of water separating the smaller island from us. The smoothness of the surface of the water and the lack of any wind allowed us to see and hear any movement that broke it and the wealth of activity was a revelation. Fur seals were enjoying themselves swishing around in the liquid crystal water. Fish of various kinds splashed in random fashion, and seabirds of many types dived and surfaced. The king cormorants appeared to work together to secure their food, forming a huge mass of several hundred and then team diving. We assumed there was a shoal of some kind under the surface, and if so, the members of it must have had a bit of a shock to find themselves attacked by cormorants en masse.

Black browed albatrosses ooze aerial competence. With an eight-foot wingspan they have an imperial appearance as they glide across the sun. They are capable of striking suddenly and decisively in spite of their relaxed air, rather like the Brazilian football team. A slow build-up, ambling at a few feet above the water, or knocking the ball around sideways in midfield, then a fish or opening is spotted, and speed replaces stooging. The fish is snapped up, the goal is scored. Everything returns to near normal, except the stomach is full or the match is won.

The rockhopper penguins march in columns, some from sea to nest, others from nest to sea. All appear to have purpose, there is no wandering about, and they seem to know where they are going. Their fish shop is always open, and they approach it in a methodical manner. They look ridiculous with their yellow crests, but then we probably look massive and equally comical to them. The birds dominate the air, the penguins possess the land, and the sea teems with life; this is one of the very best Falkland experiences.

Most winters bring snowfall to the Falklands, but never as much as the folks back in England seem to imagine. The fact that the war was fought in the depths of a Southern Hemisphere winter created the impression in sweltering London that the Falklands is dominated by tundra. It is not so, but when the snow does come, it can be magnificent. It covers the neutral colours of the grassland and it hides the untidiness of humanity. Even a rusting JCB can look attractive when laced with icicles. The snow purifies the environment and often, encouraged by the wind, it drifts into artistic shapes. It sweeps around obstacles, fills up untidy ditches and when the sun emerges after the storm, the whole place glistens and sparkles. It is worth being around for, but the tourists tend to miss it, some of the penguins miss it, and many of the inhabitants whoosh off to the Northern Hemisphere summer and miss it. Winter can be a peaceful and enjoyable time. The winds are surprisingly quieter than in the summer, and the evenings by the fireside are long and relaxing.

It is during the winter, when the wind is in the south, that the proximity of Antarctica can be appreciated. Trudging through compacted snow over low hills on a darkening afternoon it is not hard to imagine how Scott felt. The dry air is cool and crisp to breathe. On an overcast day, when the snow gusts are swirling, the sea and sky are as uninspiring as the concrete of the South Bank's National Theatre. The place has an iron spirit, the sparkle has gone and been replaced by an atmosphere that is potentially threatening. The air is biting; there is an absolute lack of cosiness or warmth. To plan to survive in such conditions requires courage and nerve as well as preparation and skill. We knew that such a scene provided an experience to treasure. So we tended to absorb the atmosphere and scurry back to the peat fire.

'It reminds me of Dartmoor,' say visitors from Devon. 'Similar to the Western Isles,' mutter the Scots. 'The uplands of Tasmania are like this,' say the Antipodeans. Those from St Helena admit it is different. In truth, it is unique. The physical characteristics serve to demonstrate that the Falklands are like nowhere else. And it isn't only the appearance that is so independent. Never mind the endless comparisons, they only convey a part of the truth. One must simply enjoy the place for its own sake.

Chapter 6

Walking through the fields of Naseby in Northamptonshire, one would be hard pressed even to imagine the charging cavalry of Prince Rupert or the disciplined behaviour of the New Model Army. Strolling around Waterloo (the one in Belgium), it is rather easier to picture the dramatic events of 1815. It is, after all, over one hundred and fifty years closer and the Belgians make a bit more of their site than do the yeomen of Northamptonshire. In their enthusiasm for history and tourism they have constructed a truly massive mound complete with plinth and lion statue. But aside from such artificial memorials, war leaves its scars on a place even though the passage of time covers and heals. In the Falklands the war is recent and the scars are still raw, both on the landscape and in the people's minds.

The task force set foot on the Falklands in the early hours of 21 May 1982. Over the next two days the weather was relatively kind to them as cloud and mist provided some cover for the establishment of a beachhead. But on Sunday 23, the sun rose in a clearer sky and rolled westward towards the waiting squadrons in southern Argentina. Lieutenant Hector Volponi slept at the air force base in Rio Grande, his mind full of dreams founded on tension and excitement. Aboard the pitching flagship, HMS *Hermes*, Lieutenant Martin Hale may also have slept fitfully.

Volponi was twenty-seven. His natural aptitude and flair had been blended with discipline in years of training. Over the last few days he had carried out several sorties from his homeland against the British and their landing at San Carlos. He had mixed feelings as he looked at his single-seater Dagger aircraft, the Israeli-built version of the French Mirage. It was no match for the British Harriers in combat, and in attacking ships at San Carlos with heavy bombs it was operating at the limits of its range. It seemed strangely lifeless as it sat on the tarmac. Yet like Volponi himself, his plane was primed for a fight.

Volponi realized that he had aged in the past few days. Suddenly war had come to him. He had been in the very eye of the storm, flashing over the barren hillsides and bearing down on British warships, delivering his deadly load from a daringly low altitude. He had learned what it was like to survive under live anti-aircraft fire. On 1 May a sidewinder missile had been unleashed towards him by a Sea Harrier (it could have been fired by Martin Hale), but he had managed to escape back to Argentina where he had phoned his young wife, pregnant with their second child. She had been mightily relieved. He knew that she dreaded every mission and longed for the certainty of his return. He had written to her the day before, 'Each mission makes me age ten years; my stomach is in knots.' In that letter he had ruminated on the experience of war: 'Sometimes I wake up not knowing where I am, or what I am doing, and sometimes I feel as if I am in the middle of a dream. But reality is harsh, fear is mixed with courage.' He concluded: 'Each time I go on a mission, I forget about me and give myself to my country, because that is the way it must be.'

In a brief episode of time he had become a hero. He had proved himself in an ultimate test of manhood. Yet in spite of all that, his job was to return once more to the savage hell that San Carlos had become for both sides. To be outstandingly courageous once is an achievement that we may ponder with awe, but to keep on being courageous when you are aware of the risks and probabilities is even more impressive. The day wore on, the pre-flight briefings and preparations ran their course. Volponi struggled into his flying suit and strapped his mission instructions and notes to his thigh. Eventually he was able to climb the familiar ladder, exchange pleasantries with the ground crew and sink into the lonely cockpit.

Over sixteen years later, on 2 September 1998, a small group sat in the Liberation Room across the corridor from my office. The mood was sombre as Ken Greenland, the Chief of Police, relayed to Keith Watson, the Coroner and Russ Jarvis, the First Secretary from Government House, the details of a recent investigation on Pebble Island. I sat in the chair. Russ, with his lively grey hair and keen administrative ability, was the senior FCO man in town. Although I was Acting Governor at the time, he did the contact work with London. Keith was our Senior Magistrate, effectively the local judge; a middle-aged likely-lad solicitor from the north-east of England with a sharp mind and a canny sense of what was right.

I glanced respectfully at the envelope containing the fragments of human bones that had been found. Although we did not yet have the certainty that could be derived from DNA testing, we had little doubt as to the sequence of events on that May afternoon. Hector Volponi's Dagger had been approaching the British along with his commander Carlos Martinez, and been made aware by radio of enemy planes in the area. They decided to make for home as quickly as they could; too many Argentine military assets were being lost. He trailed Martinez by about a mile, no more than six seconds, as they described a wide arc in banking to the left. The northern shoreline of Pebble Island was approaching rapidly. Something caught his eye. He shouted, 'Harriers, Harriers!' over the radio. They were his last words and almost his last thoughts. Martin Hale in one of the Sea Harriers fired a sidewinder. It homed inexorably in on the nearest source of heat, the tailpipe of Hector's Dagger. The explosion when the missile hit C437 almost certainly killed Volponi outright. His plane was no longer capable of flight and plummeted to earth at high speed, the thudding impact being felt by the inhabitants of Pebble Island and their Argentine occupiers alike. Wreckage, appropriately shaped as a tear drop, came to rest over a wide area and the peat bog on the side of First Mountain absorbed and hid much of the evidence as the cries of the sea birds returned, replacing the echoes of explosion. Two Sea Harriers celebrated and turned northwards towards their floating home.

It took a while for the Argentine forces on Pebble Island to extract the mangled remains from the wreckage. The notes strapped to the now lifeless thigh were read as evidence of identity rather than as mission plans. The mortal remains of Hector Volponi were transported to Argentina and buried by his grieving wife. But now, that package on the table contained additional pieces that had once formed the frame of a fighter pilot as the peat gave up some of its secrets. Peat tends to flow, it expands and contracts, and it moves objects around. Another scar had suddenly flared to claim the attention of the public.

As we discussed the most suitable course of action, I felt immense compassion for the widow and her teenage children. Hector Volponi would have been in his mid-forties, the very prime of life. In all likelihood, the fifteen-year-old son, as yet unborn on that May day, would provide the DNA that would establish identity. The thought rammed home the closeness of the past and the tingling ghastliness of war.

Rarely does a tourist come to the Islands without asking questions about the war. It is, after all, what the Islands became famous for. The bringing back to Bristol of Brunel's Great Britain in 1970 was nothing compared to what happened in 1982. Yet that tense winter is seldom spoken of by the Islanders and very rarely mentioned in talking with each other. It is as though all the local conversations have been had. Everyone knows more or less what happened to themselves and to everyone else throughout the seventy-four days of occupation. They know who was courageous, they mutter about who might have had Argentine sympathies and they also realize that the histories written and the films made subsequently were never fully accurate.

I came to appreciate that the recollections possessed a dream-like quality. There must have been an immense feeling of unreality when sudden occupation was followed by the uncertainties of an Argentine administration that was both cobbled together and systematically thwarted. Of all people, I was aware that it was hard enough to administer the place with the tacit acceptance of the population. If the Islanders were actively opposed to being governed, civil harmony would be totally unattainable. The bizarre nature of the occupation was emphasized by events such as Argentine troops pleading for food, Stanley Airport being bombed by the RAF, and one's children being evacuated to Camp. They were mightily harrowing times.

A generation has not yet passed, but even now, the memories, though easily recaptured, are somehow not so prominent. Yet if you visit the Argentine War Cemetery, then the horror and futility of the whole episode bears down on you. This is a carefully managed scar. It was visited by Argentine relatives in supervised groups until 1999, when restrictions on their entry were lifted. It is an out of the way place. A special track from the Mount Pleasant to Darwin road, itself only a larger track, brings one to an area that is effectively hidden from any nearby vantage point. The view is only of the gently rolling whitegrassed slopes and the white-fenced cemetery. The sound is of small plastic crosses, fixed by visiting relatives, tinkling and banging in the wind against the larger bare white wooden crosses, all two hundred and thirty-seven of them. They stand in lines, the grass manicured, the white fencing keeping sheep out and demonstrating to all that this is indeed a different place. There are names on some of the crosses, presumably there was identification on the bodies, but even sadder are the majority, which simply state: 'An Argentine soldier known only unto God.'

In addition, there is the immensely poignant paraphernalia left by grieving relatives: plastic flowers losing their colour in the sunlight, fading photographs of family groups or the dead loved one; even semi-political statements jarring against the atmosphere of regret. Some are blown by the wind, some rest at an angle against a white cross. Occasionally, those grieving have simply selected an anonymous grave upon which to focus their memories. The area is neat and well kept. It is a moving place, an artificial place; it just doesn't seem to belong. It is at odds with the more natural serenity of the Islands.

Retracing the journey back along the track, there is time to reflect that maybe, even for their relatives, there might be a sense that there was a great deal of good to come out of the war. For Galtieri the gamble was lost, but for the people of Argentina, although they keenly felt disappointment at the failure to secure a piece of land they felt was rightfully theirs, the defeat brought democracy and improved economic prospects.

Continuing on towards Darwin, there is a memorial by the roadside. From that verge one can walk down a small shallow valley to where Colonel 'H' Jones won his VC. The heroism of Colonel Jones will long be remembered, but it is only when visiting the site of his attack that the sheer desperate bravery of what he did in unpicking a solid defensive position can be grasped. He was running diagonally up the gently sloping side of that small shallow valley towards an Argentine machine gun position, when he was picked off by a sniper holed out on the opposite bank. The position that the sniper fired from is discernible. The distance seems so short; the closeness of the machine gun position to where Jones fell is only a few yards away. Upland geese fly over the spot, their wings beating the air provide the only sound. The very earth cries out that we should remember. The scar is real and painful.

Another VC was awarded posthumously to Sergeant Ian Mackay. Here again phenomenal gallantry was displayed in attacking a strong enemy position. This time it was on the rocky slopes of Mount Longdon. Those present at the time remember the blackness, the stench, the smoke and the noise that had come to one of the most remote parts of the world. Over seventeen years later, Sergeant Mackay's mother came to remember yet again what had happened. Many of the local people remembered with her. The driving resolve and guts of those who liberated the Islands must never be forgotten.

Ken Lukoviac will never forget, because he was there. He was a paratrooper at Goose Green. He fought under Colonel Jones. He mourned the death of his commander and many of his close friends. Ken hated the war. It made him bitter. His mind would dwell for years on the futility of the awful experiences he had survived. He wrote a harsh book about them, entitled *A Soldier's Song*. The words were penned in a manner that portrayed raw anger and helplessness. Ken came back to the Falklands in 1995 to re-visit Goose Green and to write an article for the *Mail on Sunday*. He brought a photographer with him; the photographer clicked and clicked wherever he went.

Ken began his visit by interviewing folk in Stanley, and that included me. I was astonished at the angst that was still pent up within him. He was openly resentful of everything to do with the Falklands. The questions were intelligent and interesting, but they were slanted in a manner that warned me of negative conclusions whatever I said. And all the time his photographer clicked and clicked. He clicked facing me; he clicked from the side, with the light one way then the other. He got on his knees, he stood on a chair, he took longer shots and shorter shots, and he re-loaded again and again.

Ken went to Goose Green; he visited other settlements, and he mixed with the locals. They welcomed him with an understanding warmth and friendliness that is reserved for those very special men who fought. And that reception changed Ken dramatically. He was impressed by the attitudes, by the progress, by the lifestyle, by the freedom and especially by the children and the confidence they had to grow up in a free society. He began to realize that his awful experience had really provided freedom for these people. The ubiquitous photographer clicked pictures of youngsters playing, of mothers cradling babies in their arms and Ken's bitterness was transformed into pride. He reverently placed a wreath on the memorial outside the Secretariat, and on it he wrote, 'It wasn't for nothing'.

Sea Lion Island, to the south of East Falkland, was ignored by the war. There was never any point in it being occupied, as it had no strategic value. There are no minefields and no bomb craters. But a significant scar exists. On a gently sloping hillside, just above the ruins of a Belsen–like furnace built to incinerate cute penguins for their natural oil, is a small fenced graveyard. There lie the remains of Sue Whitley, the wife of the Falklands vet in 1982. On 12 June as the British land forces closed in on Stanley, a stray naval shell plummeted into a house near the racecourse. Sue was one of three to die and the remarkable beauty of Sea Lion Island is a fitting setting for her grave, which is inscribed 'And let the winds of the heavens dance between you'.

The physical scars mature. The bits of downed aircraft get fewer and fewer. The mobile Argentine soup kitchens on Tumbledown rust away. Still, even seventeen years on, one can find twisted tins of Argentine origin in hollows in the rocks where the young conscripts must have waited anxiously for the arrival of the inevitable forward momentum of the British. The mines nestle deeper in the peat, waiting for the day when technology can locate them. The locals remember, resentful at times, forgiving at times but never forgetting.

The scars of the mind mature as well. But resentment that the whole episode ever happened is still strong and in many was as focused on the British as on the Argentines. After the first Argentine foot landed on that desolate beach on 1 April 1982, the Falklands would never be the same again.

Chapter 7

OIL – THE BUILD-UP

The search for oil started for me on a November day in 1994 when I had been in the job barely three months. As I sat in the Council Chamber eight thousand miles from home, I could hardly help wondering at the fact that my casual sifting of the *Sunday Times* nine months before had brought me to this moment. Here questions had to be answered in public and most of them were being directed at me. As the Honourable Chief Executive I was cast in the role of the chap who introduced all the legislation. My ego was being massaged so much it was sore to the touch, but my grasp of procedure and standing orders was scanty to say the least. His Excellency the Governor, David Tatham, occupied the Chair, looking appallingly well ordered. His owlish glasses gave him an aura of wisdom.

Twelve Honourable members of the legislative council sat in front of him behind tables arranged in an oval formation. The Attorney General, the Financial Secretary, the Military Commander and myself made up the non-political members. The eight who had been elected broke into two groups, the three on Executive Council (equivalent to the Cabinet in the UK) and the five who weren't. They had been warm and friendly prior to appointment and had been welcoming since arrival, yet now, as I sought a helpful smile, they looked more combative than I had taken them for. I had assumed that the underlying aggression in some of their questions was friendly jousting, but on reflection I realized that they had been keen on extracting time-constrained promises from me. Non-executive teeth can bite.

The walls around were panelled in dark plywood and behind the Governor hung large photographs of Her Majesty and Prince Philip with medals liberally distributed about their persons. The other three walls were graced with rather smaller photographs of past governors. In subsequent meetings my eyes would sometimes wander along this historic line. The images of Excellencies fell into three groups: those who would have been winners in a Tchaikovsky look-alike competition; those who had cultivated the appearance of a matinee idol; and those who had that impatient air that belies irritation with the photographer. No doubt they were overwhelmingly impressive in their day, but on these walls they looked ill at ease. Now space was running out – there had been so many governors that after Governor Tatham there would be no room on the wall. Subsequently, David secured that last place on the grid, and also stole a march by modernizing the tradition and becoming the first one in colour! Such segmentation of the gubernatorial market was opposed by some, who proposed to take a black-and-white picture of the coloured one, just to keep things in balance. The future of the dynasty was only secured by a refurbishment of the chamber in 1999 that realigned our ex-leaders by double-bunking them.

Intrusive microphones had been placed on the tables to catch every word. Bottled water was also thoughtfully provided so that the players in this drama would not suffer from dehydration. What could be more innocent than pouring this welcome fluid into one's tumbler and indeed offering to do so for others? Yet the sound was liable to be picked up by the microphones and create for all listeners the ambience of an Irish drinking club. Not only were the deliberations in this place broadcast live, they were also repeated to ensure that those who might have missed the actual performance clicked for the action replay. This was a form of torture for the participants as well as the listeners. It amplified certain small, and hitherto unnoticed, personal inadequacies. The human brain may unwittingly jump into partial disengage mode when one stands up to speak in public. This crashing of one's natural software can arrest the flow of thought. Rather than being allowed a few minutes to re-boot or scream for help, the 'ums', 'ers', 'you knows' and 'I means' are ruthlessly conveyed to all.

In order to highlight the inadequacy the supermarket would eschew musak for the local radio. Thus 'Moon River' played by sumptuous strings was replaced by proceedings of the legislative council. The rationale behind this decision was nothing to do with the quality of the speeches but based on the premise that any local material is better than none.

However incongruous the similarity, we were engaged in a law-making process equivalent to Westminster itself. Bills required three readings and a committee stage, and that was more complex for me to get the hang of than it might sound. I had to jump up and down to say the right things at the right time. In the committee stage of a bill one can remain seated. This is useful for resting the knees but only served to add to my confusion. I had imagined that for such a committee we would retire to an anteroom, have a cup of tea and a chat among ourselves, and then return to the main chamber. No such luck, we just ploughed on in situ. The participants surveyed my unease with the air of Islanders who are thoroughly conversant with the many and varied inadequacies of expatriates. It was a look I came to know very well indeed. I realized my only hope was to muddle through and reach the calm waters of the adjournment debate. I knew I had the support of the ever-helpful Attorney General on my left as well as the Clerk, Claudette, who pulled faces and beamed to indicate my aptitude rating.

This support from my learned friend the Attorney General was not to be sniffed at. Before I even left for the Islands, one of my predecessors had said to me, 'If David Lang tells you to jump out of an upstairs window, you do it.' I reasoned that nobody could be that good; I was wrong. David had the loveable untidiness of Rumpole and a truly encyclopaedic mind. His brain would have matched that of Einstein; yet his care about his appearance was more akin to that of Mahatma Gandhi. His usefulness to a chief executive was way off the top end of the scale. The consistency of his wisdom and the accuracy of his advice had become a byword.

He was powerfully and craggily built. Initially I wondered at the massiveness of his hands. They could have belonged to a prizefighter. I discovered that this classicist and legal genius had been both a swot and a boxer of some merit in his youth. I would have avoided such a kid at school. It must have been a formidable combination and David was still used to winning most arguments. Here was one ex-pugilist in whom evidence of brain damage was non-existent. His rapier mind was matched in quality by his advocacy. He had a way of ensuring that people listened to what he said and I marvelled at his technique. Normally his manner overcame even the higher thresholds of boredom. He would stand stolidly, a compact and stocky figure; then place his arms slightly behind and to one side of his body. The jacket of his dark suit was invariably buttoned, which added to the coiled-spring tension of his appearance. This penguin-like stance served to emphasize his presence. He spoke slowly and with great deliberation, often preceding what he was about to say by telling us what he was going to tell us, but we all listened spellbound. The slight sibilance of his annunciation only added to the impression of carefully weighed words and the privilege of listening to them.

It was rare for anyone to take him on in public debate and the politicians had long ago realized the futility of trying. He could, after all, run to the safe haven of the law to make his points. Nevertheless he was capable of getting excited in a discussion, very excited indeed. I could never quite work out when such reaction was part of the advocate's armoury and when it was due to genuine emotion. The sight and sound of David in full flow was awesome and I must admit to occasionally winding him up in meetings, as I felt that we both enjoyed the ensuing battle. We made it up afterwards although the prospect of mutual wound licking with David was not lightly contemplated.

He was particularly literate, both in writing and with computers. He despised the irritating discipline of all incoming software being virus checked by the internal Government Computer Department. At one Annual Budget Select Committee David had come to plead his chambers' budget for the coming year and, not unexpectedly, it included software. From the Chair I happened to mention his obligations with regard to virus checking and I was fully rewarded by the ensuing explosion. He waved his arms laterally as he expounded his well-known view with a vigour that had been dormant seconds before. Our local Krakatoa had erupted; the Mike Tyson in him was there for all to see. On David's left sat his aide – Robert Titterington, our excellent Principal Crown Counsel. As the Attorney General's massive hands flayed the air to emphasize the depth of his feelings, all in the room could see Robert ducking, dodging and weaving to avoid serious injury. His success in not being decapitated was probably due to his good eye as a sportsman; his good-humoured acceptance of such an assault was certainly due to his experiences as a Manchester City supporter.

Back in the Council Chamber I noticed that the public area was separated from us by a single rope between two posts. It would be easy to hurdle over it, but it was already too late to run for cover. I rose to my feet yet again on that November day in 1994. This time it was the big one, almost as big as it can get in a backwater – I was introducing the Hydrocarbons Bill. It contained all the legislation necessary to get the oil licensing round moving. It was the product of an enormous amount of work by David Lang and others prior to my arrival, but it was my inherited job to move the bill. The councillors were split on the subject, and public interest was running high. The chamber was packed.

I had mugged up, and grabbed hold of facts wherever I could. I tried to anticipate all the reasons why the Islands should not explore for oil and then set about concocting positive responses. We would protect the environment, we would ensure that all health and safety procedures were up to date, we would manage the pain of decommissioning and, should we strike oil, the wealth would be shared in a fair and enlightened way. The bill went through with some thoughtful opposition, but it was an unusually good debate.

We formed a team to manage the process of getting an oil licensing round going, which consisted of the good and great from within the civil service and Councillor John Cheek. John died in 1997, just as the round reached its climax, but in the three years that we worked together I found him to be indefatigable in his concern for the Islands and immensely positive in everything he turned his mind to. He was a big man with a puckish sense of humour. We were travelling together one day in Texas and due to a slight error of judgement and a momentary failure to look in my rear-view mirror, I was pulled over for speeding while showing John how cruise control worked. As the huge black traffic cop was frisking me by the roadside in between San Antonio and Houston, I glanced into the car to see if there was a supportive expression on John's face. Sympathy was in order. After all, if he hadn't wondered about the cruise control device none of this would have happened. All I could see was the heaving of John's broad shoulders as tears of merriment flowed into his beard.

Over the next two years this oil management team was to achieve something that was still a dream in November 1994. We would create a situation whereby major oil companies would spend millions of dollars exploring in our waters in spite of the lack of information and in spite of the implicit threat from Argentina. So far as Argentina was concerned, the magnificent men back in the UK Foreign Office were able to negotiate an agreement that was signed immediately prior to the launching of our round. This guaranteed co-operation and non-intervention in what we were attempting, as well as establishing a way of working together to explore the area across the notional border to the south-west of the Islands. In spite of the odd flurry of comment from the Argentine media and their opposition politicians, the agreement convinced the oil companies that the political risk had been minimized.

We launched the round with due ceremony in London and Houston. The launch itself consisted of a sequence of brief presentations, the handing out of an information pack and the answering of questions. The questions were as predictable as the answers we gave. The only really exciting incident occurred when our Attorney General accidentally found himself in a lap-dancing bar in Houston. I am sure it was accidental on his part, but I suspect that those who took him there knew precisely what they were about. I was told that he used all his advocacy and arm-waving skills to ensure that his good name remained untarnished. Some geologists can find lap-dancing joints more easily than they can locate hydrocarbons.

During the whole build-up process my fascination with geology was renewed. I had taken to it as a teenager, cycling the Yorkshire coast in pursuit of the Jurassic system. This time the geology was far more sophisticated and resoundingly practical. A field course in Utah achieved the impossible feat of being a 'jolly' that was genuinely useful. However, the five professional petroleum geologists who were supposed to be providing the answers to the questions posed by the magnificent sandstone all had individual views on virtually every puzzle. In my thirty-three years' absence from the subject, geology had become more about understanding the debate than providing an answer.

However, it was the exhibitions that provided the outsider with an opportunity to enter the culture of the industry. We sent small teams to quite a few that had oil themes. The American Association of Petroleum Geologists (AAPG) had an annual bash that gave us the chance to construct a rectangular stand and strike a pose on it to be stared at by passers-by. The British Geological Survey, who provided the much-needed technical back-up, suggested that a bowl of jellybeans would entice geologists on to the stand. They were right. It didn't necessarily mean that these geophysicists, seismologists, sedimentologists, mineralogists and petroleum geologists spoke to us. What they did was to pass by several times with arms that looped over the lip of the bowl to extract the tasty pebble-like morsels. However, professional integrity was redeemed by their curiosity over our seismic sections. We attached these to the sides of the stand along with pictures of penguins, gorse bushes, and other Falkland scenes. It was soon apparent that a seismic section to a geologist is like a light bulb to a moth. They would shuffle on to the stand chewing jelly beans, stare rather inquisitively at the variable shading on the charts and then begin to comment into thin air, to each other, or sometimes to those of us who awaited eye contact with an eagerness born of stand fatigue. The conversation nearly always involved the inadequacy of the interpretation that had been superimposed on the data. It took us a few days to realize that a definition of a seismologist is 'One who has a different interpretation from everyone else.'

We made friends, and we entertained and were entertained. At the AAPG conference at Dallas I was invited to give a paper on 'Launching an oil round – a Government's perspective'. I managed to stick to the time limit and obey the baffling sequence of coloured lights, but just as I was finishing, a kind of scuffle broke out on the floor of the hall. I was being shouted at by a chap who was saying something like, 'It isn't the Falklands, it is the Malvinas, and it isn't yours – it's ours.' With enormous mental effort I surmised that he was an Argentine, and although I had the microphone I felt that a debate regarding a long-standing territorial disagreement was not the purpose of the meeting. I waited for him to stop and said I would note his comments. The incident had substantial fall-out in that for the next two days every Argentine in Dallas made a point of coming on to our stand, ignoring the jellybeans and apologizing for the incident.

We planned the licensing round with what I would once have called 'military precision'. We hosted select gatherings of interested oil companies and explained our legislative framework, our tax plans and the existing service infrastructure. They all winged it back to their air-conditioned offices, clutching their information packs. Meanwhile, the Foreign Office kept talking to Argentina and we kept our fingers crossed. The seismic that had been interpreted looked promising, but we knew that real money had to be spent in order to prove the presence of oil.

It is fascinating to imagine the process that goes on behind the secure entrances and seismic charted walls of the oil majors. Who makes the decision to spend millions of pounds of shareholders' money on uncertainty and how do they evaluate what they are doing? Answers on a postcard please. I am not implying that they were pussycats, far from it. The problem was, as I had noted before with geologists, that they were all so different. Some wanted to take big risks simply because they knew that others wouldn't. There were those who professed to thrive on political uncertainty and others, especially for some reason the Japanese, who ran for cover at the slightest hint of dispute. They all had a surplus of intelligent managers, a plethora of information and a multiplicity of ways of bringing the two together. Normally the exploration geologists were the ones who spoke to us. The problem that we had, and they did too, was that there were hurdles to overcome before any bid could be made. Boards of directors existed somewhere in the inner sanctum and hard-nosed accountants would be giving advice. My previous experience of accountants' advice led me to believe that risks would be avoided and the unknown factors pertaining to the South Atlantic would mean a massive thumbs down.

The system that we had agreed with the UK government was that we would offer various areas of ocean around our shores. These tranches would be subject to bidding from individual companies or consortia. The bidders would submit their proposals on a set day and we would then evaluate them. The evaluation was done by way of a fairly involved points system and we would be awarding rights to tranches based on the quality of the seismic programme planned and the number of wells being offered. It sounds easy. We awaited the closure of our round and the opening of the bids with a keen anticipation and no little excitement.

The bids dropped through the letterbox at Falkland House in London. There were a few more than we had anticipated, but the spread of interest was such that my theory of geologists always reaching different conclusions was sorely tried. Almost all the bidders wanted the two tranches at the north of our northern blocks. We fielded a high-powered team for the interviews in a very summery London. Every bidder had a day to present their case and they all did so with copious detail and florid illustration and then answered our questions. We then required time to evaluate and to discuss with the Foreign Office and the DTI, whose energy department had a wealth of experience in this kind of thing from the North Sea.

The points system produced a clear result but there were political problems attached. One of the consortia bidding had consisted of British Gas and the Argentine company YPF. For technical reasons, that particular bid did not score as many points as the competition in the tranches they wanted. Yet we would dearly have liked the Argentines to be involved from the stability point of view. We were stuck with our own rules. Every possible flexibility was considered and then rejected. For the sake of consistency, we had to deny Argentine involvement. We were fearful that they would misunderstand and although some of their media did, their politicians and officials behaved creditably, as I believe they realized our predicament.

The award of licences was announced and stimulated considerable interest from the media. Shell, Amerada Hess and Lasmo were among the companies that would be the 'operators' managing drilling programmes for their respective consortia and some six wells might be drilled far sooner than we had anticipated. It took a few weeks for the excitement to die down and by that time I was safely back in Stanley, beginning the planning that would precede the oilmen coming to town.

Chapter 8

At first, being part of the society appeared to be straightforward. It was, after all, a colony and most of the inhabitants lived clustered together in a relatively confined area. There was a common purpose evident in many of their actions as well as a predictable uniformity of behaviour. When attacked by outsiders they resisted instinctively, demonstrating a strong mutual bond. However they were certainly not above a bit of petty thieving from each other if the opportunity arose. This could lead to running fights that upset the neighbours because not only did it spoil the tranquillity of normal life, but in the scuffling it could lead to damage to property – and none of them seemed to like that.

Food was reasonably abundant and although the diet would be repetitive to an outsider, none of the members of the colony cared much. They concentrated on the simple things in life: home-building, bringing up the family, and making sure that the youngsters were healthy and looked after whenever their parents were away.

Relationships between couples were strong and their faithfulness to each other over their entire adult lives was particularly touching. The harsh weather could be a problem, especially when it was cold and wet at the same time, with a Falklands wind blowing, but generally they were equipped for it. Nature had, after all, given them an amazing coat of waterproof feathers with an oily, blubbery insulation beneath. The life of the Gentoo penguin had many compensations.

The society was not quite as simple as it first appeared, but that could only be discovered by patient observation. The rewards for investing some time in simply watching penguin colonies can be immense. One laughs as one learns and there is a feeling of actually getting to know some of the birds as personalities. I defy anyone to watch penguins for half an hour without attributing human characteristics to them. And just as we find them fascinating, so they can be inquisitive about human beings. If you walk straight into a colony it will scatter in chaos, but if you just sit about ten feet away from the edge (assuming you can find a spot clear enough of guano), and stay reasonably still, in a matter of minutes you will find that there are penguins edging towards you. They do so in an almost imperceptible way, only one moving at a time, and then by a few inches, no individual committing themselves too far in front of the line.

I can well remember doing the same thing in Miss Van Der Plank's lessons at school. She was a student teacher from South Africa; she was a Boer — at the age of fourteen that seemed very funny. In drama lessons (Shakespeare being big in South Africa at that time) we all sat in rows of canvas and metal chairs facing the stage in the school hall. These chairs could be moved silently on the polished wooden floor and we would employ that technique until she was totally surrounded by spotty teenagers, her back to the stage and no escape. I doubt if she found us as interesting as Jean and I found the Gentoos all those years later.

The Gentoo is how you would imagine a penguin to be. It doesn't live underground like a Magellanic (jackass), nor does it scale impossible cliff faces as the rockhopper does. It lacks the exotic designer orange around the head so characteristic of the king penguin, but it is a bit larger than either jackasses or rockhoppers, being about two feet tall, and it doesn't go away to sea for the entire winter as they do. It is so easy to forget as one watches these black-and-white fantasy creatures living on land, that they are actually more at home in the sea. Although some of them will walk miles to get from the sea to their colonies, and vice versa, they are far more mobile and graceful zipping through waves, porpoising along the surface of the ocean, or just sporting about in the water. You don't have to watch any of them in water for long to get the impression that they enjoy being there.

Although the four main penguin species of the Falklands differ considerably in their habits, lifestyle and character, they all have one thing in common — their smell. It is not an odour I had come across before, but once experienced it is impossible to forget. I guarantee that if you played that party game where various smelly substances are placed in pots and sniffed by the participants, then penguin droppings would be identified easily even by those who may be nasally disadvantaged. If you are thinking of enlisting help in making up these pots at some stage, then count me out. The stench is fishy, ammonial and very strong. It gets into one's nostrils in a way that seems to influence the nerves there to sense nothing else for hours afterwards. I expect one could get high on it if so minded, but I've never tried to, nor ever met anyone who has survived the experience. The stench of cormorants is similar and one advantage of this phenomenon is that it makes it easy to locate colonies if you are downwind of them. I have even heard of a lone sailor on a raft who was able to navigate towards land in fog using this device.

The loveable creatures also have another disadvantage, which I'll mention in passing and then the rest will be all praise. They can bite, and bite to the bone. I admit it is rare to come across someone who is sporting a penguin bite, but I have known researchers who come to the Islands and actually put their arms down the burrows of Magellanic penguins to haul the creatures out for weighing or other scientific purposes. They always wear heavy gloves, but end up with their arms a mass of scars.

However, returning to the fascinating Gentoos: their colonies are generally within easy reach of the sea, although they can move them around from one year to the next and end up a few miles away. This may give them a bit of a walk to and from their source of food, but they waddle in a determined and resolute fashion, sometimes in groups but also singly. This ability to operate either in groups or as individuals seems to apply to all penguins. One day I watched a single jackass penguin emerge sparkling and shaking himself from the sea, waddle up the beach to be met by another individual going in the opposite direction. They stopped as they passed one another and for all the world appeared to be exchanging pleasantries. I couldn't hear anything but I could certainly imagine it: 'What's the sea like at the moment then?' 'It's not too bad actually, the krill are a bit far out, though. Has Jake patched up his problem with Harriet yet?' 'Yes, they felt they had to make a go of it for the sake of little Karl, you can't leave him to the mercy of the skuas.' 'That's all right for now but I bet they don't get back together next year.' 'Well, next year is next year.' And the seagoing penguin resumed his waddle over the silvery sand to the lightly foaming water.

The constant search for food means regular trips to sea and the penguins tend to make these at particular times during the day. Thus, if one knows the route that they take, and they generally have a favoured entrance and exit to the sea from the colony, all you have to do is sit nearby and they will stream past like commuters making their way down the Strand to Charing Cross Station.

The Gentoo walk is one of the species' characteristics. They tend to take rather larger strides than the length of their legs would appear to allow, and carry their flippers in a backwards- and outwards-facing mode, presumably to help with balance. It is also useful when they sense trouble, as they can move more quickly across land in a horizontal position. Thus, when they feel threatened, they will drop on to their starched white fronts, using their flippers as we would use arms and hands, and scurry with a motion that looks as awkward as you or I doing mobile press-ups, but is surprisingly rapid. They also feel instinctively safer in the sea and, if near to it, they belt along horizontally until they reach the relative security of water.

Returning to the colony, they seek out their own nest and, especially during the summer time, their mate, who may be sitting on an egg or two, a chick or two, or nothing at all. The term 'nest' makes the rather unimpressive earthen shape sound far more substantial than it really is. A Gentoo nest will vary from just bare surface to a built-up shallow volcano shape. They use mud, twigs, stones and any old bits and pieces to construct these homes and they are obsessively and comically proud of them. I suppose that if we built our living accommodation with our mouths we would have something to shout about too – if we could still use our mouths to shout after all that heaving of materials. A Gentoo will search for nest-building components up to quite a distance from the colony and then carry them in his or her beak with the idea of dumping the aforesaid on top of the rim of the pitiful nest while the partner looks on admiringly.

Among the many major problems facing the homebuilder is that raw materials get scarcer and scarcer as the season progresses and the dwellings are very close together, possibly a foot or eighteen inches apart. Thus, one has to run the gauntlet of envious neighbours, all sitting on their nests, all with long beaks, and all with a desire to snatch the modest strand of tussock grass from one's own grasp and place it on the side of their particular mini volcano. The problem remains that the brand new item is snatchable until it becomes bedded in. Even neighbours are not too proud to have a go at stealing when one's beak is facing the other way. Although this activity is absorbing to the onlooker, it's surprising that these creatures are not stressed out permanently.

You may think that the answer, for the Gentoo with above-average intelligence, would be to locate the family home at the edge of the colony, thus requiring less gauntlet running. The snag to this, however, is that both eggs and chicks are under constant threat from skuas, gulls and the apparently tame, but actually vicious, striated caracaras. In the centre of the colony there is a protected feeling. There are other families around diluting the vulnerability, and there is the communal head waving and guttural hissing that takes place as a predator hovers above, hanging in the constant wind. It can be quite effective in persuading the threatening bird to swoop away. On the outskirts of town, there is less protection and the skuas in particular watch endlessly for an exposed victim. Sometimes a suburban penguin will become fed up with the watching eyes and waddle aggressively towards a sitting skua, screeching and snapping. The skua will merely withdraw temporarily or select another vantage point. It takes all sorts to make up a penguin colony and they clearly have their own residential preferences.

The ground on which the colony exists is not only rich in the spasmodically squirted guano, but it is also bare. The activity of the Gentoo is not conducive to the fragile Falkland grass. Gentoo colonies tend to consist only of Gentoos, whereas rockhoppers will happily coexist with king cormorants or black browed albatrosses. In fact, they can be seen to utilize the disused nests of the others for the foundation of their own chez nous.

When Gentoo eggs are hatched after thirty-five days' incubation the small, squeaking, pale grey furry chick with its relatively long neck cracks its way through the shell and emerges to become prey. I have seen a parent struggling to undo this miracle of nature by trying to stuff the chick back into its broken shell, presumably to help in the overwhelming problem of protection. The predators watch and watch with a stillness and arrogant patience. At any moment they can swoop upon an exposed chick and whip it away for a rapid gobble. The degree of exposure may be no more than a parent turning round to chat to a neighbour and the youngster being a bit curious and leaning out of its sheltered accommodation.

Normally two chicks are hatched, and as long as they can be fed and are not seized by predators, they can survive into adulthood. The living quarters for the newly hatched penguins are dark and warm. They live underneath one parent at a time, protected by the hollow in the adult's body and a mass of soft and cosy-looking feathers. When hungry, they squeak and move about. This evidently causes discomfort to the parent, which eventually gives in and bends over the agitating chick, regurgitating part-digested squid and lobster krill into its open mouth. During this process the chick's head is well inside the beak of the adult, and both the direction of the parental puke and the ability of the chick to latch on to the idea are remarkable – there is hardly any spillage. The casual onlooker can only be grateful for such accuracy, as any further enhancement of the already pervasive odour would be most unwelcome.

There is a school of thought that believes nature should be left entirely to itself. One area that bears this argument out is Beauchene Island to the south of the Falklands, where the wildlife is prolific and where any human being would add a fresh variable to the environmental equation. I once flew low over this rocky haven on a fishery patrol flight, and the black browed albatross nests appeared to cover about one-third of the island. Is it to be left to get on with it, or should it be monitored, and if so by whom, and how? These questions are fairly profound and particularly challenging. The idea of humans somehow upsetting a balance may seem absurd when we are thinking of thousands of penguin chicks and one human being, yet it only takes a single movement by that human to distract the penguin parent from concentrating on guarding its chick and the silent watchers charge. Such an attack distracts the neighbours and in watching what is going on they cease to concentrate on their own chicks. Thus the skua may be swooping at one end of the rookery and a caracara is able to pick up a chick from the middle. The matrix of inter-relationships is complex, and a human is a massive unknown in a delicate situation.

Watching this drama unfold, one is struck not so much by the predators' ability to engineer or co-ordinate such a situation, but more by the statistical probability that favourable circumstances will arise for them if only they have the patience and the watchfulness. Be assured that they have both. They tend to stand, or sit, in a position that provides a panoramic view of the colony, so that they can strike in an instant as soon as the window of opportunity opens. To the human viewer this often exposes them, in that they are easy to spot against the skyline, but humans are not their concern. Their sustenance comes from the penguin rookery and they concentrate on their appointed role as the silent sentinels of doom. The chicks seem to sense the danger as their parents tense themselves when under attack. It must be horrific for them to live in fear of a giant winged creature diving soundlessly out of the sky above to carry them off to an instant and bloody death.

The chicks grow rapidly on their regurgitated seafood platter and the youthful Gentoo begins to spend more and more time outside the protective haven of the nest. The shape of these creatures is decidedly cute. They have longish necks with inquisitive faces on top of a triangular grey fur body and ridiculous yellowy webbed feet. These chicks congregate into nurseries where some of the adults act as baby sitters while both of the parents can go out to sea to work at imbibing more and more protein to feed the ravenous youths. In time the baby fur begins to moult and cuddliness gives way to scruffiness before the pristine adult feathers appear in all their glory. Then is the time to learn swimming and all the tricks of movement and mobility in the water that will serve to make them good hunters and help them to avoid the sea lions that may block their launchings and landings.

The rockhopper penguin is somewhat smaller than the Gentoo and carries a characteristic yellow crest on either side of its head. This gives it an appearance that is more ridiculous and punk-like than cute, but it is the rockhopper's mode of movement, both at sea and on land, that catches the eye. These creatures will swim towards a seemingly impossible cliff, joyously porpoising all the way, once again in groups or singly. The rocks are generally jagged and the sea a seething cauldron of complex currents and undertows. No human frogman could swim in such an environment for long, and no small boat could manoeuvre. The danger is all too obvious, the sheer weight and pressure of the water threatens to smash any life to bits in no time at all. The scene is one of relentless crashing, turbulent, foaming, swirling challenge. Have you ever thought that being a penguin might be fun? After all, the life can be interesting, the views spectacular and occasionally you meet interesting tourists, but this particular experience they can keep to themselves.

They float about in the turbulence standing off the point of no return, seeming to wait for an appropriate wave. Then, without surfboards but employing a technique obviously gleaned from Old Spice commercials, they zoom and flick and dash and ride until they are hurled against solid rock. They scramble, they bounce, they dive back with apparent glee, but some keep scraping and clutching and clawing, trying to obtain purchase on rocks worn smooth by generations of ancestors. As they begin to move upwards the next wave comes after them and the downwash tries to capture and pull them back into the cauldron. Their success is generally dependent on the quality of the initial ride, but their resilience is unquestionably impressive. If grabbed back by the sea, they simply go round again and again, tirelessly enjoying the fun of the fair with an exuberance and energy that is exhausting to contemplate.

When they are clear of the influence of the highest waves, the penguins stop, clean themselves up, check their pulse rate, and progress to the top of the cliff in stages by scrambling, scraping and hopping. The hopping movement is every bit as remarkable as the entry from the sea. It is the vertical reach of the hop and the judgement with regard to landing zone that impresses. Sometimes they slip and fall, but they just bounce a bit, scramble a recovery of sorts, and carry on. To be a rockhopper is to be genuinely upwardly mobile.

The Magellanics are not nearly so clustered in their distribution as Gentoos and rockhoppers. Their nests, which are in effect burrows, can be found all over the sea-adjacent grasslands of the Falklands. The young of the species do congregate together for protection, but if a burrow is more isolated than others it doesn't seem to matter. These penguins can jump, but not as impressively as rockhoppers; it is their hole digging that sets them apart. Their improvised homes often stretch several feet underground, making it treacherous to walk heavily in the area of a burrow. They can usually be seen standing or sitting in their doorways, just watching the world go by. Generally, they will wait until a human gets within a few feet, raise themselves to their full height to get a good look at you and then opt to scamper into the security of the underground system. This can be amusing if a whole family of four try to squeeze at once through a space built for about one and a half. It is one of the sights of the Islands when walking across open green pasture in certain locations. The Magellanic nests will be spaced maybe twenty yards apart in a random fashion; heads will be visible just above ground level in every direction, starkly black and white against the low greens and beiges of the ground cover. As you move near them, down they go. Once in the safety of the burrow they tend to sit there and look upwards at what is going on, and they have an astonishing head-swivelling ability through about three hundred and fifty-nine degrees which comes into play as they review the situation for danger. So one looks at them and they look back at one, first one way up and then the other. Even with such a thorough examination, they never seem to quite trust a human, but once you shuffle off, they emerge from their bunkers once again.

Late one summer, Jean and I walked to the local jackass habitation at Gypsy Cove to see if they had all set off for their winter at sea. It was 28 March and a very few remained. There they were, standing at their respective front doors, accompanied by huge offspring in a semi-moulted state. It was surprising to see how large the youngsters were relative to their foraging parents, at least one-third as big again. It was also somehow quaint to see the parents, still fussing over their overgrown youngster, waiting patiently for the feathers to drop off so that they could set off on their ocean voyage.

The local nickname, 'jackass', derives from the characteristic braying sound that the birds make. This is a strange and memorable noise that involves a build-up to the final elongated call. The Magellanic begins by raising its head, looking vertically upwards (it can swivel in that plane as well), and beginning to tremble. The movement quickly co-ordinates with a heaving of the neck and a repeated sound, which starts slowly, then gathers momentum, culminating in one long and rasping rendition of a noise remarkably like that of a donkey. When there are a few hundred of them up to this kind of caper in the evening time, it makes quite a din, but it is relaxing and fairly pleasant to the ear. It is also a sound that can carry over a considerable distance and in many coastal areas it is a characteristic feature of a still night.

The imperious king penguins are the biggest, the most colourful, the most photogenic, and in many ways the most boring of the lot. It is the king penguin colony at Volunteer Point that most tourists aspire to visit. These birds are clearly snobbish and class conscious. They stand about thirty inches high, have extraordinary dark grey leathery feet, and possess a patch on the side of the head that is a glorious orangey yellow. This gaudy but undeniably attractive design feature has a modern pear drop shape. King penguins live in colonies, as do the Gentoos, but their breeding cycle is thought to be some fourteen months. This means they get all out of kilter. There are chicks of various sizes and states of plumage all over the colony. It must be hard for them to know what time of the year it is. But as they stay around all year anyway, it doesn't really matter. In Antarctica they march miles to their nesting places and survive the winter by bundling themselves together. The Falklands is far more amenable for them.

Volunteer Point is by far the largest king penguin colony on the Islands and is also the largest outside South Georgia. It is the only place in the world where king penguins actually breed on grass. Well, it was grass to start with. Once the kings' guano has seeped into it, it does rather die off. This penguin palace is privately owned and can only be reached from Stanley by a tortuous drive that is very damp even in the driest summer. For those who find bogging a hazard, this is one to avoid. But it is an unforgettable place once you get there, another magic location where nature remains in charge and one is aware of intruding.

Penguins are magnificent, entertaining and industrious creatures. They are fun to observe and therapeutic as friends. Jean and I never gave a thought to the undesirability of keeping them in zoos until we lived in the Falklands, but try us on the subject now!

A s a total newcomer to all things military, I had foreseen a smoothly
run organization, staffed by men who were hardened by training,
tempered in battle and at the very peak of human efficiency. I was to meet
and work with the professionals from the modern fighting machine; high
flyers who were prepared to dare and to give their all for the service of
their country. They would be decisive, persuasive and direct. Their lives
would be action packed and full of sport, glamour and toughness. They
had seen it all, done it all and were raring to do it again.

Without wishing to give offence, I was more than a bit disappointed.
Most of the inhabitants of Mount Pleasant were far more ordinary than I
had expected. I found clerks going about their roles, very much as they
would have done in the Civil Service. I liaised with managers who were
frustrated by daily routine and the decisions, or lack of them, from
superiors. I encountered functionaries functioning as any public- or
private-sector employee. There were, however, three big differences.
Firstly, they wore boots all the time; secondly, they spoke almost entirely
in clipped acronyms; and thirdly, their whole culture was enclosed and
quite unlike anything I had ever come across.

Yes – boots. Even in their offices, even in their homes, sometimes at
dinner parties – boots. These were seldom the modern 'Goretex' type of
boot, although some of the infantry, who actually needed boots and were
fed up with wet feet, had bought their own. No, these were standard-
issue boots, jolly useful for all normal wear. Thanks to Doc Marten and
the fact that the social whirl at Mount Pleasant usually included other
military folk in boots, there was never any consciousness of how odd it
would all have looked to a passing civilian.

As for the acronyms, these chaps had really got it off to a fine art. For
me this was not just the occasional missing of some nuance of meaning,
this was total incomprehension. I had not been more linguistically
disadvantaged since I tried to order a boiled egg for breakfast in a small
Dutch town. The clucking noises I ended up making on that occasion
illustrated a technique that would have fitted the situation at MPA. Below
the obvious CBFFI (pronounced 'seebiffy'), who was the Commander
British Forces Falkland Islands (of course; fancy not guessing that), were

such important personages as COS (yes, we had a lettuce as Chief of Staff), COFILU, OCFIAU, OCFIAW and OCFIEU. These were the top guys. Beneath them were the really inventive roles: EORAB, TESWO, FICCO (I bet he gets a comment or two) and OC Cat and Rat Sqn. I can't really believe we had a squadron of cats and rats, but then the US Navy has been known to use dolphins and my grandfather was in a bicycle regiment in the First World War. Possibly secret intelligence reports reveal that the Argentines are fazed by this kind of combined feline and vermin assault.

Why invent acronyms when they are nearly impossible to say, never mind understand, and the emerging sounds when one does have a stab at pronunciation are all so similar as to be confusing anyway? There was also JCUFFI, which was something to do with the headquarters of the joint command, but I always had mental images of a large whirlpool bath. This may have been subliminal fantasizing on their part because although Mount Pleasant was a substantial township, they lacked baths. Showers were prolific; baths were virtually unknown. I have experienced grown men pleading for a bath in a civilian home and it was not unknown to invite military friends for 'bath and dinner – bring your own towel'.

For the humble civilian this acronym problem was at its worst when we tried to understand the orders for a parade day. Not only was the clipped form of speech adopted for such instructions, but also I had to identify the personnel involved from their wives. 'COFILU and Mrs Stanton, OCOPS and Mrs Lade,' announced the brief. I was able to work backwards to Warwick and Chris.

The theme of acronyms threads its way through my Falkland experience. I began by feeling inadequate and out of touch. Possibly I was experiencing the early onset of senility. Jean and the children had long predicted such a problem. Then I recalled the reception area of the Foreign Office in London.

Over five years I became well acquainted with this room. It is about twenty-three feet square, with a neat wooden desk that has three polite ladies in white blouses behind it who seldom seem to be fully occupied. A backlit coat of arms etched on glass graces the wall behind them. Uplighters pick out the flat whiteness of the ceiling and some comfy chairs have been provided in the body of the room so that one can sit and await the summons from the echoing corridors of the establishment. A helpful notice in a glass case is headed 'A chronology of some 20th-century developments'. The list ends in 1944, showing the FCO to be more up to date than the Treasury!

I had expected worse, possibly an endless tape loop chanting the FCO mantra, 'Never go native', or even their mission statement, 'Never know more than you need to know.' This is actually FCO speak for 'We hope you never find out more than we are prepared to tell you.' After filling in the security form containing the time of arrival and who one is hoping to see and such like, and hanging it around one's neck like a dog about to be neutered, there is always time to peruse the rest of the decor. The pictures on the wall changed rapidly after Labour's election triumph in 1997. Suddenly Conservative Foreign Office ministers meeting foreign dignitaries were replaced by more general shots of overseas happenings: Mr Nelson Mandela stepping off a plane somewhere; Her Majesty under a palm tree; Prince Charles watching belly dancers, that kind of thing. Clearly there had not been time for the new ministers to generate a suitable picture gallery. What they had been doing was inspiring people with talk of change and then sitting behind their desks reading endless briefings. Such briefings had probably been prepared specifically to head off the envisaged changes. In any event the sheer weight of reading matter would delay any pre-emptive strikes by the inexperienced political masters.

Having time to look more closely at the glass case, one could see inside what seemed to be a very battered old typewriter. The script next to it revealed that this was an 'enigma' machine. This famous piece of kit was the key to the cracking of German codes in the Second World War. It could handle the complexities of changing solutions as the code varied. Initially I wondered what the FCO were doing with it, but then I twigged that they needed it for understanding the MOD.

This code cracking was absolutely essential. Was it not the late Humpty Dumpty himself who said that words meant what he wanted them to mean? Well, the MOD had cottoned on to that with their acronyms. In the Islands we had the privilege of being served infantry-wise by the RIC, decoded in 1994 as the 'Reinforced Infantry Company'. These lusty young soldiers exercised and patrolled all day, got drunk all evening, and slept it off in time for the next patrol. The scale of the military presence was always said to be 'Matching the perceived threat from Argentina', so the more the Argies visited London, the more pressure came on CBFFI to cut back. Eventually a reduction in the scale of this force took place, but any run down in level of soldiers, being sensitive, created something of a PR problem, especially to the watchful Islanders. The RIC became, in reality, an Infantry Company, no longer truly being capable of being identified as being reinforced. Mighty brains at the MOD struggled with the problem of having to admit to only having an IC in the Islands. They solved it brilliantly by inventing the 'Resident Infantry Company' – thus the acronym never changed, the RIC remained, and the perception of downgrading was lessened; clever stuff. Subsequently a heightened layer of subtlety was introduced by a further name change to the 'Roulement Infantry Company'. Having to raid foreign tongues to keep an acronym in play may seem like cheating, but apparently this conveyed a sense of replacement and flexibility. Jolly useful things, acronyms.

As for my third point about the culture, I hardly know where to begin. For one thing the outside world barely exists. True it exists for the squaddie, as it contains more females, but mostly these people are understandably focused on the military existence. Orders are obeyed in this environment. What the boss says should happen actually takes place. This is so different from the everyday experience of most of us that it requires adjustment even to be able to realize what is happening. One more stripe or pip on an officer's arm or tunic means the world. It heralds status, recognition, formal regard for the genius one always knew one had, power (within strictly prescribed limits), and certainty of pension or a funeral with full military honours, whichever comes first.

The cultural aspect is further complicated by the tri-service dimension. The Falklands garrison is a 'purple' command. This is, of course, nothing to do with the colour purple. It refers to the fact that all three major services are brought under one command and are thus obliged to work together in this 'theatre' (military speak for 'place') of 'operations' (military speak for 'everything we do'). When I first heard 'theatre' used in this way, I thought that our military friends were putting on thespian productions for our entertainment; it was not to be so. At least not in the sense I imagined.

In this artificial environment, where three quite disparate groups of highly trained folk are chivvied together, it is entirely natural for each service to compare itself with the other two, or even for two to gang up in their appraisal of the third.

After an evening spent in the splendid company of Air Force and Navy officers, one might conclude that it is the absent Army officers who are the odd ones out. After all, one can easily spot them in a crowd, even in civilian kit. There are not all that many crowds on the Islands, but I knew what they meant. They are said to speak in an advanced form of the ubiquitous clipped tone with a pronounced public school accent. As the evening wears on, the Army may well be accused of not only speaking oddly, but also walking further, and having fewer toys. They are held to salute in a ridiculously showy and even competitive manner. But they are also said to believe that warfare is mainly about digging trenches and shooting at people. Any spouses present are convinced that Army officers' wives wear 'Alice' bands as a kind of uniform. I must admit that this particular view is substantiated by empirical observation.

By contrast, being entertained by the Army and the Navy, one is forced to admit the sad fact that the RAF is altogether dominated by their technological wizardry. They are portrayed as being so far behind the Army when it comes to drill that it is barely credible, and they are depicted as having an awful lot of officers for the men under their command. Their saluting is felt to be lacklustre and wimpish. Warfare for them is apparently about air power and air support and about having easily fired missiles that lock on to targets. They are said to be scrambling for ever newer and better toys like the visitors to Hamleys on Christmas Eve. I do not recall that RAF officers' wives wear 'Alice' bands. After what they had said about Army wives they would probably prefer a civilian style.

Time spent with the RAF and Army is rather easier to come by, as the Navy actually put to sea now and again. In fact, they are accused of always wishing they were at sea, but when they are there, longing for the home life. Their method of saluting is regarded as something of an apology for a salute, with a half-hearted action and a curved wrist. There is a sense in which the Army and the Air Force envy the Navy because of the remarkable independence that they obviously have when they leave port in their self-sufficient vessels. This stand-alone aspect of naval life generates an air of assumed superiority, often underlined by them when they endlessly refer to their status as the 'Senior Service'. Their view of warfare has undergone enormous change from being dominated by whistles and hooters to being dependent upon integrated software systems. When the heat in the kitchen gets tough, when the tough get going, and the fighting is real, one of the last things I'd want to be relying on is an integrated software system. But that is purely a personal view – I'm sure NATO, or somebody, knows what's going on. I have no idea whether the wives wear 'Alice' bands, as there were never enough on the Islands to get a statistically valid sample.

One event that is guaranteed to get all three services together is the 'Dining In' night. That is the evening when the Officers' Mess becomes overbearingly formal and they all dine 'in'. I could never be sure of where they might dine 'out', but the title of the evening possibly reflected other postings where they had more options. Such an evening demands the wearing of 'mess' dress, which translates as a special kind of uniform for the military folk that is worn only on these occasions. These uniforms are normally historic in origin, do not come cheap and are paid for by the individual officer. As they are worn only spasmodically, they are made to last a long time by the owners and it is entertaining to witness the pressure that seams are subjected to by the increment of girth due to age and modest indulgence. One meets officers who are puce about the gills and breathing in short gasps, due to the constraints of the corset-like uniforms that they are shoehorned into in the interests of formality and tradition.

And whatever you do, don't touch the silver! Never have I seen silver more asking to be touched – a model aircraft that begs for detailed examination and identification, plaques and shields that demand to be read but have minuscule print. These shining items are placed just within arms' reach on the top table. The top table might seem like the best place to be. That is not so; there is far less conviviality, as there is never anyone opposite. The choice of conversation is limited to left and right and if one is on the end of the top table the selection is the joint worst in the room. Thus, when one's conversation is lacking in military gossip, the silver becomes irresistibly alluring. But if you so much as poke it, you will be forced to pay for a round of drinks for the entire mess of hundreds of alcohol-starved officers.

A useful insight into the military psyche can be gleaned from a careful study of the in-flight magazine on the Tristar. This publication is imaginatively titled *In Flight*. It appears as new in the seat pockets four times a year. Although our forces traverse the globe in defending freedom, they fall into the trap of producing issues named after the season. Thus the spring issue immediately gets up the noses of all Southern Hemisphere readers, who know full well that it is autumn. In flicking through the pages one is again struck by the distinctive culture of the target browser. There are articles on things such as buying cars tax free, educating children at private boarding schools (not tax free), a homeopathic travel survival kit, the NAFFI, and resettlement training. The balance of the articles shows that the question of whether there is life after the military experience is of constant concern to most officers. As they ascend the pyramid, the space on the upper levels diminishes. Some are nudged off into the desert below. The threatened re-entry into real life is understandably feared. The officer commanding men is often fed the line that he has multi-disciplinary skills and will be much sought after by private industry. Most of these fellows are smart enough to find that sort of generalization hard to swallow.

There were two thousand two hundred and twenty-one civilian inhabitants of the Islands in the 1997 census, and the military presence added almost as many again. 'A soldier for everyone,' observed a rather effeminate hairdresser to me in London when I acquainted him with this simple fact. That number of personnel did not represent fighting men – the support services required for a modern tri-service garrison are considerable. However, the military presence did more or less double the population. With two equal and separate communities living on the Islands, one might have anticipated a steady flow of confrontational incidents between locals and military, a sort of 'Town and Tunic' atmosphere. The truth was that the relations were superb. It may have been to do with the sheer size of the place – there was more than enough room for everyone – or it could have been due to the enormous goodwill that existed on both sides and the proper management of the relationships.

The bonhomie on both sides shows itself in many different ways. Low flying is welcomed. Firing from ship to shore is allowed, although the sheep may object posthumously, and the crossover activities between the two communities provide welcome variety for both. The crossover king is the Civilian Liaison Officer, who is in charge of the small detachment based in Stanley. He is always selected from artillery majors, as a detailed knowledge of projectiles and explosive impacts is thought to be essential in creating any useful relationship with the locals. The EOD (Explosive Ordnance something) is based in Stanley. These are the mine sniffers, the shell exploders and the bomb diffusers. They are generally not given to histrionics or sudden jerky movements. They tour the minefields, scanning them through binoculars. It sounds silly but mines can, and do, move around in peat. If they become exposed, then out comes a cute little robot on caterpillar tracks, rather like a toy tank. This remote-controlled device sprays flame on the emerged mine to melt the plastic casing and allow the explosive to go 'phut'. The first time I heard it I was immensely disappointed to find that that is exactly the sound it makes: 'phut'.

The military are able to put on a magnificent open day at Mount Pleasant, when they seize the opportunity to show off their toys and their training. Tornados fly low and fast, generating that gut-throbbing noise as they change gear, or whatever, and arrow vertically upwards. Chinook helicopters wheel and hover as they demonstrate their flexibility, and expatriates combine with Islanders to clamber all over the UK taxpayers' military hardware.

One day in August 1998, the nuclear-powered submarine HMS *Triumph* came to town, or rather slopped about in the outer harbour of Port William. To clamber up a rope ladder lying across the sloping side of this glistening charcoal grey monster was a new experience for all those privileged enough to be invited. To descend vertically into the confined but remarkably civilized world of the submariner for about six hours, during which we dived, fired 'let's pretend' torpedoes and had a very palatable lunch, was a call of duty that was thoroughly pleasurable. Even in this canned environment we were all told to wear our TLDs, which would be issued to us by the LMA. Don't even ask what it meant – I did, and found the answer every bit as puzzling as the acronym.

The one hundred and eighteen inhabitants of that deadly metal tube operate a six-hours-on-and-six-hours-off rota while at sea and they seem to be under the sea for most of the time. It is undoubtedly smoother down there than wallowing around on the surface. The crew sacrifice personal privacy in the interests of professionalism in a manner that engenders really strong team spirit. These men live in a very prescribed environment, and they are interdependent to a remarkable degree. If ever you should begin to feel deprived of any of the fripperies of life, then think of those beneath the waves, sometimes for months on end, training, gaming and maintaining capability to be highly effective hunter-killers.

The power capacity of the nuclear plant is enormous. It could light up Southampton for fifteen years, said one crew member; Yeovil said another. Wherever it was, we could have done with this kind of silent power in Stanley. They manufacture their own air and water, make soup from the uneaten food of the previous day, share bunks, and take enormous pride in being so unusual and so proficient. Only the captain has his own cabin, and even his walls would discourage the swinging of a cat. The submariners are forced to get on with each other by the sheer physical proximity of their colleagues. Rough-edged personalities are either smoothed out, or they end up in another part of the Navy. Half the time one is squeezing past someone else.

Noise is very important to these people. There is no sound of the water rushing by outside, as you may imagine from the movies; in fact, the smoothness of diving and flying along underwater is remarkable. Sound travels astonishingly well at depth and the crew is listening for noise all the time, while being aware that its own sounds are capable of detection. The whole of the vast engine is heavily damped to avoid vibration. I was astonished to discover that these chaps can listen to conversations inside ships when they are near enough. It might be worth tracking one of those luxury cruise liners just to find out if all the stories are true...

If the Trafalgar class submarine looks a bit whale-like and ungainly above the surface, it can be excused as it is made to perform in an environment where looking like a whale is an advantage. The whale of the skies is undoubtedly the much-loved 'Fat Albert', the tubby and workmanlike C-130 Hercules aircraft. It is a beast of burden, with a long range and a useful slow take-off and landing capability. At MPA one day, the commander asked if I wanted to see one of these cumbersome giants jump-started. I thought I had misheard him. A non-RAF Hercules on its way to Antarctica had called in at Mount Pleasant for refuelling and for some reason they couldn't get the engines started. So, the canny RAF positioned one of theirs in front of its twin and with the brakes hard on, started and revved their engines. As the Hercules in front built up the power, the sheer draught of air flowing over the propellers of the plane behind it began to turn them slowly at first, and then they suddenly burst to life. The visiting Americans were delighted and jumped into their Fat Albert to ply their way to Antarctica. The thought of how they got the engines started there has intrigued me ever since. Possibly they are entombed in ice to this day. I can just see that last message to mankind scrawled in the encroaching frost by a heavily-gloved finger: 'How are yoll today?'

These utilitarian machines refuel other aircraft in mid-air. I once sat in the cockpit as the pilot steadied his course to exactly that of the Hercules flying just ahead. We closed to touching distance. A pipe with a funnel-like device on the end was hanging in front of us as it was wound out of the belly of our twin. Our probe that was supposed to dock with the funnel was on the starboard side, just above the cockpit window. The whole experience was more like an arcade game than an arcade game.

Although there was not too much turbulence in the air, the disturbance caused by the plane above and in front of us was enough to make the funnel wave around randomly. The pilot edged and cajoled his huge machine closer and closer to the device, which wobbled about like a shuttlecock suspended in an updraft. After a few 'clunks' and near misses, we achieved a solid docking and fuel could be passed from one to the other. Then, blow me, if we didn't do the whole thing in reverse. Our friendly provider of fuel became the recipient as we let out our pipe and funnel, and he came round behind us. It was particularly spectacular to watch as the pipe was run out of the back through an open hatchway. I was encouraged to lie on the hatch mechanism and watch the whole process. It became even more memorable when the Hercules broke away to be replaced by a Tornado. He was so close I could see the expression on the pilot's face. It was as though the Tornado was swinging on a piece of elastic attached to us as the sun shone on West Falkland beneath.

Islanders love the Ghurkhas – the RIC is often composed of these amazingly fit Nepalese. Stories of their bravery abound, but in the Islands there are also tales of kindness and competence. One day they arrived at Fox Bay with an afternoon to spare whilst on an exercise. Councillor Norma Edwards gave them a cup of tea and chatted. Then she left them to attend to matters in Fox Bay East while they continued to enjoy her ever-generous hospitality. On returning she found smiling Nepalese faces and some new garden paths. They had decided to reward Norma for her friendship, had found some old bricks and had carefully laid pathways around the house in a decorative herringbone pattern with serrated edges. It all looked wonderful and she was profuse in her thanks. The fact that the bricks were rather rare in the Falklands and had been specifically acquired by husband Roger to begin their house extension was a problem for the future. Norma has a big heart and appreciated the Ghurkhas' thoughtfulness. That type of happy coexistence characterizes the relationship between town and tunic (or boiler suit and tunic) and it is something to be prized.

Chapter 10

GETTING BOGGED

Every Falkland Islander knows about getting bogged. Every expatriate living in the Islands who has any spirit of adventure also knows about getting bogged. The Islander, due to many decades of natural selection and intensive breeding, knows how to avoid getting bogged; the expatriate doesn't.

When I was presented with my government Land Rover shortly after arrival I was introduced to the bumper jack. This is a hefty piece of equipment that has the ability to raise a Land Rover off the ground at many and varied points of its anatomy far more effectively than the flimsy device that arrives with such a vehicle in the UK. However, there are two snags – the 'ground' from which the vehicle is being raised should preferably be solid and level, and the jack itself has the ability to kill and maim without warning. There is a way of using it that is perfectly safe and all the Islanders know it from the cradle. It is explained to expats at such speed that, without the benefit of a slow-motion replay, one is not prepared for what lies ahead.

One of the problems is that the expatriates probably have some spirit of adventure to end up in a place like the Falklands anyway. Those who prefer the fleshpots of sophisticated world capitals, the opera, tea at the Ritz and behaving like inhabitants of *Hello* magazine, would hardly choose to live beyond fifty degrees south. Thus a breezy confidence exudes from those who listen to, rather than learn from, the instruction. The male expat knows that he can drive around Hyde Park Corner with the only damage being an angry wave, that he has generally chosen the right lanes through Swiss Cottage and furthermore he has actually driven a four-wheel-drive Sierra across a field in Scotland, so there is nothing to fear.

If one had any predisposition to fear, the warnings about always taking sleeping bags, torches, survival rations and a two-metre radio when driving across Camp would be heeded. Having a radio is one thing; being able to work it is quite another. Most Islanders have been working these things since childhood. Many have been educated on them from the Camp teachers based in Stanley. They know the wavelengths and how to find them, what words can be guessed at from the confused and random crackling sounds and which buttons to press for transmit, receive and unsquelching. These details have a fair significance if you are totally bogged, miles from the nearest settlement, with night closing in.

After the expat has been through a bogging or two, a transformation takes place. Easy confidence becomes gibbering humility; any hints on the workings of bumper jacks and two-metre radios are lapped up. Land Rovers are piled high with sleeping bags, torches, planks and bits of punched sheet metal. Whole families are allocated individual specialist roles in the event of a bogging. Those who were certain that ordinary road tyres were totally adequate for anything Camp could offer, invest hundreds of pounds in specialist wide wheels that flatten the end elevation of the vehicle. When used in anger, these succeed in spraying mud over a vast area as they extend well beyond any mudguards.

Our introduction to the world of off-road Camp travel promised to be absolutely painless. We were invited to join a commemorative drive from Port Louis to Stanley in celebration of the relocation of the capital of the Islands one hundred and fifty years previously. The overall distance by the road was a mere twenty-five miles, so even across the Camp, it shouldn't have taken very long. We turned up at the starting point at Port Louis in our long wheelbase Land Rover complete with bumper jack, provisions, planks and two solicitors, so that we could share the driving and come out on top in any arguments. There were some seventy Land Rovers attempting this drive over Long Mountain and the leader of our group was the farmer from the local farm of Estancia – Tony Heathman. Tony's lean and hawk-like appearance hides a caustic wit and a heart of gold. I now know that he knows a million or so times more about Camp driving than I do, but initially I was ignorant of that fact. The first lesson began:

'Never driven across Camp before then?'

'No.'

'Couldn't you get wide tyres?'

'I didn't realize they were necessary.'

'Well, they're not really on this trip as I'll be around, but these road tyres are too thin and cut into the peat; you're far more likely to get bogged. Anyway, remember to keep your foot off the clutch and get into diff-lock and low ratio when you need to and take narrow ditches diagonally. Watch the ground ahead for softness, you can generally tell by the colour. Just follow me, anyway.'

With that he set off in his Range Rover and we followed in convoy with various dignitaries including His Excellency the Governor (chauffeur driven at this stage), a visiting general, and the Military Commander, who had acquired wheels so wide that he seemed to be driving on both sides of the track at once. I did say track; however, it would be wrong to assume that what might look like a perfectly passable track one moment will not completely alter its character the next. It may just disappear totally; it may split into multiple tracks, all of which look equally well used and equally treacherous; it may become so obviously boggy that a detour across virgin land is the only option; or it may do the worst thing of all – simply get soggier and soggier until it sucks your wheels to its bosom and brings your vehicle to a slithering halt.

I had never really applied the diff-lock before. I realized that it locked the wheels in a manner that was not recommended on ordinary roads, but over slithering sludge it would be just the ticket. I drove gingerly. I don't believe I have ever iced a wedding cake but the delicacy of touch on the controls resembled how I imagine I would tackle that equally unknown skill. I was trying to get a feel for the surface. There were occasional slipping sensations coming through to me, as the revs appeared to be out of synch with the progress we were making. I realized that power can be an enemy as well as a friend.

For a while progress was serene. The day was sunny. Tony was driving slowly but consistently and was being followed with care by His Excellency's chauffeur. The Military Commander was immediately in front of me. He noted the steep slope ahead and decided to attack it with more speed than Tony had done. I followed rather cautiously and crested the rise to find my way blocked – he had managed to jam his vehicle on top of a piece of rock, leaving all four of his wide wheels spinning helplessly, emitting horsepower into thin air. It was heartening to see such a man of action, responsible for the repulsion of Argentine aggression and much else besides, stuck on a motorized seesaw. The picture was lent enchantment by the fact that he had selected this historic drive as the right time to appear in public wearing his novelty hat. This had a huge axe sticking out of the top, which flapped ridiculously as his family set up a rocking motion within the Land Rover in order to obtain some contact with the ground. Suddenly a couple of the whirring wheels bit and the scene changed violently. The Commander's vehicle shot off at something of an angle to the intended direction and was brought back under control with all the skill that his years as a Tornado pilot had given him.

From the top of Long Mountain we could see Long Island Farm, complete with its sweeping beach at the western end of Berkeley Sound. It was a breathtaking view. The visiting general was taking pictures. I snapped a few and noticed the trail of endeavour behind us. Obviously, the more vehicles that drive over a soft patch of land, the softer it becomes. Thus, logically, those towards the rear of a seventy-vehicle convoy might not find passage through the terrain as easy as their leaders. I put binoculars to my eyes to witness the varied stages of bogging and de-bogging being enacted on the slopes below. Our convoy appeared as a huge centipede, winding its way uphill that had acquired various deadlegs at random. Thus some parts of the body were catching up with others, but in places it was being stretched.

Tony seemed content with the picture and we restarted in order to get to the lunch rendezvous. He was being particularly fastidious, taking his leadership seriously and making sure that governors and generals were keeping up.

The younger generation of Camp drivers has a far more aggressive attitude towards the whole subject than we older folk do. Their Land Rovers are gaudily coloured and their love of spotlights is reminiscent of the moneyed Mods' Lambrettas of my youth. Some even have exhaust pipes reaching vertically for the sky above the driver's cab, as though they have some submarine capability. Their machines look oversized with their huge wheels and assume a threatening posture. It was just such a machine, driven by a shouting dark-haired local, that I noticed overtaking us across the virgin Camp to our right. No partial track was going to hold this lad. The sheer speed he was making was causing the lurid vehicle to lunge unevenly, but clearly the driver's frustration at remaining behind this bunch of old fogies was being assuaged by the thrill of surging past us. There was no denying the excitement and flair inherent in the situation. But pride comes before something. Even as I watched, the front wheels of the vehicle bounced up and then down and the whole front half disappeared in a huge splash as the whine of the engine died on the breeze. He was fished out, but not by Tony, or the Governor, or the general, or the Commander or indeed by us or the two solicitors, who had resisted the urge to make notes of the incident. We were rumbling serenely towards something that I have heard doesn't exist – a free lunch.

The convoy halted at Tony's wish in a broad valley between the bare rocked hills. There we met a large party on horseback who were covering the same historic route. The military had set up a generous and fulsome barbecue and the sun came out to shine on our celebrations as we tucked into steak sandwiches. A BV appeared over a nearby col and made for our gathering. I have no notion what BV actually stands for, but it is a wonderful caterpillar-tracked personnel carrier that is Swedish in origin. It can cover rough and slippery ground with speed and without a hint of bogging. Unfortunately, it does rather cut up the surface and is also pretty uncomfortable and noisy to ride in, but we all watched in awe as it sped up to the barbecue and a succession of uniformed men climbed out to avail themselves of this unusual temporary restaurant so nearly at the end of the universe.

After lunch, and feeling that the threat of bogging had receded, the centipede set off on its winding way out of the valley towards the goal of Stanley. We approached the town from the west down the Moody Brook valley, with Mount Longdon on one side and Mount Tumbledown the other. The bright roofs in the distance vibrated in the peaceful sunlight where only a bare hillside had been one hundred and fifty years before. Through binoculars it looked like spaced dolls' houses, with a few model trees to create interest. Several wrecks lay angular and motionless near the water's edge as giant petrels swooped around them.

The confidence of the post-lunch period was thoroughly unjustified. There were innumerable boggings. His Excellency had decided to take over the driving from the chauffeur and had managed to collect a massive puncture, with the tyre hanging from the wheel hub. Cameras appeared from everywhere to capture the moment – even Falkland Islanders have a streak of the paparazzi about them. One thing that lodged itself in my mind during the last half of the journey was the incredible usefulness of those winch mechanisms that some Land Rovers had on the front. So you get bogged; you merely summon your nearest mate with one of these winching devices. He positions the front of his Rover a few yards away from the front of yours, attaches the wire to the bumper, presses a small button, and hey presto, your vehicle simply eases its way out of the ooze.

Another thing that struck me was that in spite of the obvious skill of the Islanders, the terrain was entirely non-discriminatory in nature. Robert Rowlands was one such example. He had been a veritable Florence Nightingale of the bog all afternoon, the 'Man of the Winch', putting himself out time and time again to unstick hapless drivers. I confess he had used his red-hot winch to good effect on my behalf, yet he too found his Rover up to its mechanical armpits in the greasy Falklands soil. Fortunately, others took pity on him just as he had on them. It was that kind of a day – everyone was a loser and yet we knew we had all won. Our solicitor friends had enjoyed the change from conveyancing to being conveyed and we had all experienced at least something of the distance and challenge facing those early Stanley settlers one hundred and fifty years before. When we witnessed the runners and walkers arriving at the Community School playing field having covered the same course the following day, we realized that they must have had an even deeper appreciation of that historical hardship.

My first real bogging was a corker, within sight of our house, on Christmas Day 1994. Our children, Paul (22) and Kathy (20), were staying with us for Christmas that year and we were all suffering from late Christmas afternoon boredom. Television in the Falklands then was still only one channel (BFBS as relayed to the military), and precisely two weeks late, so the yuletide televisual feast was over the horizon. I suggested that we explored the other side of the bay by driving westwards to Moody Brook, which is at the apex of the harbour, to see if we could negotiate the track along the other side and view Sulivan House from across the water. Fairly simple, one would have thought. Kathy was not too keen on the idea and stayed put, but Jean, Paul and I ventured out in the Land Rover. On turning the Moody Brook corner and passing through a gate, the track seemed to shrink from being a 'B' category track to verging on the unrecognizable.

I explained to Jean that I fancied a bit of Camp driving in order to consolidate the lessons that I had learned on the Port Louis run. However, it has been my lot to marry a wife who has a slightly lower estimation of my capabilities in such matters than I do and she suggested that a healthy walk would be just the ticket after the Christmas lunch. Paul took her part in the debate and so I ended up driving alone. I soon pulled away from the lily-livered walkers and sorted out the semblance of a track with success. I was thoroughly enjoying the feeling of freedom. I was at peace with this wholesome outdoor environment as wife and heir shrank in the rear-view mirror. I had the whole ridge to myself. The view of Stanley over the other side of the water was fascinating and I was able to pick out individual houses. The sun shone and the logger ducks creaked; Christmas in these southern climes was not so bad after all; I'd swap a few scraggy Christmas trees for this wonderfully robust open air.

I had driven about two miles in this contented frame of mind when a depression in the ridge, giving rise to a charming little shallow bay, presented me with an interesting choice. I could mount the crest of the ridge, which was strewn with jagged rocks, or drive carefully over the inviting flat greensward around the crescent of the cove. In retrospect I now realize that this was analogous to the choice that Abraham gave Lot when he had to decide between the harsh mountainous country and the fleshpots of Sodom and Gomorrah. Unfortunately for Lot, he chose the plain and, despite having the additional advantage of some four thousand years of history to learn from, I did exactly the same. I couldn't remember exactly what Tony had said about knowing the suitability of the terrain by the colour, and I ventured on to the velvety textured green area with some caution. After all, I hadn't seen much green grass in the Falklands.

At first it was smooth and caressed the tyres with an ease that made the suspension seem like that of a Cadillac. I suspect that any reader with the remotest experience of life for what it really is can guess the outcome of my misplaced confidence. That very softness was beginning to capture the vehicle, subtly at first but then, as I realized the increasing downward component of my velocity and the escalating traction problem, I committed the unforgivable error of changing gear and slipping the clutch — Tony would have winced to see it. Well, actually, he'd have laughed, and so can I now — but I wasn't laughing then. I tried to reverse, reasoning that the way in could logically provide the way out. This kind of philosophy does not apply in the average bogging situation; I merely sank deeper. I stopped the engine and jumped out.

That was another mistake. That particular spot would be a fancied entry for the Most Misleading Place Name on Earth. It should be named the Great Grympen Mire or the Slough of Despond; the Islanders, with masterly unreality, had named it Fairy Cove. This velvety green stuff grabbed my boots in an instant, as my feet sank from sight. I managed to retrieve the footwear and heaved myself back into the Rover to try a calm and reasoned approach to the escalating problem.

I took stock. Obviously Jean and Paul would appear over the skyline in twenty minutes or so and I knew with all certainty, provided by twenty-six years of marriage, that I faced a humbling conversation. I had to de-bog this Land Rover with all speed. I had a bumper jack and although I knew it to be lethal, I had been shown how to handle it. I had a two-metre radio, but I hadn't been shown how to handle that and, would you credit it, the handbook was missing! Typical of a government vehicle! (Hang on, I was responsible for the government, so that line of buck-passing was blocked.) I even considered signalling across the bay to Stanley: dot dot dot, dash dash dash, dot dot dot... or was it the other way round? However, that was fruitless, as the vehicle was facing the wrong way and I couldn't turn it round. It was broad daylight anyway and, would you believe it, no torch in the glove compartment! My Boys' Brigade semaphore certificate of some forty years' vintage was also useless, as I had failed to take the obvious precaution of bringing two flags.

I decided to tackle the brave new world of bumper jacking and eased my way out of the driver's door, mincing meticulously across the squelching velvet to open the rear door. I could only just open the door, as the vehicle was so deeply entrenched. It then occurred to me, as I fiddled with the jack, that there was no obvious place to put it, as every possible point of jack-type contact was either below ground level or flush up against it. I crept around the Rover to see if the problem looked any better from another point of view, and it did seem that the nearside was marginally less hopeless than the offside. I managed to find somewhere that seemed likely to take the cross member of the jack and forced the jack into place, removing some of the swampy mud with my bare hands. Then I began the pumping motion to elevate the vehicle, making sure that my thumb and head were out of line should the ratchet fail. I felt the whole thing tense and my hope soared – what a feather in my cap this would be, de-bogging a Land Rover all by myself at the first attempt. My problem might be an opportunity after all. Unfortunately, what was happening was unlikely to bring about that outcome, as the base of the jack was sinking further below ground level with every effort of my arm, and the vehicle was static. I don't believe it moved a millimetre.

I was still trying to create fresh options for solving the problem when Jean and Paul appeared and the humbling process began. Yes, I should have walked with them all along; no, I wasn't a particularly gifted Camp driver; yes, even a child could see that this wasn't green grass but a lurid capturing swamp to be avoided at all costs; yes, the higher route was glaringly obvious in its overwhelming preference; yes, I should have learned the use of the radio; I should have ensured that the handbook was in the glove compartment along with the torch, and of course I should have brought a selection of spreading planks, their usefulness being universally acclaimed by all races from the cradle to the grave. Goodwill towards men, I thought to myself. I was, after all, the senior man present. I knew that it was best to let this storm blow over, and when it had subsided and my chastening was complete, for the time being at any rate, I consulted Paul to see if he had options up his sleeve. He took the view that he was merely a guest in a foreign country and that his father generally knew all the answers that were to be had, so why ask him.

By this time it must have been around 4.30 p.m. on Christmas afternoon. We were within sight of our house, only half a mile away across the water. To walk back there would be at least five miles, and what could be done then anyway? Although my AA membership didn't run out for six days, I didn't imagine that their international reciprocal arrangements stretched quite this far. I felt that, with Paul's assistance, I might just stand a chance of levering the Rover out of its resting-place given time, but I had to admit that it was a long shot. We decided that Jean, who had been so keen on walking all along anyway, should walk back to the house and see if she could summon some help from somewhere, even though it was Christmas Day afternoon. None of us were in particularly good humour when she set off, and I began to introduce Paul to the bumper jack with the vague idea that a slightly different angle of attack might produce movement.

We struggled for a few minutes as Jean disappeared and then I heard the sound of an engine. It was faint at first and came and went on the wind but it became clearer and was obviously heading in our direction. Surely Jean would see them and tell them of our plight and maybe they would help. The last thing I had expected was another Land Rover out for a spin on Christmas afternoon.

An old vehicle hove into view with Jean alongside. It contained two brothers, Thyssen and Martin Smith, sons of the much-respected museum curator and our near neighbours. To our amazement and everlasting gratitude they had actually witnessed my bogging through binoculars from their front room while digesting their Christmas lunch. We were later to learn that nearly half the population of Stanley had also witnessed my bogging through binoculars while digesting their Christmas lunch. However, these two worthies were the only ones to react and come to the rescue and they set about their mission of mercy with a sure touch. They confirmed what I had come to suspect, that this was a notorious bogging place and that they would have to be careful not to become enmeshed themselves, so we used a long rope and several hard tugs before lurching out in a forwards direction. Unfortunately, the whoops of delight were curtailed by a fresh bogging about ten yards on, but once again the Rover responded well to a few harsh tugs. Then I followed the Smiths on a tortuous course out of the bog, which actually entailed some beach driving, and I was back on the semi-track, facing in a homeward direction, humbled, gratified, thankful and somewhat wiser.

Our next bogging adventure was very different in nature and took place as we were en route to Salvador in order to spend a night with the very hospitable Pitalugas. Robin and Gene are members of the landed gentry in Falkland terms. These are not farmers who are strapped with a recent mortgage following land reform; the Pitaluga family have been farming at Salvador for several generations and Robin is an ex-councillor and man of considerable experience. He had argued long and hard that his settlement should have priority in the road-building programme. Thus, Jean and I knew that we were going to be driving over rough Camp and that the route was far from easy. In fact, we had a lengthy and well-written set of instructions that were heralded as idiot proof (more of that as the narrative progresses). I had by now learned how to operate the two-metre radio and had included spreader planks, a tool kit, a torch and any instruction booklet I could lay my hands on in the Land Rover.

One of the reasons that this Camp journey had to be taken seriously was that the existing track ended a full twenty-five miles short of the settlement and the route thereon crossed many streams and skirted several bays. The instructions indicated that we could drive around the beaches when we came to the bays if the tide was out, but the blue clay was to be avoided at all costs as not only would it entrap the vehicle firmly, but also the tide would come in, cover the vehicle and thus ruin it for all time. There were other helpful hints on the instructions, such as 'Follow the fence'; every time we thought the phrase might have a relevance to our position there were multiple fences to choose from. Another was the use of the word 'pass'. In country that is relatively hilly I would naturally conclude that a pass is a gap between two hills. Not here it wasn't! It meant a crossing of a stream in a valley. Almost the opposite interpretation, I'm sure you'll agree.

We progressed slowly along the designated route by adopting an ultra-cautious approach. If I wasn't absolutely sure that the Rover would traverse the next section, we would get out and walk it so that we could judge the hardness of the terrain and the optimum line to take. In reality this meant that we made about the speed of one of those early steam trains which were preceded by a man with a red flag; the man in this case was Jean. The fact that many of the wettest areas are on the tops of the hills rather than in the valleys then came into play. We arrived at the summit of what is known as the King's Ridge and although I was concentrating on making the Rover caress the ground like gossamer we ran into an area that simply got softer and softer without any warning. As forward motion declined and engine revs increased, that awful awareness that one has literally driven oneself into trouble hit me in the pit of my stomach. Yes, I'd done it again – we were unable to move in either direction. This time

I felt rather better prepared for what must surely lie ahead and we were not embedded beyond jackability.

I prepared for the work in prospect by donning Wellington boots and gloves. Then I removed the wooden planks from the Rover along with the bumper jack. Even Jean appeared impressed by the sheer professionalism and I can remember that we both felt guardedly optimistic. I selected the worst-looking side and placed the plank under the base of the jack. I began to pump the arm of the jack, ensuring that the ratchet mechanism engaged properly and that the cross member of the jack located under the optimum part of the rear bumper. So far so good, the vehicle lifted from the mire with every thrust of the lever. First the body lifted on the suspension and then the wheel itself followed and was elevated above the deep furrow it had created. This was most satisfying and although the pumping was rather hard, I was able to gaze at the spectacular view from the ridge as the hills swept away to the south and east. I can remember admiring the clouds as they sped across the sky. Then it began to rain, lightly for the moment, but enough to make one damp.

So, one quarter of the Rover was out of the bog; now, how should I move it forwards? The obvious thing was to place some of the other planks under the hanging wheels so that when I let the jack down, the wheels would locate on the load-spreading plank and then I could drive along the plank to the security of the rather damp-looking patch a few yards ahead. I forced a plank into position, let the jack down and asked Jean to watch from a safe distance as I tested the method. I started the engine, engaged the very lowest gear ratio and eased my foot off the clutch.

A slight forward movement was followed by a thumping as the plank smacked against the underside of the Rover. The whole thing just slithered along a yard or so and formed a new rut. On examination I realized that only the front wheels were actually in this new rut – the rear ones had merely taken up station where the front ones had been. Telling myself not to be discouraged, I tried again. The technique was similar, with a few refinements that came to me as I was pumping, but the result was startlingly similar. This happened a few times, probably half a dozen. We had moved about twelve yards and were just as bogged as we had been at the beginning. Over an hour had passed and it was still trying to rain.

I relinquished any pride I had ever had and decided to seek help on the two-metre radio. I turned it on and said something like, 'Hello, hello, Andrew Gurr calling. We are bogged on the King's Ridge, can anyone hear me?' Having created this mayday of the bog, I tried it several times, waiting in between to see if anyone would reply. I had heard that the police keep a listening ear on this frequency, but nobody seemed to be there. Then, to my surprise a voice came over the ether, 'Hello, Tony here...' 'Tony who?' I enquired, aware that it is a popular name and my tenuous link with possible survival could be anybody anywhere. 'Tony Heathman,' said that lean, helpful, and at that moment, wonderful man. I explained to Tony the depths of our predicament. Jean muttered that as it was Tony that had taught me all I knew about Camp driving, maybe he should feel some responsibility for this situation. I felt that mentioning that fact to Tony might be looking a gift horse full in the mouth, so I simply sought his advice.

'There's plenty of diddle-dee up there,' he said confidently. 'When the vehicle is jacked up, stuff as much of it as you can under the wheels. Do both sides, and then you should be able to drive out.' I thanked him profusely for the intensity of his local knowledge and his technical wizardry, indicating that we would immediately employ this new strategy.

Diddle-dee is a heather-like plant, prolific in the Falklands. It has a wiry and woody character and Jean spotted straight away that the diddle-dee on this particular part of the King's Ridge was not all that prolific. In fact, there were one or two bushes visible on the horizon about five hundred yards away. Jean noticed the distance, particularly because she was the one that had to walk backwards and forwards collecting the vegetation while I set about jacking first one side and then the other. I was just managing to elevate the first side when there was a pinging sound and a spring clip spun off a joint on the jack and spiralled away into the mud. I considered the construction of the jack and whether this event would endanger my life and or limbs. I realized that it could do if I wasn't very careful, as the whole thing could fall apart. It seemed the safest thing to look for the clip in the mud.

I don't know whether you have ever spent time on a darkening and wet afternoon in the middle of nowhere, searching in mud for a minute spring clip while your wife is collecting a pile of diddle-dee from a source some distance away. If you have, you will know exactly how I felt. Jean was particularly silent throughout this period and I realized what that meant – a great deal of muttering was going on, but very much under her breath. However, I managed to find the spring clip, or half of it anyway. I used pliers to push it back into its little hole and bend the ends so that at least the jack would be passably safe. I continued the pumping.

The diddle-dee method was slightly better than the plank method. We may have moved an extra yard, but remained well and truly unable to get out of this remarkably gripping situation. Back on the radio, Tony agreed that he would have to summon help. The nearest settlement at Douglas Station was devoid of men, who were all at some Camp Sports meeting or ram sale or something, but I was assured that the ladies would come and rescue us. Sure enough, within the predicted time, we could see through binoculars two Rovers climbing out of the settlement towards us.

Leona Whitney and Carol Phillips are the very salt of the Falklands earth: farmers' wives who know about so many things that town folk could not even guess at. Cheerful women and I suspect, on this occasion, rather amused. They brought ropes and chains and the large wheels on Leona's Rover looked capable of driving across blancmange. After trying the simplest option of one vehicle towing us out, Carol became bogged as well. Worse than that, the rope between our vehicles was as tight as a rope can be and neither of us could move in either direction. This was my first double bogging. Leona then had to pull Carol's Rover backwards slightly to get the rope undone and we were able to connect our stricken machine to both at once for the mammoth pull. It worked! I relayed the happy news to Tony, who remained calm and equable as ever. He was amused as well, I could tell.

Carol and Leona would not trust us to negotiate the rest of the ridge without them and they helpfully guided us to its end, where we waved a thankful farewell and set off across an area of beach. The instructions warned of a dreaded 'blue clay', which must be avoided at all costs. Thankfully, this particular hazard did not manifest itself. The day was darkening as we made slow progress and we came to a desolate area surrounded by hills known as Rattley's Flats. In the pilgrim's progress that is life, this place will always be embedded in our minds as a symbol of supreme adversity and unfair trial. It was traversed by ditches. Small ditches, admittedly, but not the sort of ditch a Rover can get across without some help. The help was in the form of bits of metal. The idea is to first find the ditch, rather than stumble into it unawares, then find a handy bit of metal and place it horizontally across the ditch. Then find a second piece of metal and place that across the ditch too, ensuring that the gap between the two pieces is identical to the gap between your wheels. Then drive over it while your wife guides you flawlessly from the other side.

Here was yet another process that sounds simple but was fraught with snags. Bits of metal of the required strength and configuration do not occur naturally in these parts. Thoughtful travellers along this route had deposited such items in a seemingly random manner. Thus, the metal was not always where we were. Having found a ditch we then had to move up and down it, either on foot or slowly in the Rover, looking for pieces of steel that had rusted to the same colour as the surrounding grassland. Once discovered, the precious bit of metal was likely to be bent rather badly and would require considerable effort and leverage to bend it back into a flattish shape. We stuck to our task as there wasn't a lot of choice. By the end we were actually searching for the wretched bits of metal by torchlight. However, we triumphed; we were now not far from the wonderful security of Salvador and the equally wonderful hospitality of the Pitalugas. The headlights of the quad bikes searching for us were balm to our ditch-sensitized eyes. No oasis in the middle of a desert could have

Above: Myself and Jean, shortly before we left for the Falkland Islands.

Below: Sulivan House, the home of the Chief Executive.

Above: The view of Stanley while landing at the airport.

Below: Stanley again, this time from the west. The roof of the hospital and the tower of the Cathedral can be clearly seen.

Above: Magellanics emerging from the sea.

Below: A Gentoo feeding a chick.

Above: Sunset over Mts Tumbledown and Kent

Below: Argentine field kitchen remains on Mt Tumbledown, overlooking Stanley.

Above: The Land Rover, stuck in a bog on King's Ridge, on the way to Salvador.

Below: Battle day-this picture shows the military band marching past Government House, where the Governor is taking the salute.

Above: Jean.

Below: The peat shed at Sulivan House: Jean soon made our peat shed the envy of the other islanders!

Above: Penguins emerging from the sea.

Below: Port Howard.

Above: The *Greasy Pole* competition in Port Howard.

Below: This shows Governor Richard Ralph, with a Striated Caracara, on the uninhabited Jason Islands.

been a more welcome sight to a weary traveller.

The mindful reader may wonder how the return journey turned out, as the very next day we had to retrace our route. The fact is, we arrived back at the beaten track without one bogging, feeling rather pleased. The self-satisfaction was rather muted, however, as we called on the Phillips and the Witneys as we passed through Douglas Station. Mr Phillips and Mr Witney were smiling a mite too much as we thanked their wonderful wives profusely.

I rather wish that the story could finish there. A partial success had been achieved and I genuinely felt that I had conquered the Camp driving problem. However, a desire to convey the complete truth can sometimes be overwhelming and therefore I must tell the tale of the most ignominious bogging of all.

Neil and Glenda Watson farm at Long Island. It is the very farm that we could see from the mountain on our first Camp drive from Port Louis. The farm itself is not far from the road, possibly five miles, but the track to it is described by Islanders as a bit 'soft'; the Falklanders' penchant for understatement has long been acknowledged. We arranged to visit the Watsons for lunch and I made sure that the Rover had wide tyres fitted so that any disaster could be averted. In addition to that, Neil described the track in detail and promised he would keep a look out for us if we informed him of our leaving time. All went well, the wide tyres seemed to make a great deal of difference and we glided across bog and mire with an ease that I, for one, found impressive. Admittedly we were a trifle slow, and Jean did a fair bit of walking in front, but we were determined to claim a victory at last.

We arrived intact and had a wonderfully tasty lunch, good conversation and a tour of the sweeping silver sand that is Long Island Beach. The beach curved gently between sloping hills and the breakers heaved lazily on to the shore. Logger ducks and seabirds took little notice as Neil drove us around. As the afternoon wore on, I was careful to bring the excellent hospitality to a close in time to be sure of avoiding darkness. Neil sensed my nervousness and volunteered to accompany us across his ground to the road. We accepted and left around 3.30 p.m., with at least an hour's good daylight ahead of us.

We traversed the most lethal areas and within about three-quarters of a mile from the road, Neil asked if I wanted him to come the whole distance as the worst was now over and we had easily covered this section on the outward journey. I encouraged him to return home in the confidence that all would be well. It was unfortunate that Jean did not overhear this exchange with Neil, as she later assured me that, had she heard Neil's kind offer, she would have insisted that he stayed with us until we were firmly on the road. However, although such post–event wisdom can be a great blessing, Neil did go and we eased our way cautiously over the remaining yards of Camp.

A small stream that we had glided across earlier that day had a rather muddy crossing point, but the wide wheels were showing no signs of slipping; they had been more than enough to rise to every challenge. I drove down into the slight depression and as we began to ascend the other side, that ghastly, and ominously recognizable, stomach pit feeling hit me. We were losing traction – then forward motion ceased. Previous experience had prepared me for this moment. As traction ceased I stopped and jumped out to evaluate the position. It didn't look too bad: we were not in very deeply and all it needed was some coaxing. Jacking was out of the question, owing to the slope. The coaxing merely increased the depth of the wheels in the mud. We quickly rummaged for diddle-dee, and this time it was abundant. However, even that was of no avail. I reviewed the situation once again. The bed of the small stream seemed to have stones in it and to be reasonably solid; if I could reverse into that, then I could exit at a different angle and that should provide more traction. By this time I was aware that the daylight was beginning to fade, so I felt that the risk would be worthwhile. I engaged reverse and the Rover moved backwards and deeper into the bog. It was still a good two yards short of the stream and would not budge in any direction.

With embarrassment and shame in my heart, I reached for the two-metre radio – this would cause another stir in the Heathman household, as they were one of the nearest farms. Unfortunately, I couldn't raise anyone at all. In spite of apparently being on the right wavelength and in spite of my being experienced in its use, the wretched thing wouldn't deliver any response. I could only conclude that we were in such a valley that the radio signal simply wasn't getting out. I had to admit that it did seem unlikely, but what else could it be? When all the possibilities have been exhausted, the one that remains, however unlikely, must be the right one, to paraphrase Sherlock Holmes.

I was getting close to a decision that would stay with me for the rest of my life. Those who know and love the Falklands regard this particular set of circumstances as demonstrating beyond any reasonable doubt that their Chief Executive possessed no competence whatsoever in the essentials of Camp driving and probably everything else. We had no sleeping bags, no compass and not even a map. I knew the way in any case and we had left Neil's long before nightfall – that was why we had no need of a torch either. The prognosis was grim. In less than an hour darkness would be total. There was ten-tenths cloud cover, so no helpful moon was likely. We couldn't stay the night in the vehicle as we might get extremely cold and there was little chance of moving it by ourselves. The options were:

a) Walk back to Long Island Farm – but we knew that nasty peat banks were in the direct line. A torch and a compass would have been useful as no farmhouse windows faced in this direction, so no source of potential light would be forthcoming.

b) Walk to the road and stay there to thumb a lift – but we could not be certain that anyone would pass that way that evening.

c) Walk to the road and turn right – towards Port Louis and Green Patch Farm. But I knew that Port Louis was a fair distance; as for Green Patch, I had only ever been there in a helicopter and had no map to indicate its whereabouts.

d) Walk to the road and turn left – towards Estancia, home of the Heathmans. I knew this to be a fair distance, but I was at least certain of the route and almost confident that they would be in and could help.

I felt the chances of a vehicle on the road were high and the safest bet was to go for the lowest risk and start the walk to Estancia. So we set out.

In the first few hundred yards I let slip to Jean the fact that I had refused Neil's offer of help to get to the road. I knew I would regret this revelation, but I had no idea that it would be used so forcefully to illustrate my total lack of judgement, both then and since. We reached the road, only half a mile away, without mishap and realized straight away that any thought of standing there with our thumbs in the air would not be sensible. The ribbon of man-made track stretched away in both directions, brown against the beige of the whitegrass and becoming increasingly grey against the blackening sky. We accepted the infinitely long option of walking towards Estancia.

It was quite fun at first; we identified a milepost and that gave us a fix and an incentive. The fix was not all that useful without a map, but at least we would be able to tell how far we had walked as we progressed, if there was light enough to actually see the mileposts. This one looked ominously like a small headstone to me.

The first challenge was a long incline to the summit of a hill. I dared to hope that as we mounted the crest we would see a snaking line of Land Rovers with their headlights beaming happily in the darkness, but it was not to be so. When we reached the top, the road merely continued down and up again; and even that we could hardly see in the gloom. It was solitude at its best – we were bereft of any other human contact and the hillsides mocked us in their stark and rocky arrogance. Jean took to shouting insults at everything and everyone; this seemed to help her a bit.

It reminded me of a game that we used to play at school, in which the boy who could shout 'Boots!' the loudest in a lesson and get away with it would win. Roger Wholley, who was a friend of mine, was awarded a detention for his effort, but it was worth every moment of the imposition. His 'Boots!' was of such a volume that, even today, I can visualize the veins standing out on his neck as he shouted. I believe it was a French lesson, so possibly we should have translated the word, but it might have lost its impact. Why the word 'Boots' should have been chosen I cannot recall, but it stayed with me as a challenge into adult life and on many occasions, when shopping with the family, we have held just such a competition. I must admit that middle-class respectability has meant that as soon as other pedestrians begin to look at us, we generally stop. However, at that moment we were especially privileged to be in the middle of nowhere with nobody around and we shouted 'Boots!' with great volume. Roger Wholley would have been proud of us.

By now it was changing from pitch-black to the kind of night that would have been the answer to Macbeth's plea for cover of darkness so that he could murder Duncan. It was so dark that we couldn't make out the puddles in which we were walking. As the road was uneven, progress slowed. The route seemed to go on eternally, the dual-purpose headstone mileposts passed, ever more dimly seen. Surely Estancia should be over there to the right somewhere? I shared my concern with Jean that possibly the Heathmans were out and that we might find that we had to go on to the next settlement. That would explain the lack of a light. Maybe there was a whist drive at Teal Inlet and all the neighbourhood had joined in (an unlikely thought, but the mind plays tricks in these circumstances). Jean was not overly pleased with this line of reasoning. If, perchance, the Heathmans had decided to go out for the evening, we would just have to walk to the next nearest place. I worked out that this was either Teal Inlet, goodness knows how many miles to the west, or Mount Kent, at least another eight or nine miles to the east. But first we had to reach the road junction and see if Estancia was alive.

We had trudged about six miles when we first saw the light, exactly in the direction I had estimated, just miles further away. It grew in intensity as we struggled on. Being perverse, the road, didn't go straight to Estancia. In fact, it now seemed to turn away from it. We decided, wisely I'm sure, to stay on the road, as plodding across unknown Camp towards a pinpoint of light would be even less fun. Possibly the light was just a security light that had been activated by a passing sheep, and the Heathmans really had gone out. We reached the junction that we had driven through that very morning, aeons ago. We took the right-hand turn towards our goal. The light now disappeared as the natural contour of the land took us behind a ridge. The road was fairly rutted at this point, which increased the unwanted challenge. Estancia hove into view and we could pick out the window from which the light beamed. At least it wasn't a security light. How ridiculous – what on earth would Estancia need a security light for, anyway?

At last we reached the driveway and made our way along it. The wonderful light that had been our target for so long now began to be a hindrance, as it was blinding us. We could see even less walking towards that light than we had been able to on the dark road. We then heard the dogs, and they didn't sound very welcoming. Did Tony let them roam at night? Were they vicious? In our blind state we imagined them hurtling towards us. Then we heard chains rattling and knew that they were on long leashes; but were those leashes long enough to reach the path? We held hands for mutual support and stuck to the middle of the path, rather like Bunyan's Pilgrim passing between chained lions. On a few occasions I fancied that the dogs were so close I could feel their hot breath and sense their expectant fangs. We survived to reach the house and could see the welcome figure of Ailsa Heathman working at her sink.

Jean knocked on the door. It must have been unusual for the Heathmans to receive visitors unannounced in the middle of the evening. There were sounds within, Ailsa appeared, her friendly form silhouetted by the light behind. 'You're bogged,' she said. 'You've been to the Watsons, and you're bogged.' We were both taken aback by this stunningly perceptive greeting. 'How could you know that?' Jean asked.

'Well, everyone knew that you were going to the Watsons, what other explanation is there?' Although there was an obvious logic to this answer, I suspect that Ailsa has such a naturally kind disposition that she didn't like to add, 'And we all know that Andrew gets bogged as soon as his wheels hit the Camp.' She ushered us inside. There was Tony, who had, after all, given me my first lesson in Camp driving, fixing something or other on the kitchen table. I described the circumstances of our predicament and as I was Acting Governor at the time, I offered to summon help from the Governor's chauffeur in Stanley. 'I'll come and get you out,' he stated as a fact. I had total confidence that he could and would. But first the normal hospitality: cakes and coffee and convivial conversation. Then, when we had recovered somewhat from the adventure of the past two and a half hours, Jean stayed with Ailsa while Tony and I set off in a suitably large-wheeled vehicle laden with ropes and chains. It was 7.2 miles back to the site of the deserted Land Rover. It lay at a crazy angle, the helplessness of the position all too apparent.

We attached a chain and tried a straight pull, which failed to have the desired result. Even Tony was slipping. Inventively, he tried an alternative method. He traversed the slope in front of me so that he had adequate traction. Then, as he passed across the front of my Rover and the rope became taut, I came out forwards, turning the wheels to the right to follow him. Yet again the Heathmans had come to our rescue, and we came to regard them as the guardian angels of Camp driving, a reputation thoroughly deserved.

A few days later, Neil Watson was attending a meeting of farmers in Stanley that I was addressing. It got to about 4 o'clock in the afternoon and I was pontificating happily when Neil stood up and said to the assembled company that he had to leave early to ensure that he didn't get bogged on the way home. The laughter was raucous! I knew that any eye contact I had with those farmers for the rest of the afternoon was going to be accompanied by a knowing grin.

Getting bogged is tremendous fun in retrospect. It produces more stories among the expatriate community than golf or fishing. The locals tend to take it in their stride, dismissing the psychological damage and life-threatening challenges as being no more than commonplace. I suspect it is character building. It will be sorely missed when all the Islands are served by roads.

Chapter 11

They came spasmodically, mostly in the summer months. They came for all the very best of reasons – on fact-finding missions (jollies), as influential and opinion-forming guests of the Falkland Islands government (more jollies), and as scientists, explorers, yachtsmen, musicians, golfers, darts players, swimmers, scramblers, marksmen, drummers, entertainers, politicians, consultants, ministers, bishops, Foreign Office sub-Mandarins, businessmen, peers of the realm, adventurers, war heroes, tourists and last but by no means least, as royalty. If they were not on a jolly, they generally vowed to return on one as soon as possible.

Some had a fabulous time, enjoying every minute and getting on well with everyone in sight. A few found it all a bit dull, and couldn't wait to get away, in spite of the rigours of the return journey.

Everywhere must have visitors, even places like Vladivostok and Withernsea get a few. But the magnetic attraction of the Falklands, aligned with the small population, meant that visitors stood out. They probably imagined they were anonymous as they dined quietly in one of two restaurants, but most of the other diners knew precisely who they were, where they had been that day and probably what they had ordered for breakfast.

Over the years, patterns of dealing with these visitors had been established. Those who qualified for the official dinner in Government House were in for a very special experience of civilized entertaining with more than a smidgen of colonial formality. Those who wanted to go fishing came back with cups full of happiness and conversation loaded with mind-numbingly boring stories. They had pitted their intellect and stamina against a sea trout. They had risked their reputations in a game of hide-and-seek against small, silvery opponents and they tended to savour their triumphs and near-triumphs as though they were returning to ancient Rome with Caractacus encaged.

Those who wanted to pay respects were taken to battle sites and memorials to imagine the horrors that even the grass was beginning to forget. Those who wanted to watch or photograph wildlife generally found that someone could arrange it. All creatures great and small then obliged by proving that in the Falklands, nature itself is a poser. Those for whom a government briefing was deemed appropriate found themselves being talked to by senior officers of government. Most of them managed to look awake and interested and I tried to make such sessions more discursive than formal. Those who came to gather news found a myriad of unrelated stories and ideas that generally appeared far more exciting to them than to their editors back home. The fight for column inches can put pressure on the truth, and reality can become much less important than perception.

The local media, on a day when it wasn't busy creating news from the scrap heap of small-society ambitions and misdemeanours, would take an intrusive interest in almost any visitor at all. An innocent bird-watcher from Utrecht could well find a microphone shoved under his nose while questions about Argentina and sovereignty were posed. One definition of an expert is 'anyone more than twenty-five miles from home', and most visitors were eight thousand miles or so away from anyone who could vouch for their common sense, never mind their grasp of international politics.

The Islanders had developed a colourful sport – 'goading the visiting politician'. A whole folk history had grown up around it. Some MPs had been known to lose their credibility, and in some cases their cool, by underrating the intelligence and the perception of the Islanders. The Tory Minister who said on a phone-in that the 'wishes' and 'interests' of the Islanders were the same thing had not read his brief thoroughly, and was savaged by a dour Camper. Prior to the war, Nicholas Ridley had visited the place to try to instil some kind of understanding of the fact that the UK government considered a compromise with Argentina to be a good idea. He returned to Mrs Thatcher having achieved absolutely nothing except confirming in the minds of Islanders that a sell-out mentality existed in Whitehall. He had spawned a decade or more of mistrust and suspicion that even the triumphs of 1982 could not erase.

The Princess Royal came in February 1996. She was greeted warmly and responded with immense professionalism. That gift of making people feel that they have had a meaningful conversation with one, even though it only lasted for ninety seconds, is not easily acquired. Of course, she said wonderful things about the Islands – nearly all visitors do. Her ancestor Queen Victoria would have been proud of her 'We are not amused' posture when I pointed out to her that her father's photograph in our Liberation Room had been subject to the ravages of time and had provided him with a halo.

One of the least-expected visitors, whose importance was not to be acknowledged, was Mrs Paula Gaul – the daughter of Guido Di Tella, the Argentine Foreign Minister. She applied to come on holiday with her Swiss husband and three young children and as they were all travelling on

Swiss passports, she was able to come. There was some debate as to how she should be treated. The conclusion was that as these people were tourists, they should be treated in exactly the same welcoming manner as all others. That is precisely what happened. I was Acting Governor at the time, and was approached by our radio station to see if there would be any objection to her being interviewed. A twitcher from the Netherlands may respond with insignificant banalities, but whatever Mrs Gaul might say could have real political impact. However, by carrying out such an interview we were in a sense admitting an element of diplomatic significance to her holiday.

All this may seem sensitive and irrational in the cold light of a European day, but as the Islanders had been subjected to varying kinds of propaganda from the lady's father for many years, it was a very live issue. I felt that we could play it safe, by carrying out the interview but not guaranteeing to broadcast it unless we wanted to. The radio station readily agreed and so did the charming Mrs Gaul. Events turned to our advantage. Senora Gaul spoke excellent English, was transparently honest and may well have embarrassed her father by admitting that the place was far more British than she had been led to believe.

I had always mixed up the Banks boys in my mind. They were both individualists, but one was a Labour MP renowned for his wit, the other presented *The Clothes Show* on television and knew a thing or two about fashion. Tony came to Stanley one morning from a cruise ship; he just wanted a quiet saunter around the streets and a pint in the Globe Tavern. He didn't realize that we were hosting a Commonwealth Parliamentary Association conference and that two Westminster colleagues would be greeting him with gusto. The Sports Minister-to-be was a good sport.

Unrelated Jeff didn't realize that the attractive 'Falklander' jumper that he designed for the Islanders to manufacture was simply too labour intensive for us. He should have, because he had to make the prototypes all by himself. We didn't need the employment and just couldn't match production efficiencies elsewhere, but we did enjoy the recording of *The Clothes Show* in the town hall. The pride of the local feminine gender was flattered into walking a televised catwalk for what must surely be the only time in their lives.

When it comes to important visitors, they don't come much bigger than the heir to the throne. In February 1999 we were engulfed in a hectic phase of pre-royal visit planning, painting rusty buildings and waking up in the middle of the night suddenly seeing possible unforeseen problems. The Prince of Wales was coming. He would be taking in the whole of the southern cone of South America in a week. Well, most of it – Argentina, Uruguay and then our own significant backwater. Chile was considered to be off-limits, due to the fact that General Pinochet remained in the UK awaiting his fate. The detention of Pinochet was popular or unpopular in Chile depending on how you may have fared under his iron fist.

St James's Palace (I hadn't even realized that the Prince of Wales lived there) sent an advance party/recce team on an anticipatory visit. Our small organizing committee juddered all over the Islands with the four of them in a helicopter. Expectations of His Royal Highness meeting everybody, seeing everything and having plenty of time for relaxation were unrealistically high.

To achieve all the proposed objectives would require a visit of about three weeks, or a prince who was capable of travelling at the speed of light while shaking hands and making people feel they had enjoyed a royal interface. We got out the pruning pens and soon concocted a programme that we thought had a balance of major interests and would optimize the impact of the visit. Put another way, it might minimize the complaints. It was, of course, timed to the minute.

A royal visit is one of the very best devices to divide a society and set families fighting. If you really enjoy causing bitterness and resentment, just volunteer to select who is going to shake hands with the most important visitor for years. Initially you will discover that enemies suddenly become friendly and, much worse, so do friends. After the selection process certain changes may take place; I leave you to fill in the blanks.

Breeding obviously has a great deal to do with being royal, and these days they must undergo special genetic engineering so that they are born with resistance to painter's colic. Everywhere they go, everything has just been painted so that it looks wholly unnatural and gives off health-threatening fumes. Even the helicopter was to get a new carpet. The carpet was entirely non-controversial, but the helicopter-landing site made up for that. Would it be the playing field, in place of the specially constructed pad? After all, the Princess Royal had landed on this self-same field in 1996 and the Prince of Wales was a close relative. This very field had been hand-picked by the new-broom COS who condemned the pad.

However, we discovered that the lives of those who regulate these matters are very fraught. The goalposts had shifted. Clearly, helicopters had become more dangerous over the last three years, as this time even the playing field was forbidden. The military were convinced that the rugby pitch some half a mile away was the answer. There they spotted goalposts that hadn't moved for years. We were planning a storming welcome – cheering, flag-waving, walkabouts and so forth. That pitch, which had not seen a rugger match for a while, was normally a quagmire and the idea of serried ranks of waving children being up to their armpits in mud while they burbled greetings at HRH was not elevating for the Islands' image. In the end the Palace changed their minds, but not before reducing the numbers to be carried in the whirring monster. That decision had a knock-on effect on the logistics of press movement.

I don't suppose the average person sitting on the Clapham omnibus ever gives a thought to those unfortunate people who have the responsibility of ensuring that the press who follow royal activity are in the right place, at the right time, with the right gear and the right technology to hand. As Mr Normal of Gravesend reaches around his newspaper for his marmalade or glances past his wife to the breakfast television screen, is he looking for evidence of crunchy sound bites and spectacular photo opportunities? I doubt it. Does he really want his news so red hot and up to the second that reports must be composed before the event actually occurs? And is he so picky that he refuses to buy the paper that has clearly missed out because its reporter could not be in two places at once? How does he know anyway, unless he spends the working day at the office or lathe, chatting with his mates about the comparative merits of media organs?

Nevertheless, the Prince would be bringing a large selection of journalists, presenters from radio and TV, photographers and cameramen with him in his chartered plane; all had to be catered for. Then there were others who would be arriving from South America or via the Tristar. We predicted that there might be eighty in total.

Now, the Falklands is a wonderful place, but it does lack certain resources. Stanley boasts about thirty-four hotel bedrooms with en suite facilities and telephones. The normal annual tourist cycle indicated that there are not many to spare in March. The aircrew from the royal flight demanded a mere nineteen. Take a tip from me and get in to the safety business; nobody can argue with you when you are on the side of safety, especially when it is the safety of the heir to the throne. The fact that nineteen folk from British Airways happened to have the very best rooms in town was entirely to do with safety and nothing else.

A telephone line is to a reporter as oxygen is to a normal human being. Such lines must exist wherever the said reporter goes and they must function properly. We knew that we didn't have enough lines to be able to guarantee the ability to file copy at any time. Squaddies tended to chat to their families on a Sunday afternoon without a thought for the deadlines faced by Monday mornings' papers. To add to the problem, over the past few months I had become used to dialling MPA around three hundred times before getting through; in fact, we installed an office junior to do little else. Cries of triumph went round the Secretariat when we managed to get through to a voice at MPA, however faint. This was because of the clapped-out nature of the installation and cutbacks on military spending. Not being able to raise the armed forces in time of war is bad enough, but when the media become involved it gets serious.

The press also demanded to go everywhere the Prince went. The Prince's Press Secretary (what a job she had!) indicated that His Royal

Highness would prefer it if the press did not scurry around after him. They must be in situ before the royal arrival and leave afterwards. A kind of reporters' leapfrog was envisaged.

These requirements provided a recipe for public relations disaster. Treat the Prince badly and you'll probably make the headlines; treat the press badly, and you will make bad headlines. I pictured chain-smoking editors toying with gems like: 'Prince in the Pits', 'Fed up in the Falklands', 'Kelpers refuse to help press' (*Buenos Aires Herald*), 'No phone in Lafonia', and 'This is a nice mess you got me into, Stanley.'

Yet our planning was thorough – it had to be. New phone lines were laid and the Court and Council Chamber became a press centre. The watching eyes of the ex-governors lining the walls surveyed an unusual scene. The contractors' camp, built the previous year from a Hungarian kit, was adapted to house the demanding 'rat pack' of reporters. One of the adaptations was to leave half a bottle of whisky on each bed. We had ideas about photo calls and even began composing sound bites. We desperately wanted to get across the message of the new, burgeoning Falklands, with thriving businesses, healthy, well-educated youngsters and money in the bank. I was particularly convinced that if we could expose the press to the wildlife, some powerful images would result. We must avoid minefields, sheep, bad weather and Benny hats and we mustn't talk about the war! Of course, there would also be wreaths to lay, and rightly so.

I had attended a briefing session in London where the canniest of the hacks had kept pushing the question, 'Why is the Prince making this trip now?' It was not easy to imagine an answer. Islanders were secretly fearful of a devious Foreign Office plot, and although they welcomed friendship between the UK and Argentina, they remained nervous about it becoming too developed.

The Prince ended such minor considerations by lobbing a grenade. In Buenos Aires, at an official dinner, he read a speech that asked the Argentines to '... live amicably alongside the people of another modern, if rather smaller, democracy lying a few hundred miles off your coast'.

For the journalists and diplomats who live on words, the impact of this humane request was surprising. Although Islanders were astonished that the Prince had been so positive, their reaction to the words was overwhelmingly favourable. At last, a Prince who said what he thought and cut through the fudge of the FCO and their dreaded diplomatic language! The problem was that the speech had been written by that same Foreign Office. Treble bluffs are far too complicated for most of us. Maybe by shooting oneself in the foot, one proves to the world that at least one can shoot.

The great day dawned. The courageous Prince was on his way. His Boeing 777 touched down at MPA in bright and windy sunshine and a delay in the form of tea at CBFFI's house had to be conjured up as the Uruguayans had let him leave early. I bustled into the back of a Chinook helicopter with the pool of press selected to get to Stanley first.

I have never been in the company of so many people carrying aluminium stepladders. Either they were trying to gain advantage in the leapfrogging or they were going to use them to gain the advantage of height over their competitors. But then if they all had them... We stuffed yellow plastic foam bits in our ears and the frenetic drama that was to last for forty-eight hours began. It was all new to me, but Nicholas Witchell and Jenny Bond opposite looked as though they had seen it all before – as indeed they had.

The first evening went more or less as planned. His Royal Highness shook many expectant hands and looked into eager faces. He did, too – he looked calmly at people in an interested manner and exchanged smiles and banter that he might not remember but others would. The journalists quite liked the press centre. The phones worked, the staff were zippy and polite and, to our surprise, they didn't mind the contractors' camp too much. The one that said it was better than the hotel in Buenos Aires had either experienced an extreme form of Islandization – or had possibly swigged the whole of the half bottle!

The next day dawned mistily, but being Sunday, church was the first port of call. We had hoped that the sun would burn off the moisture; it refused to do so. At around 1030 hours I received a call in the press centre from the military to say that the helicopters couldn't fly and we would have to convert to the 'No-Fly Programme'.

Contingencies are there to be looked at and admired. They are normally one of the things you file for future reference. Having to actually implement the hastily conceived no-fly programme was quite another matter. For one thing, nobody had realized that the decision would be made so late on. Coaches and Land Rovers had already set off for the far-flung reaches of the itinerary. Well-known faces and voices from UK television networks were already scaling the Sussex Mountains in a dusty mini-bus on the way to San Carlos. Little did they realize that the Prince was not going there today. Some newshounds would have nothing to sniff. Aluminium stepladders might not have to be used after all. They were none too pleased. There was nothing for it but to tinker with the no-fly programme so that it would provide optimum cover from now on. We convened a small group with pencil and paper and, after ten minutes of argument and redrafting, I addressed the press – no Chinooks, no Sikorskys, only coaches and mini-buses. We might get through half of the programme. They took it very well, but then they had had a petrol bomb thrown at them in Buenos Aires, so this was by nature a fairly minor crisis.

Cellular mobile phones would not work in the Falklands. Thus, any traveller on our uninhabited tracks had no way of eliciting the latest news concerning where they should be. I set off in a coach with twenty-two reporters and photographers. These ladies and gentlemen of the media would have pushed the apostle Thomas to the bottom of the all-time doubters' league. We were en route to Goose Green some two hours away beyond MPA. I deduced that the Prince would follow in the Governor's Range Rover, with the royal standard fluttering in the mist. After about an hour, as we neared MPA, the sun came out. The press was not slow to spot this, in spite of last night's whisky; their powers of deduction anticipated helicopters flying long before we made it to Goose Green. I offered to stop off at the military police station and call up the Chief of Staff to check out the situation. He had, after all, given me a number to ring.

I burst into the police station to discover that their world was travelling at a far slower pace than mine. I was set on sorting out a dicey situation. My heart was pounding. These Mr Plods in combat uniform were in tick-over mode; thinking slowly, reacting slowly and moving barely at all. There was nothing I could do to speed them up. I explained who I was, who was in the coach, who I wanted to reach on the phone, and asked to use it. A girl carrying a cup of coffee who probably thought she looked like Private Benjamin, but didn't, waved idly towards a phone. I dialled the number. It rang and rang and then was answered by a very sleepy sounding male. 'Can I speak to the Chief of Staff please?' I asked politely. 'Who?' came the weary reply. I repeated my request – didn't these chaps even know that they had a Chief of Staff on this base? 'He's not here,' said the lugubrious one. 'I'm sorry it must be a wrong number,' I said putting the receiver down convinced that my adrenalin had caused me to slip a digit. I tried once more.

Those of you who have received and made wrong number calls will realize that almost always the error is repeated. It happened on this occasion. 'Well, what is your number?' I asked the man, who had almost gone back to sleep. He gave me the one I had written on my bit of paper and rung.

I turned for help to a military policeman munching his way through a roll with his feet on his desk. 'Could you tell me how I can get in touch with the Chief of Staff please?' I asked him.

'Who?' he enquired.

Considering that he had been within a few feet of me throughout the previous exchanges, I found his question barely credible. I kept what cool I could and repeated the rank and name of the man who was in charge of the whole base and all the flying and to whom I desperately needed to speak. I was only too aware of the press hounds outside. They were not baying at the door – far worse, they were coming through it in dribs and drabs to use the loo, giving me 'Get on with it' looks as they trundled past.

'I don't know, try the operator,' suggested the roll eater.

'What is the operator's number please?' I asked through tightly clenched teeth.

'Zero,' replied the uniformed one.

I dialled zero and explained to a helpful girl that I wanted the Chief of Staff.

'You won't be able to talk to him, he's in a meeting,' she informed me.

'He asked me to disturb his meeting and gave me a number to ring in order to do so,' I replied – with remarkable patience, I thought.

'What number was that?'

I told her.

'That's a fax number, you won't be able to speak to him on that.'

I tried to explain that it couldn't possibly be a fax number as I had just spoken to a rather tired man who had answered it twice. But life was passing, the sun was beginning to blister out of a blue sky and the intrinsic farce of the situation was beyond belief. The girl put me through to some juniorish chap somewhere, called David. He obviously knew something of what was happening, said I couldn't possibly speak to the Chief of Staff, but that there were not going to be any helicopters flying for a while yet. He advised us to go to Goose Green; by the time we arrived they would have sorted it out and maybe a Chinook might come and pick us up. If it hadn't been for the clarity of the sky, what he was saying would have made sense. I returned to the coach to find the press sunning themselves on a grassy bank and muttering darkly.

I ordered the driver to drive to Goose Green and picked up the microphone, normally used to address information-hungry tourists. 'I am reliably informed by a military man called David,' I began, 'that there is no helicopter flying at present and they will be sorting it out shortly.'

'Well, what's that then?' said the man from the *Sun*. He prodded at the sky and I followed the line of his finger. To my horror there was a Chinook hovering away to its heart's content in the crystal clear air. Quite clearly David had misled me. The twenty-two massed cynics mumbled and muttered.

I then had the bright idea of getting at the truth by asking the driver to take the coach round to Heliops – that is where the military helicopters are controlled. There the answer would be obvious. The driver obeyed, the short journey taking a couple of minutes. I skipped off the coach and pushed through the doors into the innermost sanctum of the helicopter world. There was not a soul there. I shouted; I wandered through doors that said 'Death on Entrance' and made as loud a noise as I could, yet nobody appeared. Clearly Heliops were not operating any helicopters, yet I could hear the Chinook flying around in the sky above. I was losing touch with reality.

Next door to Heliops was the building used by Brintel, the private-sector contractor to the military. They were responsible for the Sikorsky helicopter that the Prince should have been flying in – they should have known what was going on. In a lather, I burst in to their office. There they were – about half a dozen chaps in flying suits and other appropriate garb, sitting around, sipping coffee and reading books. It could have been Biggin Hill before a scramble.

I explained who I was and what I was trying to achieve. 'Can you tell me what is going on?' I asked politely.

'Can you tell us?' they responded.

'But I can't get any information from the military,' I continued plaintively.

'Tell us about it,' they answered. 'We are only the private sector.'

'Could you find the COS on the phone?'

They managed to get through for me and the Chief of Staff was as friendly and efficient as ever. He promised that if I was a good boy and took the coach to Goose Green, then they would bring the Chinook there to pick us up if there was to be any flying at all. This was the kind of assurance that I felt might just stave off the Islands' first coach passenger mutiny and minder murder. I mentioned the blazing sunshine and clear blue sky, but was told curtly by the COS that the met men had other information that indicated that the weather wasn't always what it seemed. I rejoined the reporters, whose chat reduced to silence as I approached. I insisted that the driver rejoin the track to Goose Green.

The weather continued to improve throughout the day and towards 4 p.m. I ended up on Sea Lion Island with a load of journalists and photographers. The weather was superb. The wind and cloud had dissipated and the scene was breathtaking. Elephant seals were slumped on the beaches, penguins were scurrying about their business or just hanging about in clusters and it was shirtsleeve warm. The cynics in my charge loved it. They chatted amiably, watched the killer whales blowing off shore and began to take pictures of each other. In fact, they were enjoying the whole experience so much that it seemed almost incongruous when the Prince arrived and started doing his photo-call duty. It had been a Waterloo after all – victory snatched from the jaws and so forth.

So, the extremely royal personage came and saw and re-conquered for Britain. He managed to be normal yet special, reactive yet proactive, listening yet talking, serious yet humorous, informed yet questioning. He was impressive in public and in semi-public. In organizing his press followers one could appreciate something of what he has to contend with. There were no real moments of privacy and the occasional eccentricity was to be expected. His personal artist made up for the fact that his watercolouring time was reduced to zero. She would arrive at a location in a breathless state, set up her easel and gaze at view and canvas in turn, then hastily create some kind of foundation for later, more detailed work.

I was fascinated with the magnificent crested silver stirring stick, placed so neatly beside His Royal Highness's drink at dinner. I felt it would give him something on which to settle his mind and fingers when bored by our gauche conversation. But if time lay heavily upon him, he never showed it. Maybe he is a brilliant actor, or possibly he really did enjoy his visit.

Chapter 12

A lone sheep stands stolidly on the Islands' crest. In some depictions it has five legs due to an error by the Computer Department when toying with the graphics. Although inhabitants are a bit sensitive about the sheep jokes that come thick and fast from visitors and the UK press, the humble sheep gambols through the Islands' culture in a thoroughly dominant way. It represents the heritage of the Falklands. Most Islanders would allow the pungent smell of the woolshed to conjure up mental images of home and a sense of belonging. Yet for the past quarter of a century the wool business has been dying a slow death.

The stockpile of fleeces in Australian warehouses and the increasing popularity of substitutes have lead inevitably to the fact that there are too many sheep in the world. No matter how hard the average sheep farmer works, the market for his product gets smaller. His goal of financial self-sufficiency remains over the horizon. Generally he hates to beg from central government, and the government, in turn, is well aware of the problems associated with subsidy. But there is a fundamental political point to be made. In order to maintain the claim to the land there is a sense in which one has to inhabit it, at least that is the doctrine that has emerged. Thus the will exists to keep people living in the vastness of rural Falklands, no matter how meagre may be their ability to sustain themselves or how thin may be their distribution.

In the good old days that glowed golden in the national memory (but which nobody ever really wants to go back to), the sheep farms tended to be large. These settlements, of sometimes well over one hundred souls, were virtually self-sufficient communities and they managed the sheep over a vast area. Shepherds used the option when necessary of staying away from the main settlement in outhouses and shanties and the task of gathering and driving the sheep to be shorn was done on horseback. Many Campers became highly accomplished horsemen. Today the sound of the quad bike has replaced the heavy breathing of the horses. Some of the shanties still exist and are used as holiday cottages by Stanley folk. You originally came to Stanley to get away from it all – now you can get away from Stanley as well!

The social calendar and even the clock were geared to the natural needs of the ovine population. Only when shearing was over could the farms relax and have their festivals. The innovative Camp Sports and the 'two nighters' were born of this harvest celebration. Never volunteer for a 'two nighter', unless you are all set up for a liver transplant and enjoy not remembering what happened last night and tonight as well.

Prior to the war the balance of new immigrants came from the UK to work on these large farms. The reasons for deciding to take a chance on a robust life at the end of the world were many and varied. Some sought adventure, some were frustrated by lack of opportunity elsewhere, some wanted a fresh start and others may well have been escaping from situations, or even from themselves. Many came and went, but others stayed and integrated into the existing fabric.

After the events of 1982 there was another flurry of immigration and this time the emphasis was more on business and Stanley, but the Shackleton Report had said a great deal about the future of the Camp and land ownership. The revamped administration began to work on breaking up the large farms and eroding the respected but hated grip of the absentee landlords. Local people clamoured to have their own farm at last and the government helped in creating that opportunity.

This process of subdivision looked like a good idea at the time. Indeed, if the world wool price had held and if somehow farms could have varied their scale and specialization, it would have worked quite well. But it hasn't. Many of the subdivided farms were of similar size – big enough to make a profit pre-1982 but too small to generate enough turnover subsequently. In addition farmers have tended to want their farm to be a microcosm of the historical model. Thus the settlements fragmented as individual outhouses became farms. Houses were moved – yes, moved – over many miles. Woolsheds were built to cater for fewer sheep than could possibly make a return on the investment.

This kind of economic problem was not unique to the Falklands; small rural communities throughout the world have struggled with the same issue. Thus, the package of answers was unsurprising and related to the twin objectives of diversifying into other products and markets while improving the efficiency of the core product – wool.

After a great deal of thought and consultation we set about achieving the necessary changes, realizing that we had to stay with it over the long term to reap benefits. The measures required a great deal of work and culture shift. We had to build an abattoir, as no meat could be exported, or even sold to the local military, for as long as it continued to be slaughtered in the old-fashioned manner. The abattoir was to be funded by European money.

Pause there to utter a brief incantation for the Brussels gravy train. The legislative and bureaucratic mesh in which we became trapped caused the far-seeing Governor Ralph to bet the optimistic General Manager of the

FIDC that the abattoir would not be completed before he left the Islands. The bet was placed within days of the Governor's arrival in January 1996. Governor Ralph left via the public jetty following a ceremonial goodbye with guns and ostrich feathers in May 1999, his £1 winnings firmly in his pocket. The contractor had not even been appointed. The eventual decision was to build it with local money. Even the UK civil service can learn a thing or two about delaying tactics from Brussels.

The number of suitable beef cattle had to be increased significantly and pigs needed to be bred. We had to reinforce existing research programmes into grassland improvement and find ways of changing the scale of certain farms and the options for keeping more unusual livestock, such as guanacos, deer, goats and even ostriches, needed study. Needless to say the idea of ostriches came in for particular criticism from the denizens of the Camp. The Government's Agriculture Department was sharpened up and we found scientists from Australia and New Zealand scrambling for the jobs.

One of the most interesting and challenging problems was that of the grassland, as the natural whitegrass lacked the quantity and balance of nutrients necessary to increase sheep or cattle production. We were averaging less than one sheep every four acres. The obvious piling on of fertilizer would have solved the problem, but there was no local source of calcium, nitrogen or phosphate and importing these things added an impossible premium. Thus we initiated a search into the possibility of improving the soil naturally by introducing plants that would fix nitrogen in the soil as they grew. I was to learn that types of legume have this ability and that some would be better adapted to our climate than others. We needed to find out which was best and this meant a dedicated research scientist. One of the 'discoveries' was a type of seaweed that the locals had known about for years. It had a high calcium content and was washed up on the broad beaches of parts of Lafonia. There were substantial beds of the stuff just offshore and all that we had to do was to reduce it to a dust, in which form it could be used as a first-rate fertilizer.

Many attempts had been made since the beginning of the 20th century to grow trees, but apart from the rather ambitiously labelled 'forest' at Hill Cove, which was no more than a couple of acres of woodland, they produced nothing. The benefits promised to be substantial. The prospect of natural shelter from the wind for animals and crops was attractive to both. A carefully managed programme was introduced and thousands of saplings were squidged into the peaty earth. Time will be the judge of the plan's success.

Life is singularly challenging for the farmers of the Falklands. Existence is a strange mixture of idyllic self-dependence and personal economic struggle. They may own the land as far as they can see, but their mortgage could well be larger than their ability to pay and the value of their holding only equivalent to what it can produce as fleeces. This can be less than the shearers' wages. The stress and worry can be severe and the loneliness can be intense. The nearest neighbour could well be thirty miles away across very rough country.

One evening I was at Port Stephens in the remote south-west, home of the Robertson family. Leon Berntsen, the farmer from Albemarle, had ridden his motorbike over the mountain to meet and discuss farming issues. Such conversations were always enjoyable. The issues were fundamental and practical. I sometimes felt that we were debating points that had been around for generations, if not centuries. We may not have solved many problems, but we improved our mutual understanding of them. When he left for home, our host, Peter Robertson, stayed up for a couple of hours until he received a call over the two-metre radio from Leon saying that he'd arrived. That was normal courtesy in Camp, but to me it spoke volumes about the constraints of being so isolated. Men have been known to just disappear. The areas are so large and once one is off a recognized track or routeway, it is possible to be covering ground where no human has ever set foot and may well not be planning on setting foot for a long time to come. Camp is a place where spares are rarely stocked and the bodge may be the only form of repair, yet there is little margin for error.

To say that the Campers are resourceful is to understate their incredible ability to live under a self-help regime. An advert for an average farmer might well say:

ENJOY THE FREEDOM OF BEING YOUR OWN BOSS

Applications are invited from the Falkland Islands Government for experienced sheep farmers who must be fully conversant with all the options for diversification. You must possess proven skills in plumbing, carpentry, mechanical and electrical engineering, painting, gardening, cooking, tourism management and fishing. The ability to butcher your own meat will be essential to survival and experience as a wildlife warden and entrepreneur would be advantageous. A working knowledge of wind turbines and remote telephone systems would be more than helpful.

You will be required to live many miles from anyone else and your social life will be at best spasmodic. A hard-working, thoroughly supportive wife who is prepared to be part teacher to the children, hostess to unannounced visitors and farm labourer is an essential prerequisite. Experience in writing letters to the press and lobbying politicians would also be useful.

There is no salary but you might be able to acquire a mortgage that will be far higher than the actual value of your farm.

Yet these folk are among the most hospitable in the world. It isn't just that they never see anyone; even those who enjoy the mixed blessing of farming near Stanley, who have far more than their fair share of callers, are warm and welcoming to strangers and acquaintances alike. It is quite common for a squad of squaddies to drop in for tea and be given a spread of home cooking they will always remember.

In a sense it was the war that created the extreme freedom of Camp life for most of the inhabitants. The ability to farm for oneself, to be unconstrained by all the paraphernalia of town life, to have all other humans at multiple arms' length – those that did it loved it. But the economic pressure has proved relentless. Not all have been, or will be, able to attain or afford the exquisite freedom offered by one of the most isolated existences on earth.

Chapter 13

At 8 a.m. I struggled with the two viciously sprung doors that created an airlock against the Falklands wind in one direction and bureaucracy in the other and entered the Secretariat. The office junior was hoisting the flag. The pulley squeaked and the rope resounded against the hollow metal pole as it flapped about in the wind. This sequence of events took place every weekday morning. The day was overcast and the forecast was uninspiring. Tuesday, 14 July 1998 had all the makings of a mundane working day.

I slogged up the steep and gloomy stairs towards the rarefied air of the top floor. Many a colonial administrator had started their working day as unimpressively as this. Even the Argentines had run the civil side of things from the Secretariat during those seventy-four days in 1982.

Maria, my PA, greeted me civilly. Her neat appearance matched her administrative skills. She was absolutely brilliant at her job and had become indispensable in the way that PAs rapidly do. Her accuracy and her ability to sweep up all the loose ends that I generated were matched only by her sighing and shrieking. She would emit plaintive noises of varying volumes at regular intervals related to the work in hand, my own many shortcomings, the idiocy of the computer, or the state of the world in general. Her Latin temperament added spice to this endearing characteristic.

I didn't so much as glance around the room or at the view from the window. If I had, I would have seen a Korean doll in a glass case that I had inherited from my predecessor. I subsequently ditched this rather inappropriate ornament by offering it to the general office. They took a liking to it and kept changing its clothes. Once it appeared with a photo of my face stuck on it, which caused disproportionate merriment. On one wall I had placed an upside-down map of the world given to me, yes you've guessed it, by an Australian. And as luck would have it, Australia was in the middle and at the top although the Falklands was right in the top left-hand corner. Southern Hemisphere folk loved this map and all those who studied it were surprised at how unfamiliar well-known shapes become when they are the other way up.

The international issue of the week was de-mining. It had been debated in the House of Commons and Carey Scott, of the *Sunday Times*, was visiting the Islands to give local colour to her journalistic efforts. I had already had some lengthy discussions with Carey, who was both professional and perky, but in one hour's time our local radio station was going to interview me on the de-mining issue. So I spent my first fifteen minutes mugging it up from an FCO briefing supplied to me as Acting Governor.

There was nothing particularly contentious. The overriding fact to my way of thinking was that nobody could guarantee 100% clearance from peat or sand and all our thirteen thousand or so landmines were in either peat or sand. What was the point? The local folk were well used to the problem and just worked around them. OK, they blocked off a graveyard at Fox Bay and captured sliced golf balls on the first hole at Port Howard, but they were only taking up 0.16% of the underused landmass anyway. In any case, some of the inhabitants of Port Howard had been accused by golfers of putting up the minefield fence simply to ensure that they would never have to buy a golf ball again. Now I come to think of it, I didn't see many in there when I was looking through the fence for mine...

Feeling that I had absorbed the brief sufficiently, I glanced with awe at the 'in tray', which had assumed the proportions of a stratigraphical column. I thought that in the interests of time management I had better have a go at it, so I began the process by dictating some necessary documents. The previous afternoon, in following up an instruction from the Islands Planning Committee on the unbelievably complex subject of privatization, I had had a chat with the half-dozen employees in the computer section to see if they might be interested in a management buy out. They had been universally opposed to the suggestion. Even raising it with them had made them feel vulnerable. They had exuded an air of dark suspicion and mistrust that all my attempted bonhomie could not overcome. Maybe my positive enthusiasm had made it worse. Such emotions in a community the size of Stanley always have a knock-on effect, so I felt that a sensible record of the exchange was necessary. I moved on to create a brief paper for Executive Council on the proposal for a renewal of contract for the managing director of Falkland Landholdings Ltd. As the government owns all the shares in the company, it was my job to keep councillors informed.

I then phoned the general manager of the Development Corporation to discuss the various options for restructuring Consolidated Fisheries Ltd. That company, known as CFL by its friends and 'Confish' by its detractors, had been through a switchback existence. Financial success had come easily at the beginning, as they had had an exclusive licence from government to longline for the valuable toothfish (sold in Japan as 'mero'). Subsequently, investment in their own ship had eaten capital and government had been trying for some time both to stimulate and help in restructuring. As some councillors owned shares in CFL, I had to be especially circumspect. I then spoke with the Director of Mineral Resources over the possible visit of some journalists from the UK, believing that September or October would be the best option, both in terms of the oil-drilling programme and the possibility of them being able to see some wildlife.

I had only been at work for fifty minutes and by then I had moved on to some organizational aspects of my forthcoming business trip to the UK. Maria was busily sorting out the inevitable juggling with my itinerary and was seeking agreement from many different parties at once. We needed to wedge in discussions with both of our investment bankers, meetings with our PR people, dinner with some Japanese fishing supremos, job interviews for a replacement deputy financial secretary, the normal chat with the FCO and an assortment of other appointments.

I then brought myself up to date on the possible disbandment of the Wrecks and Hulks Committee by picking up the top file in the 'in tray'. I didn't get very far with that before 9 a.m. heralded the arrival of the radio reporter for the interview on de-mining. I waded through it and the words escaped on to the tape, to reappear on radio's news magazine and then be lost for eternity as fresher words usurped them. I couldn't remember saying anything too gauche and when I heard it the following day, it sounded unspectacular – possibly a good target to aim for.

Another Executive Council paper then received the dictation treatment, this time an altogether more substantial effort on the coastal shipping service, which needed some political decisions on future structure. Once again, a councillor was involved, being a director of the company that had the current contract with government. I followed on with a memo on the salary of one of our folk in the London office and then a reply to the Deputy Director of Public Works (the Director being away) over his rather snotty note to me because I had been less than serious when giving his draft answer to a 'question for oral reply' at the last legislative council. More was to follow, as I was in a flowing vein: a rebuke on the use of government vehicles for transporting one's own children, a clarification on the terms of reference for the vehicle working group and a recommendation that our financial secretary attend a conference in Ottawa. He subsequently declined, as I knew he would. It just isn't possible to attend all those events that many of the senior people get invited to.

Ten o'clock was the time for a committee in the Liberation Room across the corridor. It was the FIPASS Logistics Working Group. FIPASS is one of our very own acronyms – Falklands Interim Port And Storage System. It had been Interim when it was put in place after the war and logic decreed that it had fewer years left in it now than it had then. I had set up this small committee to deal with the issues surrounding the use of our port by the oil industry for the support services to the rig. We managed to get through the business in forty minutes. Hopping back to my office, I dictated yet another paper (it was that time of the month) on the setting up of a temporary road safety working group.

There was an on-site meeting at 11 a.m. behind the Upland Goose Hotel. There the Falkland Islands Company had kindly offered to allow us to use some of their land, along with some of our own, to enable children from the Junior School to be picked up by parental cars without being exposed to the potential danger of street parking. The idea looked a good one and all seemed to be in agreement. We thought that we might actually get something positive done. In fact, the whole project foundered subsequently, traffic-flow problems being put forward as the major reason. I ask you – traffic-flows! In a place where a ten-second wait for another vehicle is considered an imposition!

I returned to the office in a mood of unwarranted buoyancy to be confronted by a petition with some two hundred signatures under the heading 'Support for the Government Housing Crisis'. I knew that the creator of the petition had not intended it to say the opposite of what she had wanted, but that is what had happened. Had the signatories realized her mistake too and jokingly signed it? How was I to know? I dictated what I considered to be a witty letter to the *Penguin News* on the subject, but later withdrew it, as it really wasn't on for the Chief Executive to poke fun at an individual, or even a whole section of the community. By this time the 'in tray' was approaching the Cretaceous, and I had hopes of getting to the Cambrian by close of play, but the First Secretary at Government House soon put paid to my feelings of complacency when he raised the problem of the forthcoming joint commission meeting due to be held in Buenos Aires.

This joint commission had been set up in 1995 as a result of the agreement that allowed the Falklands to explore its own waters for oil without frustration from Argentina. This commission was also responsible for developing exploration in an area to the south-west of the Islands, which straddled the notional boundary with Argentina. It had held regular meetings since inception and was getting through piles of essential work. Normally we sent two delegates, our Attorney General and the Director of Mineral Resources, but recently Argentina had been getting pretty sensitive over our exploration activity and there was a real move within their parliament to repudiate the agreement. Certainly the opposition in Buenos Aires had made no secret of their intention to ignore the agreement should they come to power, and elections were next year. Our politicians felt that it could be sending the wrong signals if delegates were to attend, as the Argentines were being so negative. The FCO advised that they should, until the talks actually broke down. Our officers felt that they would like to avoid a wasted week. Any decision was delayed until the return of the Governor. I was grateful.

As I pondered this particular problem two Tornados flew right past my window at about two hundred feet. The clouds were breaking up and the sun was glinting on the harbour. It was a stirring sight for the eyes and good exercise for the ears.

Come lunchtime (noon), I hurried home to change for my Falklands Tennis match. I was up against our very best player, Paul. He was a mere twenty-three years younger than me, considerably fitter and had topped the league for some months. The fact that I beat him has nothing whatsoever to do with why I chose this particular day to be worthy of recapturing for posterity.

I returned to the office to read through the dictation of the morning. The papers had been networked through to my computer, and the letters and memos were for signature. Then it was time for a review interview with the General Manager of FIGAS, the Government Air Service. We had spent a great deal of time revamping our method of personal appraisal and remuneration and I was experimenting with a new way of handling objectives and personal development. We managed to feel our way through the interview and move on to discuss some strategic matters surrounding the operation. Were we cross charging enough for the fishery patrol activity? Could we instigate a system of having standby passengers or would that cannibalize our existing clientele? How could we generate more customers when there were so few people to start with and there was no competition to beat?

Towards the end of the afternoon I began to concentrate on Stanley Services issues. This company was a joint venture between government and two private-sector companies from the UK. It operated a monopoly on the supply of fuel, both onshore and offshore. The private sector in Stanley rather resented the monopoly and politicians were always wary of the situation. There were two councillors on the board and there was to be a board meeting the following day. Four other directors had arrived in the Islands that morning and were flying back to the UK after a board meeting the next day. They were only able to achieve this incredible feat of rapid movement over sixteen thousand miles because they had cadged a lift on a 747 that was involved in a crew changeover on the oil rig. As chairman of the company I needed to do my homework, and getting up to date was essential if the meeting was to bear fruit.

The sun was beginning to set over the hills to the north-west. The clouds were high and scattered. They drifted gently across the view, bathed in orange and rose hues for several minutes, before the light began to fade. I glanced across the harbour as I turned the pages. The view was a good deal more attractive than the minutes of the last meeting. The phone rang. The two senior directors from the UK wanted a pre-meeting meeting. I invited them to Sulivan House for tea as one was staying with us anyway. The two councillors also felt that a separate pre-meeting meeting was necessary. Thus I had two pre-meeting meetings, one slightly more pre than the other. There was no time to change before the whole board met along with available spouses for dinner at the Malvina House Hotel. I was feeling hungry and managed to tuck away a mixed grill. The conversation was fairly general but enjoyable. Both Jean and I were ready to make our farewells at around 10.15 p.m. and get home for a reasonably early night.

It had been a fairly mundane day. It had contained no really high-level stuff, nothing international or strategic, no major committees and no lively public debate. Yet at no time had it been in the least bit tiresome or frustrating, the sheer variety of activity in both subject and level keeping any boredom threshold well at bay. Had it all been worth it? Were the steps forward outnumbering the steps backwards? Who can judge? Who actually cares? Does it matter anyway? Operational managers are always confronted with the problem of tackling the essential and delaying the discretionary. I felt that if all my mundane days were equally enjoyable, then I had reason to feel content.

Chapter 14

The Falklands is the natural gateway to South Georgia. Being the gateway to somewhere that is one of the most inaccessible places in the world has the potential to create some interesting moments. Passing through that gate are supplies for the temporary inhabitants, occasional tourists, private yachts, the British Antarctic Survey (BAS) scientists, and military folk either doing their job or pretending to while they indulge themselves as tourists.

South Georgia is an island shaped like a shallow crescent. It lies at around fifty-four degrees south, which makes it about two degrees nearer the Antarctic than the Falklands. It is just over one hundred miles in length and up to eighteen miles wide. More to the point, it has real mountains, the highest, Mount Paget, being just short of ten thousand feet high. It is a paradise of wildlife and dramatic scenery.

There is no easy way to get to South Georgia. It is six hundred miles to the east-south-east of the Falklands and no airport exists, nor, arguably, could exist there. The provisions for the base are naturally organized through the military, who parachute supplies in on a regular basis. If you do not have your own ocean-going yacht and want to visit, there are only three options: 1. Book a passage on a cruise liner (pricey); 2. Pay for a trip on a private yacht (even pricier); or 3. Persuade the military administrative machine that they can shoehorn you into a fully laden naval vessel. I managed to strike gold with the third when I was offered a passage on HMS *Somerset* in September 1997.

HMS *Somerset* was the newest ship in the navy. The very latest type 23 frigate and housing by far the most impressive collection of warfaring capability in the South Atlantic (unless of course a nuclear-powered submarine happened to be prowling in the area). I had met Commander Martin Westwood socially, and was looking forward to the voyage under his captaincy. I had spoken at some length with others who had sailed the same stretch of ocean and the message was consistent – a wonderful place to see, but if you suffer in any way from travel sickness you may well be totally incapacitated for three days in each direction.

People with sound judgement had spoken enthusiastically of the high snow-capped mountains, the translucent blue glaciers, the prolific wildlife and the fascinating ruins with contented smiles playing around their lips. But when they began to speak of the voyage, faces went ashen, lips tightened and the slightest recollection brought obvious pain. One told me he had eaten nothing for five days – and he went as the cook! This evident downside to the equation had dissuaded Jean from attempting the journey. But I turned up at the naval port, complete with cameras, cold weather gear, brand new sleeping bag and a substantial intention to always obey any orders as I was the only civilian on board, apart from two BAS scientists that we were to deposit on Bird Island. I had also already taken my seasickness tablets precisely as directed. I believe that this sudden burst of enthusiasm for obedience to authority, although marginally out of character, was entirely logical in the circumstances.

I carried my gear along a level walkway on to the quarterdeck at the rear of the ship. There was about half an hour to sailing and this rather gloomy enclosed deck was a hive of activity. Sailors were shouting orders at each other, there were various last-minute supplies being loaded and a group of men in combat dress were looking nearly as sheepish as I felt. I deduced that they were the exchange batch of Royal Engineers for the garrison in South Georgia. I was clearly invisible, but nevertheless I stood still in the sure confidence that someone would take some notice of me eventually. I had learned that this is always a good ploy with the military. It is superior as a technique to butting in when they are busy, as they simply do not recognize the existence of civilians at such times. Sure enough, I was rewarded with a nod of acknowledgement and after ten minutes or so a young sailor arrived to help with my bags.

He led me through doors, which were actually more like openings where the door doesn't reach the floor, along a long corridor and up several flights of very steep steps. They were certainly not stairs, but they were not quite ladders and I was most grateful for the portage as I would probably have missed the view of the departure if I had been trying to heave all my own stuff around this labyrinth. I noticed that the decor was rather basic; none of your *marinite* wall panels with tasteful depictions of Mediterranean scenes on this ship – all the pipework and wiring was exposed. It was meticulously clean, and neat little notices provided fresh acronyms or warned of something being too dangerous to tamper with.

The bag carrier left me in a cabin on the starboard side one level down from the bridge and one level up from the wardroom. This postage stamp of a cabin was a double, and was the abode of an officer called Richard; he was one of three Officers of the Watch. As it turned out that the other two such officers were Rachel and Emma, I had obviously been deposited in the appointed place.

It was small, very small, and unfortunately for unpacking, my half of it was still taken up with someone else's gear. Toby, the observer on the Lynx helicopter, had been asked to relocate in order to house me. I felt embarrassingly intrusive, as this cramped windowless space was regarded as the height of luxury. I was learning fast that luxury is relative on a warship. Toby took it very well, but the alternative fragment of a postage stamp that comprised his new quarters did not provide him with many storage options, so it was another twenty-four hours before I could unpack with any sense of sorting things out. In a confined space, keeping things sorted is of paramount importance and I never quite mastered it, finding some items on my return home that I knew I should have taken but could never find on board even though I had them with me all the time. As one was a rather ridiculous fleecy hat, such inefficiency was probably a blessing.

I made my way to the bridge to watch the departure and there I discovered that apart from standing on a very cold deck, there was no other way of getting a view of anything outside. HMS *Somerset* only has one porthole (another luxury), and that is fairly high up in the Captain's quarters. Even he had to stand on a chair to see out. I was told that the reason for this lack of facility is that the ship is built for fighting and not for passengers. Some months later on another type 23 I was told with equal authority that it was a cost-saving measure.

I quickly came to appreciate the uniqueness of my position, being able to live as a naval officer without having to know the first thing about seamanship. (Members of the other services may feel free to insert a comment of their own at this point.) The bridge was crowded at the wings by the few spectators from among military hangers on, as we weaved our way out of Mare Harbour behind the much smaller HMS *Leeds Castle*. *Leeds Castle* was apparently undergoing some kind of inspection. It had senior chaps from the UK on board and so was taking a most erratic course in order to trace the correct departure route, which we dutifully followed. I could see from the detail that was being studied and the care being taken over every nuance of direction, that steering a frigate is a bit more advanced even than navigating the Shropshire Union Canal in a sixty-foot narrow boat. Sightings on insignificant promontories and rocks were checked regularly. Richard, as Officer of the Watch, was walking around with headphones on, talking in a loud voice occasionally and checking the engine speed and direction constantly. I noticed a chart table at the back of the bridge with a bright dot on it, which turned out to be our location as identified by the satellite positioning system. This was useful so long as we had taped our chart in the right place. A further officer was manning these charts and there in his own chair, just to the right of centre at the front of the bridge, was the Captain.

That chair is the only chair on the bridge, and nobody else sits in it, ever... well, hardly ever. It is a rather comfortable-looking swivel chair and has ergonomic access to, or sighting of, all the significant information for manoeuvring and fighting. Martin sat in it impassively, occasionally asking a question, concentrating on what his crew was accomplishing and ensuring that all was as it should be. There could be no doubting the authority implicit in this situation; the chain of command was clear and unambiguous. I had been told that if a naval vessel runs aground, the career of the captain generally does exactly the same a few months later.

We cleared the harbour and I wandered around the deck, bracing myself against the wind and noting features not remembered from my cross-Channel ferry experiences. There was a threatening-looking hatch with a notice on, warning one not to stand near it as a missile may emerge at high speed. I moved on quickly, just in case! There were alcoves in the superstructure that appeared to have been built for chaps to slip into for a furtive smoke. There were guns of various shapes and sizes and significant-looking lifeboats. The pervasive colour was light grey and the whole thing confirmed the impression obtained below decks of functional readiness for modern warfare.

However, the bridge was warmer and more inviting. I spent a great deal of time there over the next eight days. It was in many ways the most interesting place to be. My questions were willingly answered by any of the crew present and I began to understand something of the sophistication of this remarkable craft. Equally fascinating for me was the management process, both in terms of the rule of the Captain and the ready acceptance of the professionalism and skill of the female officers.

The Captain I knew to be a personable and intelligent man, able to give and take a joke. However, at sea his perceived demeanour changed substantially as his role hardened. He became set apart from his officers by the design of the accommodation, which meant that he had to eat in his own cabin, only venturing into the Ward Room (a kind of officers' lounge/dining room) if invited by the officers. Would the single porthole compensate for the loneliness? Did he spend hours standing on a chair, gazing out of it? I doubted it. This physical segregation clearly existed to underpin the fact of the Captain's authority, which is paramount. There could be no question that the system works very well and has done so for centuries, but it is a far cry from modern participative and consultative management.

I clambered up a stairway on the second day at sea to find that a queue had formed in the passageway. Having been queue conditioned from my earliest years, I naturally wandered along the line of rather solemn-looking men to find the end in order to join in. A rather craggy sailor informed me that all the men in the queue were 'on charge' and were waiting to be disciplined by the Captain. I looked back up the snaking line and there at the head, standing behind a high desk, was the Captain with his First Lieutenant at his side. He was hearing pleas for clemency and dishing out punishments. I sauntered off to the Ward Room, trying hard to look invisible and failing miserably. If only one could manage in the civilian world like that. Corporate locations could have a brig and various privileges could be denied recalcitrant middle managers...

As for Rachel and Emma, without wishing to be in any way sexist they were every bit as effective as any man could have been. However, I could see that their acceptance by the male officers and crew was based on the fact that not only were they manifestly competent, but they were also well able to handle all the harmless badinage that flew around because they were female. The whole atmosphere on a warship is essentially masculine and these ladies had mastered the art of beating the males at their own game whilst maintaining their essential femininity. I admired them greatly for it.

The evening meal was most palatable and no alcohol whatsoever was consumed in the Ward Room. What had happened to the sun going down over the yardarm and all that stuff? What about splicing the main brace? Did they all know something I didn't? Was it the weather forecast? They explained that they never imbibed when at sea. Eventually, tired by my own inertia, I retired to the cabin and opened up my new sleeping bag for the first time to discover that sleeping bags had changed since I last used one some centuries before. Not only did mine guarantee that I could sleep in a temperature of minus ten degrees and still be warm, it was also very shiny on the outside and thus threatened to slip easily over the edge of the bunk depositing me on the floor under the influence of the slightest motion. I could have coped with that had the bunk not been six feet above the floor and the movement of the ship was already beginning to pass the threshold of tangible awareness. The bunk itself had a rail that could be specifically located at its top, its middle or its bottom. Thus I could be sure of falling out feet first, head first, or becoming wrapped around the rail at stomach level as my feet and head dangled helplessly above the moving abyss. Why on earth hadn't the navy the sense to invent a rail that secured more than a third of one's body? I had some trouble in relocating the rail, but with weary tuition from the ever-civil Richard, who had to get up at some unearthly hour to 'watch', I opted for the middle position feeling confident that my head would not slide over the edge so quickly that I could not grip the rail and arrest the descent.

However, the new sleeping bag, in order to ensure its guaranteed performance at minus ten degrees, was designed in such a way as to captivate one's arms and hands. In fact they were tied in by a series of loops around the neck and head. I was a helpless slippery chrysalis about to be subjected to the roughest seas in the world, whilst balancing on what might as well have been a polished table, high above a rock hard floor. I tried to jam my knees against the rail and wedge my body across the bunk. That technique gave me some sense of solidity, but sleep was not knocking at the door. In the ever-present subdued night light, I noticed for the first time the thick complexity of cables and pipes only inches from my recumbent head; I mused on their function. Then someone pulled a lever in the 'heads' next door and at least a proportion of the problem was solved. Applying all the dexterity I could muster, as the deserving Richard appeared to be sleeping and I would have hated waking him up, I moved the retaining rail to cover the top part of my body and felt more secure immediately. Although my head might bang against the rail, and it did, at least it could not be thrust into space to be followed by my frictionless torso. The motion of the ship was irregular and thus unpredictable, but a drowsiness that was probably caused by the seasickness pills gradually overcame me and I slept like a baby.

A whistle blew in my ear and the impact was rather more decisive than my normal radio alarm. This is how the navy wakes up in the mornings, so I dutifully woke up, washed, dressed and experienced my first breakfast in the Ward Room. There were no sittings as such. At all other meals there were two sittings, which matched the capacity of the table and the staff. Breakfast, however, was just a matter of arriving in between about 0730 and 0800, serving oneself with cereal and ordering whatever cooked items tickled the palate. All very civilized as we made twelve knots eastwards through choppy seas.

The degree of roughness seemed worthy of study. How does one measure whether this is a force four or a force five; is the 'sea state' something different, and if so, how is that determined? I hung around the bridge asking this sort of question for most of the morning. Irritating though that must have been, I was always answered with immense patience. The force of the wind was measured by an anemometer and could clearly be seen on one of the many instrument panels as long as one could remember where to look and the sea state was a matter of judgement based on experience and a little book. This book was housed in a small cubbyhole and contained photographs of rough seas. All one had to do was to compare the view from the window with the photographs to obtain the score. Unfortunately, that exercise was not as simple as it might seem. The sea outside appeared to be moving in all directions at once with no real pattern. The reason for the turmoil in the sea was to do with the permanent and substantial 'fetch' in this latitude. A swell is built up by the action of wind on the surface of the water (some geography from over thirty years ago was still housed in the labyrinth of my mind) and south of Cape Horn there is nothing to stop the prevailing southwesterlies building up a particularly large swell as no land exists anywhere at that latitude to break it up. As the wind at present was coming from the north with some strength, there were two quite distinct forces at work creating the confusion.

I watched in fascination, trying to predict the movement of our ship from the shape of the sea ahead of us. There was a kind of spirit level device in the centre of the bridge that provided the angle of roll and pitch and at times the roll was well over twenty degrees each way, although the pitch was considerably less. With nothing in particular in my diary for that day I was able to amuse myself by trying to forecast the extent of movement by analysing the sea immediately ahead. It was not really possible. Some of the officers said that very experienced sailors might take hours just watching such a sea to get a feel for its pattern before making a manoeuvre. Thus the juxtaposition of the two forces continued to take me and, more importantly, HMS *Somerset*, by surprise. Our existing roll and momentum at a particular moment had a considerable influence on the next horrifying lurch. The most telling movement for the whole vessel was the smacking sensation when the bow had obviously lifted right out of the water only to come crashing back down with considerable force. This created a shudder that ran throughout the ship and brought a crashing impact of water against the front of the bridge several seconds after the bow swept downwards into the foam.

The sea state that appeared so wild to me turned out to be a miserable five rating after lengthy discussions and perusals of the little book with accredited experts. All agreed that the cross seas created an uncomfortable environment on the ship, so possibly this really was quite rough and I could bore my friends back in Stanley with tales of heroism.

That evening, after dark and after dinner, someone in authority decided that the Lynx helicopter should go for a sortie. The Lynx was located in a rectangular hangar that dominated the aft of the frigate. It was suggested to me that it might be worthwhile to go and watch from the hangar doorway. I was wholeheartedly impressed by this experience. Here we were, literally beyond help or assistance, well on our way between the Falklands and South Georgia, with no other vessels in our area, about to launch a flimsy and very valuable helicopter from a plunging deck, in a mountainous sea, in total darkness. I watched with awe as the very Toby I had inadvertently turfed out of his bunk, donned his helmet and sat beside Paul, the young pilot. The ground crew undid the strapping that held the Lynx to the deck and the revolutions of the blades increased. I noticed that the darkness was such that even my camcorder's low-light setting couldn't obtain a smidgen of a picture. The Lynx hovered for a second or two and then whipped away into the night and the noise that had dominated without my noticing suddenly ceased. All I could hear was the vibration of the gas turbine engines and the swishing of the creaming sea against the hull. Apparently the helicopter was to describe a circle around the ship and return to land on the unstable deck.

The blackness was total. The ground crew had lollipop-type lights that they could wave in the air to mean something or other, but to the uninitiated their efforts seemed futile. I asked the flight deck crew if the pilot had night vision with the aid of special glasses; they assured me that he could see only what we could see. I had hoped that this was not quite the case, as I could see virtually nothing. I waited in a state of some tension. I liked these people. Paul the pilot I knew, the observer's bed I had slept in, and I wanted them to survive this monumental test. The ground crew stood motionless by the hangar entrance. The Lynx reappeared flying in a wobbly fashion – no, it was *Somerset* that was whooping up and down in the high sea. I tried to focus on the dim red light of the helicopter and I realized it was holding a course parallel to our stern, moving forwards at our speed, but maintaining a consistent height above the swirling sea. Thus it levitated on our port side, steady in forward motion but moving up and down in vertical motion relative to us. This was the technique they had all been trained to perform under exactly these circumstances. Wait for the right moment, then slip the Lynx to the right and slam it on to the deck. How on earth could Paul see what he was doing? He held it, and held it, and seemed to hold it even longer and then, just as the sea relented for a moment, the Lynx slid sideways and downwards and it was on the deck. A harpoon device leapt out of the base of the helicopter to grip a grille in the deck and secure the machine until the ground crew had moved out of the protection of the open hangar to fix the strapping.

I could feel the tension and sympathized that no hot baths were available for after-flight relaxation. Then it became clear to me that this was just the first sortie, they were going to do the whole thing yet again, but this time with dummy ammunition. There were threatening-looking bomb–type objects cradled nearby in the hangar and the crew began to fit these to the helicopter with all the skill and dexterity that thorough training brings. No sooner had they finished but the Lynx was off to do another giant circle around our surging ship and approach once again hanging noisily in the raging air on the port side. Paul did it, he managed to get the Lynx down on to the pad once again and the harpoon secured the landing, holding the valuable helicopter with its war-like fittings fast against the deck. The palms of my hands were wet and I was merely a bystander. Did these people do this kind of thing often, and if so, why? The question answered itself over the course of the week. A warship like *Somerset* lives on training and a constant honing of preparedness for aggression or defence. Training has to be as real as it can be; there is no point going through the motions half-heartedly, as the crew need to be able to perform their duties in the most demanding circumstances.

In spite of the relentlessly unpredictable motion of the ship I had another good sleep wedged in my slippery bunk. On the following day I was shown the Operations Room, with all its technological wizardry. I had been impressed by the bridge but this experience transported me into the world of technological warfare. This was the nerve centre. As a gadget man I would opt for an ops room in my Christmas stocking. This is where conflict is conducted. Massive deadly weapons must heed the instructions coming from the dimly lit keyboards. The probability of it ever being used in anger must have been low, and I suspected that in spite of the many hours of training, the operators hoped that they would never have to play the real game.

While I was there they were going to simulate a 'cat and mouse'-type situation with a submarine. I was given a chair confronting a screen and told not to touch any buttons. I obeyed, just in case. All kinds of imagery appeared on the screen, having been generated from the software's imagination. Apparently it was certain that the let's pretend submarine was in the area but we were unable to detect it. There was an atmosphere of intense concentration and competition, in spite of the fact that this was merely a training exercise. The team manning the room wanted to find the sub and zap it if they could. The electronic beeps and voices distorted by headsets were the only sounds in that metallic basement shimmering with cathode tube light; then, suddenly, a shout – 'Submarine!' Someone blew a whistle and we were in a middle game situation of chase and conquest rather than one of being hunted. I pointed out to nobody in particular the incongruity of blowing whistles and shouting when so much electronic help is at hand. The response came back that it was the most effective way of relaying the information quickly and I was forced to agree.

The evening passed with another Ward Room dinner, a video and watching the endless playing of uccas – or uckers, or however it is spelt – a game with the superficial simplicity of ludo that in the hands of these experts became a re-run of Caesar's conquest of Gaul. I was quite unable to decide whether it really was enormously subtle or merely the ocean-going version of Mornington Crescent.

The next morning we were to arrive at South Georgia and I made sure that the whistle did not catch me unawares. I was up early and on the bridge to see the sight; initially, it was rather disappointing. As the land emerged from the misty morning it was just a rocky area with a covering of snow. Gradually the sky began to clear, the sea became far calmer and an impressive vista opened up. All along our starboard side was the northern shoreline of South Georgia – mountainous, snow laden, and grey in the swirling cloud. As the sun began to shake off the low cloud, the perspective changed. The view could have been mistaken for a giant, slowly melting ice cream with dark chocolate layers (if you were given to that kind of fantasy). Ahead was the mouth of the inviting Cumberland Bay with the snout of a glacier at the left hand, appearing as a vertical wall of pale blue, easily studied through binoculars. We moved slowly into the jaws of the bay and small icebergs appeared all around us. These translucent glacier-blue chunks of ice wallowed in the dark blue water. With nine-tenths supposedly below the water line, I wondered how long they would last before finally melting.

After a while that telltale evidence of humanity's presence appeared in the shape of some uniformity against the randomness of nature. Some buildings could be made out, namely King Edward Point, the military barracks, and then beyond, rust coloured at the base of a towering white peak, sat the ex-town of Grytviken. I had not expected it to be so enclosed or the surrounding mountains to be so high. We approached the fixed buoy in order to moor – by no means as simple an operation as it sounds, especially with a bit of a wind blowing the ship away from the fixed point. Swimmers clad in substantial protective rubbery suits were in our sea boat and eventually managed to secure the vessel, but not without more than a hint of impatience from the otherwise impassive Captain.

In no time strange craft were buzzing around us at high speed. These were the commando landing craft used by the garrison on South Georgia. They skimmed the surface of the water like flat stones, whilst the dozen or so occupants hung on to handles having placed their feet in stirrups hoping that their lifejackets would not be needed. The Royal Engineers riding these fun machines were clearly delighted to see us. But then I suppose that was no big deal as we had brought fresh food, mail, videos, beer, and a relief detachment. The sun was trying to burst through the cloud layer at a higher altitude now and the peaks were assuming their true alpine proportions.

I squirmed into the proffered lifejacket and negotiated the steps down to the commando craft. There I made sure I tucked my boots very firmly into the stirrups and sat awaiting the skimming sensation that did not disappoint. We zipped across the bay to a cluster of buildings partly hidden by snow but all part of King Edward Point, some distance short of Grytviken itself. This snow was impressive. In England one always dreams of snow up to the rooftops and of the necessity to wear snowshoes or skis; here that dream was reality. This was serious snow, drifting well up to the first-storey height of many buildings and almost impossible to walk through without some kind of assistance. We were ushered into the post office.

The presence of a post office may give the impression that here was a civilization with a population and some sense of community. Possibly the mayor would greet us in the village hall with a short speech and we could exchange pleasantries over a warming tot or two. But there was no mayor; in fact, there was no population. The only inhabitants of King Edward Point were the Liddles (Gordon and Alison) and the small military detachment.

Surely there would be a deputation from Grytviken itself? Actually no; it was never to materialize. The only inhabitants of Grytviken were the Carrs (Tim and Pauline). They lived on a small yacht and Tim was away somewhere anyway. Where on earth could he be? Pauline would be manning the museum for us during the afternoon. It all became more and more amazing and improbable.

Gordon and Ali lived in the post office. I fancied I could hear a solo guitar playing a tuneful ditty – it sounds like, and indeed it was, a kind of truncated Trumpton, where the animation budget had been cut back by snowfall leaving only Gordon and Ali to act out the entire drama. This they did with considerable dedication. Gordon was the harbour master, so he dealt with the cruise ships and fisheries matters. Ali was the postmistress, so she was responsible for the postcards and the franking. Of course, that is all that happened to the postcards – they were franked and then handed back to us. They could only begin their journey through the arteries of the postal service when HMS *Somerset* began its voyage back to the Falklands. The living room in the post office was immensely cosy and warm. Ali purveyed delicious soup while I quizzed her about life under such unusual circumstances. This had been a kind of elongated honeymoon for them as they had not been married all that long, and as a beginning to a marriage I could see that it had a great deal to commend it. No running back to mother, no going for a stroppy walk around the block, no night out with the lads, no working late at the office; in fact, an enforced proximity that might iron out any wrinkles in a relationship. That said, I doubted that Gordon and Ali needed such assistance from the environment.

We set out to walk to the Shackleton memorial. The memory of Sir Ernest Shackleton is fused into the history of South Georgia and the sheer heroism and guts of the man deserves every remembrance. On 3 December 1914, just five days before the Battle of the Falklands, Shackleton and his men sailed from Grytviken in the *Endurance* in an attempt to traverse the Antarctic on foot, calling at the South Pole and carrying on straight through to New Zealand. *Endurance* encountered unseasonable ice conditions in the Weddell Sea, and became helpless as the ice drifted northwards. For nine months they withstood the phenomenal weather of an Antarctic winter without all the breathing fabrics and scientific underwear of today, only to find *Endurance* cracking up due to the sheer pressure of the ice. In November of 1915 the ship sank, leaving the men marooned on melting ice and drifting ever northwards, with only those things they had been able to rescue from the *Endurance* before she succumbed. Thankfully this included three small boats. During that austral summer they were able to sail and drag those boats further northwards, and come April, as winter closed in, having been forced to eat their dogs, it was decided to risk it on the open sea. They reached Elephant Island, where at least they had the security of land, but the lack of food was critical. Shackleton decided to set sail for South Georgia in one of the small boats, the *James Caird*, taking five others and planning to return to Elephant Island to rescue the rest.

It was the only possible chance of survival for the whole party, but the thought of travelling eight hundred miles in a virtually open twenty-foot boat, in the worst seas in the world, in the middle of winter, did not fill any of them with genuine optimism. Realism would have declared that the odds were heavily stacked against them, but after seventeen days of what Shackleton himself described as 'supreme strife and heaving waters', they made it.

Unfortunately, they were on the wrong side of South Georgia, all the settlements being at the heads of the northern-facing fjords. So after the momentous sea journey they set about walking over mountains and glaciers, actually extracting nails from the now-abandoned boat and hammering them into their boots to improve the grip on the ice. On 20 May 1916 they made it, and subsequently all the party on Elephant Island were rescued. It was the essence of legend, an heroic effort that thrilled a nation. Less than six years later Shackleton was dead. He suffered a final heart attack at Grytviken in January 1922 at the age of 47 and although his body was taken to Montevideo to return to England, his widow knew he would rather be buried in South Georgia. So he was finally laid to rest at Grytviken in March of that year.

We made our way to a memorial cairn sited on a small promontory across the harbour from the grave that had been erected by Shackleton's shipmates in 1922. In order to get there we had to venture off the semi-cleared track beyond the barracks and I found myself like Wenceslas's page, placing my feet in the deep holes made by the leader in front. One couldn't actually lift one's legs out of the holes totally, so our enforcedly balletic strides made progress slow. We moved forward on trust; Gordon assured us that the path was hereabouts, but for all we could see there could be a deep crevasse underneath our feet. After much huffing and puffing we reached the cairn, which was rewarding in its sheer simplicity. I surveyed the staggering view. *Somerset*, in the middle of the bay, swung lazily as the wind shifted about the buoy, the snow and rock peaks glinted and vanished as cloud and sun waltzed around them. The snout of the glacier looked like an artificial white wall across the gun-grey water and to the right the silent Grytviken itself was dwarfed by the massive mountain towering above. At every point of the compass there was snow – deep snow, drifting snow and swirling whipping snow as the wind chose to gust and rise. It was deeply and wonderfully memorable, incapable of adequate description and way outside of the scope of photography. Ignoring that fact, we all busied ourselves taking pictures.

We did the Wenceslas page in reverse and returned to the post office to catch the skimmer to Grytviken. Here was a place worthy of consideration, a ghost town of surprising scale – a magical snow palace at one glance and a heap of rusting junk at the next. This was one of the most beautiful locations I have ever seen and yet in its heyday Grytviken was a huge butchery. I can remember as a child reading adventure books based on the daring exploits of the men who sailed in these waters. They were action packed and the whales came across as being fair game, I loved them. But perceptions change with time and fashion, the horror of what had happened here gripped me as I saw the uniform smooth slope on which the massive creatures had been cut up. I stood on the slipways and gangways that were the production line of death and I wandered and wondered among the giant vats and pipework that had bubbled, boiled, processed and stored humanity's pitiful exploitation of this vulnerable species. Apparently, when the whalers first arrived Cumberland Bay was so full of whales that the production capacity of Grytviken, Husvik, Stromness and Leith was easily satisfied without the need to go further afield. Now, we didn't see one sign of a whale on the whole voyage. I was told that they were increasing slowly. Maybe our heirs will allow them to do so.

We staggered through the snow to the museum and, true to her word, Pauline was there to introduce it and let us saunter around. The museum pulled no punches in terms of detail. Ghastly implements abounded, but it also told the story of the people, their families and their way of life in this extraordinary place. There had been love, marriage, children and sports and there still was a useable, but unused, church. The overwhelming racial influence was Norwegian, but the British had been involved too. The best year for whale killing had been 1925/6 when seven thousand eight hundred and twenty-five had been dragged up the slipways; seals had suffered slightly more, with seven thousand eight hundred and seventy-seven being done away with in 1952/3. One thing that kept hammering home was that all this had happened so recently, the last whales were butchered in the year England won the World Cup, 1966.

Naturally, the only visitors to the museum that day, or indeed that week, or probably that month, were the selection of sailors and myself from the frigate. Yet of all the unlikely things, the experience was just like that of strolling around a local museum in the UK. Even a souvenir shop was there at the end of the tour offering the ubiquitous T-shirt (where do they all go?) and various memorabilia.

Outside, I was offered snowshoes by Gordon. He said they would help if I wanted to explore. I certainly did, so I strapped on something I have never worn before. They were not the tennis racquet type, but a modern version with canvas webbing. I flopped along behind Ali, who was obviously pretty handy on her skis, and we progressed towards the church – Ali gliding gracefully as the skis kissed the glistening snow, me lurching like a fly that has inhaled killer spray. The sun came out. I looked upwards towards the peaks and upwards and upwards yet more. The Himalayas could not have been more dominant. More inadequate pictures were hurriedly taken and we entered the church.

Inside it appeared to be a building that had been translated from Norway – which, in fact, it was. 'Beam me down a wooden church, Gunnar.' However, the rest of the place was not nearly so civilized. It had been once, but vandalism had virtually destroyed this industrial archaeologist's dream. Not a window remained unsmashed, corrugated iron had been bent and kicked, equipment that may have had a value had been ripped away. What is it with human beings? Senseless and gratuitous destruction in one of the most remote places on earth by people who must at the very least have realized how unique it all was. Nobody seemed certain of the identity of these seafaring vandals. Russian sailors were mentioned, but without much conviction.

Every door yawned open; some had gone completely. Beaten-up metal buildings contrasted with the virgin snow that embraced them. Inside, apart from the snow that had drifted through every wind-facing aperture, it was like being in one of those deserted warehouses or old factories in which perilous chases take place in the last fifteen minutes of a thriller. I half expected John Thaw and Denis Waterman to run past shouting and waving guns, looking overweight. They didn't, but we did stumble across something that did look very overweight – a young bull elephant seal in a dark corner. The smell had been a bit of a giveaway. For some reason this creature, of about ten feet in length, had chosen to heave itself along a railway track into the large dilapidated corrugated iron shed and was resting contentedly until the snapping antics of our party encouraged it to emit a guttural growl and wave its head in a manner intended to threaten. We could see that it had followed the curving tracks from the slither marks in the snow. I have met some unusual railway buffs in my time, but the affection this huge seal appeared to have for narrow-gauge railway tracks was a first. Had the lines actually helped his progress? What would he have done if the points had been set in the other direction? No problems with the wrong type of leaves in a place like this!

We explored in and out of this ruined metal graveyard and tried to picture what each part had been. It was not too hard to imagine it bustling with activity, work to be done, schedules to meet, the ever-present stench of blubber and charnel and a cosy white painted cottage with a warm stove welcoming at the day's end. We weaved our way through exits and narrow gaps, sometimes finding a dead end or an impassable drift of snow and eventually ended up on the narrow beach moving towards Shackleton's grave.

Ali had fitted her skis back on, and was swooshing along effortlessly, while I still had problems with walking in the snow with the new-fangled snowshoes. I hoped that it was the texture of the snow that was at fault rather than me. Sometimes the snowshoe would hold fast on the surface, I could trust all my weight to it and it would indent no more than an inch. No sooner had an acceptable pattern established itself than the imprint would become twenty-four inches as one of my legs simply fell into a hole! It provided a new form of exercise, which probably did some muscles good somewhere. The famous man's grave was similar to the memorial in being a sombre and understated edifice, but well worth the visit. Mission accomplished, it was time to return to the ship, which was accomplished by bouncing across the dark grey waters in a swirling snowstorm.

The next morning we were still moored in Cumberland Bay and I sauntered on deck as everyone else had something to do, noting the indifferent weather, drinking in the view and enjoying the cold, bracing atmosphere. *Somerset* is a curvaceous ship. Trying to get an autofocus camera to focus as your lens picks out a navy grey surface on a type 23 can be a monumental waste of time. It won't settle. Whatever achieves the stability of picture just bounces around as rays deflect. The man-made beauty of the ship contrasted with the wild mountain bowl that scaled us down. Petrels swooped and levitated in the breeze, then a couple of sailors came on deck to enjoy a smoke and spoiled the atmosphere. I sympathized with their plight – it can be very hard to get away from people on a crowded ship. We had come into a desolate environment but we had brought our own version of society with us. To me it was a novel society, but to these ratings it was the main part of their lives.

Gordon and Ali came on board in order to sell cards and stamps while we cast off and set a course for Husvik. They spent the whole time dealing with the front of a long queue that had formed in the middle ranks' mess area, while I swapped between bridge and upper deck depending on the view and the wind. We hugged the coast as we moved slowly north-west, turning into the next bay. This bay contained the other three ghost settlements and we could just see Stromness and Leith as we slid through the water to the buoy at Husvik. The snow showers were persistent and seriously damaging to the perspective. We arrived at the buoy to find that its location did not suit us. The mooring would have been too shallow particularly if the wind had swung us about, so we let down our anchor.

We then went through a period of decision-making with regard to landing as doubts emerged about the safety of the rotting jetty. Not possessing any skimming craft we had to use our 'sea boats' – the equivalent of the tourist industry's 'zodiacs'. These could not land us on a beach. An exploration party was sent ashore in a howling blizzard to discover that the jetty was indeed rotten. Gordon said that there was a safe place to walk, about eighteen inches wide, that ran the length of the jetty. As the whole structure was laden with snow one had no way of being certain as to which particular eighteen inches this might be. However, this was the Navy, not a namby-pamby cruise ship. So the officer who had investigated thought we could get ashore without mishap. I wasn't quite so confident as this time the rope ladder was being used to get from the frigate to the sea boat and to my horror one of the two sea boats had a puncture where it had struck a nail on the jetty. I queued to take part in the ordeal of getting ashore and was much relieved to notice Martin in the same sea boat.

Husvik was in many ways a repeat of Grytviken. It had more of the huge vats, but essentially it was just another whale cutting-up centre. It too had been vandalized, but there were some buildings that left me with a lasting impression. They were full of echoes, echoes of our voices, of the wind and of the past. A packing area still had the cardboard boxes with printing on them ready to receive the whale product. There was a *Marie Celeste* feeling to such evidence of occupation. Another shed twinkled inside with the driven snow and frost in a way that would have forced David Lean to include it as a set in *Dr Zhivago*. Elsewhere, the icicles were of giant proportions, hanging as translucent stalactites from the rusting gutters.

The following morning we dropped Gordon and Ali back at Grytviken and began the journey back. I was immensely frustrated and satisfied. Frustrated at not having the time to see any more and also at imperfect weather. Satisfied at having had the privilege of seeing it at all. During that afternoon we were to have a gunnery exercise and I would be allowed to stand on deck to watch, as long as I wore flash protection headgear. I duly donned the equipment and waited, camera at the ready.

It seemed interminable as they checked and double-checked everything and then I noticed that something had caused them to stop just at the point of firing. What could it be? I noticed an officer hurrying up the ladder towards me. It transpired that the delay was entirely my fault. In order to get decent control of my camera I had taken my gloves off and thus exposed my hands to the risk of flash. The gun crew had been very observant, very safety aware and also very polite!

The firing was noisy, but dull. Hammering shells into water was not all that exciting. Then, just as my interest was waning, the largest iceberg we had yet seen hove into view. It was about fifty yards wide by fifty feet high and as we approached we could see it swaying drunkenly in the swell. *Somerset* manoeuvred so that the berg was at the right distance to present an appropriate target and we let fly. The loud crack of the gun was followed by a significant splurge on the iceberg, with bits of ice being hurled looping into the air. We circled in order to be able to test the gun on the port side as well. Once again the accuracy was impressive, but in spite of the pounding the berg remained intact and appeared just as big. Rather disappointing, as I had at least expected a modest explosion and the berg breaking up or disappearing in a huge cloud of smoke; instead, it simply continued to wallow in the water. We left it there and turned westwards once more into the rising swell. An officer remarked that it would have been unfortunate if there had been a scientific base on the other side of the iceberg!

The forecast was not good for the next forty-eight hours. The wind was coming from its prevailing direction, the south-west, and thus it was combining with the natural swell to generate some huge waves. I stood with some difficulty on the bridge as *Somerset* smashed its way across the surface of a foaming and threatening expanse of black ocean. I learned that normally under these circumstances the degree of roll and pitch could be reduced by judging the speed in such a way as to make the forward progress in sympathy with the amplitude of the waves. However, we had a rendezvous with *Orange Leaf*, a supply vessel, and in order to be at the right place at the appointed time we had to crack on a bit. A speed of around eighteen knots was calculated. The lurching and plunging increased noticeably.

To make the situation even more exciting, or frightening, depending on your point of view, ice was beginning to form all over the deck. It became difficult to see out of the windows on the bridge as the windscreen washers (just like a car) were not able to remove some of the salt spray that was forming a crust on the glass. Ice began to grow everywhere, from the wire rails each side of the fo'c's'le, from the heaving gun turret on the foredeck, from the launch shield surrounding the Sea Wolf missile housings in front of the bridge, from the signalling lamp out on the deck at the side of the bridge – everywhere it could get a hold. With each downward pitch of the bows a wall of deep turquoise water would curve up on either side, shaping itself like softwood dropping from a sharp plane, changing colour to a shimmering green just before it whitened into spray and hammered against the bridge. As the spray touched any surface a part of it froze, adding to the weight of ice. The effect on the wire rails was astonishing. It was as though they were draped in a ragged cloth and unpredictable frosted-glass shapes grew like crystals in water glass.

I had heard of the problems that this kind of icing causes. The ship becomes overweight and then capsizes. I wondered if naval officer training dealt with this issue, but I didn't dare to ask. The deck surface itself was by now as slippery as any ice rink and treacherous in the extreme. All personnel were banned from it, but two of the officers were detailed to clean the bridge windows, which they achieved by edging gingerly around the superstructure, holding on to any iceless surface with heavily gloved hands and rubbing the windows vigorously while we watched from the comfort of the bridge. If they pulled a few faces at us as the freezing spray clobbered them, it was only to be expected.

The second day of the return voyage was one when the sea was really rough. On the bridge we referred to the little book and the sea state was classified as being seven. The wind was gusting at well over fifty-five knots and we were still making seventeen knots or so into a sea where the peaks of the oncoming waves were well above the level of the bridge. I watched the spirit level device in fascination to see how far we were leaning over and it was often exceeding thirty degrees from the vertical as far as roll was concerned and over twelve degrees pitching. With this kind of movement being largely unpredictable, it was very difficult to carry out most normal activities. The floor appeared to move both towards me and away from me. The steps were not easy to go up and down as one moment I was almost weightless and the next I found myself exceedingly heavy in relative terms. Most objects needed to be secured so that they didn't suddenly take off and smash. However, the ship was designed to cope with this kind of treatment, and there were fixing points for most things. In the Ward Room the table was fixed to the floor by bolts, there were friction mats so that plates could not slide, and everything appeared to be well housed. I was told that if one stood at the corridor level where a long passage ran the length of the ship and looked aft, one could see the flexing of the whole ship as she plunged and snaked around. So I went to look. It reminded me most of being in an empty tube train and looking down the carriage through all the central windows of other carriages. The movement was both sideways and vertical. This was a design feature, the Engineer informed me. It helped to pass on the stresses this way, as a rigid structure would be far more vulnerable in a rough sea. I tried hard to be convinced.

It was during this period that I visited the engine room. The movement down there was not nearly so bad. I saw the gleaming Spey engines and praised the spotlessly clean surfaces. Chris, the Engineer, believed quite firmly in keeping everything in pristine condition. He explained that if there is no oil on any surface and you find some, then you can trace the problem. I had visited some fishing vessels where the practice was at the other end of the philosophical spectrum. Down in the engine room was the mechanism driving the stabilizers. These are like huge flippers that stick out of the ship's side below the water level and react to movement to create an opposing effect. Their sheer mass means that there is a considerable time lag built in to the activity, but I was assured that it does reduce movement and watching the hydraulic device moving them, I could see they were clearly very busy.

During the first sitting of lunch I was on the bridge, doing the involuntary aerobic exercises that were becoming instinctive due to the enforced plunging and hurling of one's environment, when a combination of wave and aspect threw the ship way beyond the worst angles we had experienced already. There was a loud smashing noise from down below and a bit of shouting. I scurried and lurched down the steps in the direction of the noise to find that the table in the Ward Room had come adrift from its bolts. The first sitting of lunch, namely half the officers on the ship, had made rapid progress towards the wall of the Ward

Room, arriving against the wall around the same time as the table in question, the matching chairs, the food and any soup or liquid that was being drunk. In short, the mess was in a mess. Thankfully, no one was hurt. Even as I watched from the open doorway, admiring the spirit of these highly trained individuals as they extricated themselves from the wreckage, the ship went through a reciprocal motion, rolling an unwarranted amount in the opposite direction. Thus, the whole circus – bodies, table, chairs, food and liquid – inevitably travelled the eighteen feet or so to the opposite wall. It was a captivating spectacle and I would have liked an action replay, but the participants were not receptive to the idea and there was a great deal of clearing up to do.

The storm abated slightly towards evening and we approached *Orange Leaf* for our appointed RAS (Rendezvous At Sea). We began to flash our lamp at them and they flashed in reply. This conversation in Morse went on for some time. Was this really the best way of communicating? Apparently it was, though I never found out why.

The whole purpose of our RAS was to refuel and to do so by steaming on parallel courses pretty close together. We were to fire a line across to them and then they would send back a probing device along the line, which was at the head of the flexible tube through which the diesel was to flow. It sounded fairly simple, but it was explained that two vessels sailing closely together actually affect the steering of each other. There are outward forces and inward forces acting and it all depends on the size of the ships, their speed, the state of the sea and exactly where they are in relation to one another.

The technique of arriving at the correct position involved us approaching the wallowing tanker at speed from behind, pulling out to one side, moving rapidly ahead to become parallel, and then stabilizing the situation prior to the line firing. The rapid movement is necessary as diagonally backwards from any ship is a suction zone where we would be in danger of slamming towards them if we made a pig's ear of judging the distance. Martin took charge as any damage to the ship would be his fault and I waited expectantly as we approached the huge tanker. The ice had melted by now and I stood on the deck, clinging to a rail as we smacked about. The closer we got, the more I could appreciate that *Orange Leaf* was considerably larger than we were and even more impressive was the way in which she was plummeting around and bursting through the huge waves. I wondered how we appeared to her crew, who must be watching our approach with interest.

We carried out the procedure with dexterity, but as we closed in on our parallel courses it became obvious that neither of us was having much success at actually holding our relative positions with accuracy. The sea was simply too rough to refuel. After several attempts going in several different directions we called it off and decided to have another go the following morning. All that scything and smashing through tempestuous waters at breakneck speed had been for nothing.

The following morning the sea was somewhat calmer, though by no means a millpond. However, we approached again and managed to fire the line across first time. After some delay on *Orange Leaf* – where we could clearly watch the action, as they were less than eighty yards away – the probe came easing its way across the line. It ended its hesitant journey by thumping home into its housing and being secured by some large clips. The oil ran from them to us, but the roughness of the sea was still a problem and the probe undocked itself, snaked around for a bit and deposited a considerable quantity of diesel over the deck and the nearby sailors until the flow was staunched and the whole thing got back under control. Exciting to watch; lousy to be involved in.

This was the last day and already time was flying by as we flashed farewell to the tanker. It was not only the time that flew. As the sea was calmer we decided to have a real burst of speed, with both gas turbines at full throttle. I was advised to visit the quarterdeck to experience just how quickly we were moving, as on the bridge it all seemed rather smooth. The quarterdeck was immediately underneath the flight deck and just above the screws. It has two large openings at the back from which one can see the wake. I made my way along the corridor of the ship to the deserted quarterdeck.

What I saw came as a complete surprise. The wake was in fact a swirling wall of water that towered above the openings. The quarterdeck itself vibrated and shuddered as we belted along. The noise was deafening. It was like being at the back of a speedboat, and yet this ship had over one hundred and sixty people on board. Our actual speed was just short of thirty knots but it felt as though we were endangering the world water speed record. The atmosphere was exhilarating.

In just eight days I had gained an enormous respect for the Royal Navy, for its equipment and above all for the sheer dedication and professionalism of its men. They were magnificent to be with, cool under simulated pressure and, I would wager, would be almost equally cool under the pressure of a real-life drama. South Georgia had been amazing and, in spite of the roughness and the confined space, I had enjoyed my whole seagoing experience hugely. I was sorry to leave a ship on which I had come to feel at home.

Chapter 15

Back in May 1997, apart from the private sector's entrepreneurial capturing of some South American TV, we were living in the non-live era. However, the cost of satellite connections was reducing over time. The military station provided us with our diet of two weeks' delayed soaps and gratuitous violence. There was, of course, a programme called *Soldier*, which looked as though it was life as they knew it and thus rather short on being a broadening experience for Her Majesty's forces. However, the executive council had agreed the year before to help pay for a few live sporting events. Thus, for several thousands of pounds shared with our uniformed friends, we could get the FA Cup Final, the Wimbledon Singles Finals, the Calcutta Cup, and a few other potentially exciting matches. The money apparently found its way through the British Forces Broadcasting Service (BFBS) corridors at Chalfont into the pocket of the owner of a satellite.

At the executive council that May, the Military Commander, who was a suitably assertive brigadier, outlined an offer from BFBS whereby we could actually hope to receive 'same-day' TV. This was all being made possible by a new satellite to be launched shortly by an Arianne rocket, and all we had to do was contribute £75,000 per annum, and hope the Arianne made it into orbit. The more satellites up there, the less the cost of using them. Thus, we could at last join the serried ranks of boot wearers in Croatia, Germany, Honduras, Cyprus, Northern Ireland and wherever else we had any influence left, in seeing news that would only be a little bit out of date. However, the major philosophical issue of when news becomes history surfaced to enliven the decision. We had to have some kind of time lag. To transmit the programme truly live would mean it ended almost before the evening began. In the winter our time differential with the UK was five hours, but because most of Britain's troops were in Germany, BFBS ran on Central European Time; thus, we could be six hours adrift. In addition there was the problem of the adult watershed. Programmes that may be considered unsuitable for children are only shown after 9 p.m. This would, under live conditions in our winter, change to 3 p.m. – the optimum watching time for kids. I was reasonably sure that most of the youngsters in the Falklands watched this kind of programme already anyway, but the principle was sound enough.

The councillors liked the proposal, as it had 'This will please voters' written on the packaging. So we accepted the offer, opting for a time lag that changed during the year so that we always got the 9 o'clock news at 10 p.m. We were asked to contribute half the cost of the timeslipping device, a mere £45,000 as a one-off payment, and were assured that we could retain the ability to watch specific sporting events live if we so wished. (Remember that last half sentence, it plays a part in the ensuing plot.) The world was a great place to be; we were all happy. It was announced with as big a fanfare as we could muster (do not be lulled into being impressed) and in December 1997 same-day TV began. It was launched by the Governor and the CBFFI jointly. If I hadn't known better, I'd have sworn they both claimed it as their personal intitiative in subsequent interviews.

Everything was tickety-boo until the week before the Cup Final in May 1998. It then became clear from the programming that the military had no intention of transmitting the final live. It was going to be time-slipped like everything else. There were a number of reasons given for this: a) it wasn't technically possible to show it live; b) if it was shown live, then it would have to be shown time-slipped in the afternoon as well, and who wants to see it twice? c) the trusty squaddies had a great deal of work to do on the Saturday morning and it would be too big a temptation for them if the match should be live; and d) there would be complaints from the many who watched the normal programming on a Saturday morning. I doubted that the *Teletubbies* lobby could be that dominant, but this was the rationale of the military men of action.

There was an instant surge of complaint. What began as mere zephyrs of whinges gained strength and pace until the overworked Stanley Whinge Centre issued a hurricane warning. This was, said the popular view, regression. We had enjoyed the final live in 1997. Now we were in this bold new age of 1998, with only one more year before a new millennium, and it was back to the old ways. I was well aware that these very same people would have argued vehemently for a return to the old ways over an entirely different point, but that was a leaf of thought lost in the gale. After all, there was substantial unity and clear perception on this matter and Falkland folk do enjoy their soccer.

The arguments a) to d) were countered with: a) it really was technically possible, a point conceded subsequently by the manager of the station; b) nobody minded about seeing it twice, although football should be live in the first instance; c) whatever happened to military discipline? and d) let them complain, they'll be in the minority.

A new Military Commander was in post. He lacked the boisterous approach of the gunnery-trained brigadier, but had replaced it with the tough, though normally reasonable, attitude of an air commodore. He looked at the situation in a logical manner and felt that although technically the match could be transmitted live, it would be too inconvenient and therefore it wouldn't happen. Sure enough it didn't, and seething resentment was felt by many. The battle lines were being drawn for the next encounter. We didn't have long to wait. The World Cup, being staged in France, was just around the corner. There was also a cruel twist to come.

At the executive council at the end of May, the Military Commander, under Any Other Business, put on the table a proposal that rather wrong-footed our politicians. He revealed that Mount Pleasant was just about to receive a load of equipment that would enable them to transmit an additional channel. Thus two channels could be received simultaneously, one live and one time-slipped. This would mean that the whole of the forthcoming World Cup could be watched live as well as time-slipped, so folk could choose for themselves. Bliss for the soccer hooligans who could actually smash furniture in the Falklands while it was being simultaneously smashed in Marseilles. (Only joking; the military are not hooligans, their aggression is channelled.) The snag was that this could only be done at Mount Pleasant, unless councillors coughed up a further £20,000 for similar equipment for Stanley. That would not benefit the rural areas, where the cost would be prohibitive. It was also clear that there wasn't time anyway for Stanley to get the whole thing in place before the World Cup, as the option had been presented too late.

All the civilians had rather naively assumed that the assurance made at the executive council the previous May would hold for the World Cup. (Remember that half sentence a while back?) And that it would be transmitted live for them under the original agreement. The agreement could be interpreted as implying that, but was tantalizingly unspecific in its wording. As the Commander was not the same individual who had made that apparent suggestion, and as all his paperwork implied to his satisfaction that no such undertaking had been made, when we all thought it had, there was some choppy water ahead.

Councillors immediately decided that the £20,000 for the second channel in Stanley was a non-starter. They had two pretty good reasons for this: a) they didn't want to be seen to favour Stanley above Camp, where football followers were just as committed; and b) they felt that the 9 p.m. watershed problem was far more relevant to the civilian community than to the military. Thus it was no deal on the new equipment, and it couldn't have been in place in time anyway. The Stanley public, when they heard, was livid with fury. Well, that's not entirely true. Some of them were, but in a small place a few people can make a very big noise. The situation was exacerbated by the fact that the *Penguin News* thoughtfully gave programme timings for all televised World Cup matches under the headings, 'Live at MPA', and 'Time-Slipped Stanley'.

Enter Mr Mario Zuvic-Bulic, a most engaging man who was an absolute wizard when it came to communications technology. A Croatian who had been brought up and educated in Chile and married an Islander, Mario was the entrepreneur who had brought live satellite television to Stanley. He reckoned that with a relatively modest amount of financial assistance and the co-operation of Cable & Wireless (our local telephone provider), he could legitimately capture and re-transmit the World Cup games live. This had the makings of a good solution. I set about talking to councillors, who were smarting from the ear bashing they had been getting from football fans in Stanley ever since their council decision. They were sympathetic to assisting the private sector in this instance and gave me a financial ceiling to work with. I knew I could beat it, and it didn't take long to obtain sponsorship from some private-sector companies for what Mario was setting out to do.

He did it. Well, he did it after a fashion. The reception at Sulivan House was so awful it was virtually unwatchable, but it was live, and there were pockets in Stanley where it could be received with clarity. Football supporters crowded into those ghetto areas to share the good fortune of those who were thrice blessed by being able to pick up Mario's signal cleanly. The final itself was the big event and Mario worked with Cable & Wireless to use an enormous, recently decommissioned Earth Station dish to produce a superb signal, even for those of us in Sulivan House. Not only did the football lovers get this feast, but after the sums had been done, it became apparent that the private sector had coughed up so much that government had nothing to pay. So the private sector got their advertising and a feeling of being public spirited, Mario earned Brownie points galore, government could be seen to have achieved something at no cost, and above all, the fans saw the match. This was a rare win–win–win–win scenario, seldom seen in the Islands, or indeed anywhere else.

However, the underlying problem had not been solved. I knew that sooner or later, councillors would pick up the strand that had been laid earlier. Under 'Matters Arising', they would remember that a real-time service had been promised by the military, and they would get a bit tetchy about it not being available. I wrote to the Military Commander, keeping the Governor in the picture, suggesting that we should discuss the options so that we could head off confrontation.

One of the problems was that military men are trained to deal with confrontation. These days that can be pretty sophisticated and very nasty. Handling three slightly upset councillors and a neutral governor, was a cakewalk to this air commodore, and he knew it. The Foreign Office are always looking for a positive meeting of minds, the military for victory in battle and the councillors for votes. A chief executive flaps about between them.

I knew that a confrontation would not be helpful. Even if the civilians won their point, the result would be Pyrrhic in nature. While musing on the situation I stumbled across the blindingly obvious solution. Only one channel could be relayed across the Islands – the original time-lagged one. Mount Pleasant had both that channel and the real-time channel; could they not merely throw a switch and send the real-time picture out over the Island-wide network for however long the event was to last? The Commander researched this solution and discovered that it could.

He presented it with a flourish, and credits, at the next executive council. Another multiple-win solution – this kind of thing just had to stop. We were left to ponder which of the many possible events we would actually require live. A small sub-committee was set up to discuss the matter. As for the World Cup, England ended up having to play Argentina. If only they had concentrated against Romania... but then I'd watched football for too many years to fall into that ghastly 'if only' vortex.

I was awoken early on a Saturday morning by a phone call from the *Sunday Telegraph* – what did Islanders think about England having to play Argentina? What a crass question. I answered remarkably politely in the circumstances. The pubs with live television were heaving with supporters when the match started, even though it was the afternoon of a working day. The Beckham sending off and the penalty shoot-out were watched in horror, silence, elation and dismay. England had lost. Nowhere in the Southern Hemisphere can the result have been greeted with such disappointment. But life went on, Holland knocked Argentina out in the next round, and we set about trying to consult over the issue of live events.

We held a radio phone-in. This is normally a rather predictable affair in which the same half-dozen people ring the studio to make the same general points whatever the issue in hand. However, on this occasion it turned out to be a very different cadre, all taking the view that time-lagged was OK. They were particularly positive about the worth of the military channel, and their desire not to have it mucked about. Thus we were confronted with the other end of the spectrum from the live sport lobby, which had not got its act together or were probably playing football at the time of the phone-in.

Eventually we set out a compromise. Some carefully selected major sporting events would be shown in real time: the FA Cup Final, the Wimbledon Singles Finals, the Calcutta Cup and a few other potentially exciting matches. But wasn't that where we came in?

Now for the crunch. The military refused point-blank to respond to our request. 'It can't be done,' they said. I pointed out, with all the respect I could muster, that it was they who had agreed that the throwing of a switch was all that was necessary. 'Yes, we did say it can be done, and technically we were correct, but we haven't got a switch. We'd have to buy one and it isn't in our budget,' they countered. I said that the government might well offer to pay for such a switch. 'It could be very expensive,' they warned. I asked for a ballpark estimate. 'Around £20,000,' they replied. I refused to be fazed by this knockabout and said we would consider such a sum seriously. 'But we haven't got the manpower available to actually throw the switch,' was their next obstacle. I offered, in a moment of almost obscene recklessness, to provide manpower. 'Your people wouldn't be allowed to handle the equipment, it is a military asset,' retorted the brick wall.

This encounter led me into thinking that the issue might not be that important after all. Life, at best, is only seventy to eighty years and the argument was clearly going to outlast me or anyone else alive in the 20th century. I put this rather hardened and cynical view to councillors, and bless them, they agreed with my analysis. 'So we can drop the whole issue?' I asked. 'Until the next time,' said a councillor with considerable wisdom.

Chapter 16

Sixteen years to the day from the signing of the conditional surrender, the dawn sky was as clear as a bell over the eastern horizon. The colours turned from light grey to palest pink and then into raging yellow as the sun burst over the hill opposite. The waters of the harbour were unusually still as Stanley exchanged the sloth of a Saturday night for the ceremony of a Liberation Day morning.

By 9.30 a.m., Jean and I were seated in our formal position in the cathedral – the second row on the right-hand side. The Band of the Royal Logistical Corps (no kidding) was playing fittingly solemn music from beyond the partial wooden screen. The choir stalls beside them were seldom bulging with choir, as only a skeletal one existed. Half a dozen stalwarts rotated in order to keep the thing alive. Generally their mouths moved more or less in time but I had never heard it make a noise except when augmented at Christmas.

The cathedral is undeniably splendid, considering the distance that most of the construction materials have travelled. Inside, it is every inch a replica of an English parish church. Built of stone and brick, it has a high vaulted roof, finger-shaped stained-glass windows, a small pipe organ, oak pews and stalls, and plaques on the wall. The plaques mainly witness Island worthies of the past, although some commemorate military events. One in white marble fittingly recalls 'Rear Admiral Sir Christopher Craddock, killed at the battle of Coronel on 1st November 1914; remembered by the men of HMS *Canopus* and His Excellency the Governor at a service on 29th November 1914'. Little did they realize during that service that they would avenge that defeat so decisively at the Battle of the Falklands only nine days later.

To our right, a tattered White Ensign flown by HMS *Achilles* during the Battle of the River Plate in the Second World War hung limply above us. Beyond the screen was displayed the colourful Garter Banner that once belonged to Lord Shackleton. Its original home had been with the Garter Banners of all knights of that order in St George's Chapel at Windsor. I had seen it there, little realizing I would subsequently be reunited with it on the other side of the world. Lord Shackleton, a great visionary as far as the Islands were concerned and son of the heroic Sir Ernest, had died in

1995 and his daughter had fulfilled his wish for it to end up in Stanley. It added to the formal atmosphere on this 14 June 1998. Reverence was in the very air we breathed as the time allotted to the living ticked by. The annual service of commemoration for the trauma of 1982 was about to begin.

With one minute to go, the Military Commander, his aide de camp, and his wife, took their place in the front pew on the left-hand side and then His Excellency the Governor arrived in all his regalia to take his seat, along with his ADC, right in front of us. On this occasion the Governor was also accompanied by Mrs Jennifer Barker, the widow of Captain Nick Barker and her son, Ben. Nick Barker was the notably independent captain of HMS *Endurance* during the Falklands War. His recent death had been mourned in the Islands.

The back of His Excellency's uniform dominated my forward vision, the blackness of the tight-fitting jacket (they make them that way) in colourful contrast to the bright red pockets with intricate silver piping. The Governor's pew has certain benefits that are not available for every worshipper. The wooden floor is carpeted, there are highly decorated kneelers, and there is a little cupboard attached to the low screen in front. I had always wanted to discover what was in that cupboard – could it be a hip flask? A pack of cards? A Walkman maybe, for when the sermon gets really boring? Once, when I was Acting Governor, I dared to have a look and found an odd glove, some rather tired tissues, and a leaflet about a missionary society.

The service began with the Commander making a brief statement focusing our attention on the reality of the sacrifices made in 1982. Then a member of the local Defence Force walked slowly up the aisle with the Book of Remembrance containing the names of all those who died liberating the Islands. The service proper began. We sang some well-known hymns and then a small plaque to Captain Nick Barker was unveiled by his widow. The incumbent delivered himself of a brief sermon and then we all lustily sang two verses of the national anthem. Why we always sang two verses on such occasions was never made clear to me, but it may have been something to do with being twice as patriotic. In any event, I challenge any English person to recite the second verse – many Falkland Islanders can.

Liberation Day is one of the four formal celebrations, and is both sad and happy. We were, after all, celebrating a victory, and a victory that many of those present could remember with great clarity. But we were also there to think about those who died and were wounded and of the shattering aftereffects of those seventy-four days of occupation. How does one do such a thing? Can we conjure up in our minds a picture that is meaningful, a memory that somehow helps? I could sense gratitude, relief, almost awe, in the face of the courage and determination that was demonstrated by the British. I had been on those bare hillsides where, for me, the wind had howled a memory all its own. It looks glorious in retrospect, but it was harsh and unforgiving in reality. While singing I looked down at the limp ostrich feathers on the Governor's hat placed on the pew before me. Right at the crown is a little brass ring (not many people know that), which I presumed might be used to hang the thing up in some way. The formality of the metallic braid on his uniform and the off-white holster for his ceremonial sword hanging at his side, spoke somehow of my homeland, of its pride, of its colonial past and above all, of the astonishingly loyal and tight relationship between the Falklands and Britain. It may be old fashioned – my own children would call it jingoistic – but for decades the British Empire held sway over a well-organized world. Should we demonstrate pride or shame at the fact? Having marched round a playground at the age of four waving a Union Jack on Empire Day, I am hopelessly biased. It was a privilege to be present during this passing of empire in what must surely turn out to be the last outpost ever fought for by Britain.

The congregation shuffled out into the sunlight, warm on our faces even within one week of the shortest day. The band assembled on the crumbling concrete of Ross Road to march westward to the memorial to 1982. Few of the population like going to church for anything, but a quick outdoor event is fair game, so the crowd began to swell as the monument was approached. We drove the back streets to beat the band. The sun decided to hide behind the multiplying cloud layer but astonishingly, the atmosphere remained as still as it was at dawn. As we took our places for the ceremony, within and outside the semi-circle of the monument, a hush descended. Not a breath of wind distracted from the sound of a cough or a footfall. There must have been at least four hundred people present. No children cried. People communicated in whispers, if at all. Even the muted clattering of a camera shutter seemed noisily out of place. The youth organizations lined up in silence, the four Defence Force sentries around the monument itself were as motionless as their granite background. I noticed their rifle barrel ends resting on their boots. All was respect, solemnity and overwhelming dignity.

The Governor, who had been back to Government House for a coffee and a spruce up, was driven up in his official Range Rover. This vehicle had replaced the world-famous taxi some two years before when the taxi's brakes became dysfunctional and the bodywork irreparable. I tried hard to persuade His Excellency to go for a new taxi as the public relations benefit would be very positive, but he resisted. The whole point of the taxi in the first place was so that he could wear his hat inside the vehicle; now he had to fix it in position as he clambered out. His chauffeur, Kevin, held the door. Kevin had fought as a para at Goose Green; I wondered what he was thinking at that moment.

Another playing of the national anthem – only one verse this time. A prayer, a hymn, and then the bugling of the Last Post followed by a minute's silence and Reveille. The silence was enormous, even the ducks seemed quiet. A cormorant flapped busily across the still water, but nothing else so much as trembled. I looked up at the crowd, hardly daring to move even my eyes. I saw a collage of faces, each one thinking something different. I recognized so many. Some were filled with tangible grief, some caught in the memory of the moment and some thankful for deliverance. Some were hopeful for the future and others were recalling a childhood time when armed Argentines in scruffy uniforms dominated these streets. Others, being visitors, simply watched the spectacle. The Governor laid the first wreath as a lone piper began to play, the sad wailing sound entirely fitting to the occasion.

The Commander's wreath was laid and then the sequence of wreath layers began. I was about seventh in line, laying one on behalf of the government. I was not able to salute, as I had no uniform, but stepping back, I bowed towards the wreath as was the custom and resumed my place in line in front of the girls from the Brownies and Guides, who handed us the wreaths. Other wreaths followed. Some were personal, some corporate, all had poignant meaning. Some were laid against the wall where the name of the individual remembered is inscribed. Three non-commissioned officers from the resident guardship HMS *Edinburgh* laid a wreath with 'HMS Glamorgan' on it; they were veterans of the war. The swirling lament died, a blessing was given and people began to move about a bit, cough and hold conversations as life returned to normal.

In fact, it became super normal. Free drinks for all in the town hall. This was a public reception, and it was crowded. There were people there I had never seen before; either the population had grown inexplicably or these were seafarers or oilmen gate-crashing. I later found out that this was a crew change day for the oil-rig and after two weeks without booze these chaps could hardly believe their good fortune! Nobody minded at all on what had become a joyous occasion. Light rain began to fall outside, but the Royal Logistics Band played tunefully on and throats became sore in shouting above the hubbub. I suspected that the fire limit was being exceeded, but the thought of draconian measures to enforce it on such a day passed quickly.

Liberation Day is in many ways the most telling of the ceremonial occasions, but there are three others. And they all have their own character. Each one is held at a different location. On Remembrance Day the citizens gather around the Cross of Remembrance to the east of the town. Here we stand solemnly again as the piper plays and the Chief Executive reads the names of all forty-three Islanders killed serving Britain in the two world wars. I always found the moment particularly moving. It is somehow so close when serving military men are part of the ceremony and the surnames of those who died clearly show that they were relatives of many present.

On the Queen's birthday and Battle Day the RAF provides a fly-past with whatever they can muster – normally a Hercules or VC10 and a couple of Tornados. The Tornados show off their ability to thrill and deafen by suddenly surging into a vertical climb, with the orange flame of the afterburners emphasizing the drama of the occasion. Where else in the world would a handful of people be treated to a fly-past on a regular basis?

Falkland folk have a love of ceremony. They tend to regret that as time passes, the relevance becomes diluted. The rationale behind the pomp is not immediately obvious, but it was something to do with confirming the history, emphasizing the links, remembering the obligations and underpinning the stability. One new governor tried to adapt the Queen's birthday ceremony by changing the location. It was one of those ideas that seem good at the time when they are discussed in committee. There was an outcry – letters and phone calls flowed. Being a diplomat, His Excellency was quick to realize his mistake, cut his losses and revert to tradition in his second year. One incumbent at the cathedral tried to revamp the service. The fact that he remained unrepentant for this obvious lack of judgement only added to the opprobrium. He had not been to the FCO school.

During our five years in the Falklands the colonial traditions melted before our eyes. The behavioural patterns that had managed a massive empire, the protocol of calling the Governor 'Sir', and all such things were passing. This change was dubbed modernity, but in truth it was the Falklands catching up with the outside world. It was also Britain making sure that it wasn't caught in a time warp, being accused of colonialism long after it was acceptable. Could I really feel sad at being so close to the end of a glorious era that had encompassed India, most of South Africa, Australia, Canada and, in its heyday, even the United States? The handing over of Hong Kong was moving and significant. In the Falklands we lived through a similar process. The iron grip had long gone, an imitation velvet glove remained, and in many ways that was welcome. But a degree of uncertainty was the price to be paid.

One of the most evocative moments of the year was always the beating of the retreat on Battle Day, 8 December. Expatriates and Islanders turned up to watch this in some numbers. The visiting military band would march up and down the playing field, which was helpfully sited between Government House and the Community School. The culmination was always the playing of the Last Post by the full band while the Governor and the CBFFI took the salute. Listen to the strains of history, of bloodshed, of heroism, of careful administration, of a legacy given to a huge proportion of the world by a small island nation. There were always lumps in throats. It was more British than Britain itself had become.

Chapter 17

On Monday, 15 June 1998, the very day after the Liberation Day celebrations commemorating victory over Argentina sixteen years before, Señor Ernesto Barcella made sure that his Piper Apache had a full fuel load, and took off from Comodoro Rivadavia. He flew south along the eastern coast of South America and then, in contravention of the flight plan he had filed with the Argentine authorities, he headed due east towards the Falklands. He faced at least three hundred miles of open sea before he would sight land.

The policy that the Islands had adopted with regard to visits from Argentine nationals was particularly well known and very clear. If they were travelling on an Argentine passport, they were simply not allowed in. Special concessions were given to bereaved relatives on authorized group visits to the Argentine graveyard at Darwin, but that only happened a few times a year. Otherwise, virtually without exception, they could only enter on a foreign passport. Argentina particularly disliked this stand taken by the Falklands' councillors, but as many Argentines were able to obtain second passports, it wasn't totally restrictive. However, it stimulated the often-held argument: 'Surely in this day and age you should let them in?' Versus: 'We will only do so if they drop their claim.' Now the claim to the sovereignty of the Islands had only been voted into the Argentine constitution in 1993, some eleven years after the war, so the Islanders' position was not that they were being picky about a dusty and outdated situation. Far from it, they were objecting to something particularly current and using one of the few real weapons at their disposal to make the point.

Sr Barcella had only his Argentine passport with him. He checked his fuel gauges and realized that he was taking a heck of a risk. He may even have used those very words as, although an Argentine national, his current home was in Bakersfield, California. His hands moved over the controls nervously. He kept his video camera running for a while, lodging it on the co-pilot's seat so that he could smile with affected courage into it. He might just be shot down; he could hardly have doubted the ability of the RAF to achieve such a task. He would have to land in any case in order to refuel, and he had no prior permission to do so. Possibly he could land on a grass runway, but he had little idea as to where they were and there was no certainty any fuel could be purchased. It is doubtful that he even knew that there were two main airports, Stanley and MPA. He was carrying over two thousand tea bags, some oranges and some flour. He had persuaded himself that these would be worthwhile gifts to the underprivileged locals. So he flew on, into monumental uncertainty and international irritation.

Needless to say, his presence was detected on the military radar screens. His direction and the lack of an agreed flight plan, along with the slowness of his progress, alerted the uniformed watchers to something that was the most realistic and feared threat – an unauthorized 'cowboy'-type incursion that can lead to an international incident. It had happened in the Falklands in the Sixties and Seventies, and here it looked as though it was about to happen again. An F3 Tornado was scrambled and in no time was flying around the Aztec. It had to be content with a sequence of passes, as it could not fly slowly enough to stay alongside. Sr Barcella was delighted. He turned his camera towards the Tornado and felt even more daring than before.

He spoke some English, and a good job too, because much of the Islands were covered in cloud and he had to be helped to lock on to radar beacons in order to land. If he hadn't been talked down he would certainly have crashed. The landing was achieved with some difficulty, but he managed to carry out what the experts felt to be a rough landing on the huge MPA runway. A few hours earlier that same runway had welcomed the fortnightly Boeing 747 carrying the crew change for the oil rig working to the north of the Islands.

His small plane came to a halt away from the military buildings. His radio contact had directed him there as, although he had said he was alone, our lads were taking no risks in such an unusual circumstance. It was 3.30 p.m. and, as luck would have it, it was a bank holiday in the Falklands. The previous day's liberation celebrations normally took place on a bank holiday, but that had been Sunday in 1998. Most inhabitants were watching England's first game in the World Cup, time-lagged or live as available.

Sr Barcella emerged gingerly from the Apache and jumped to the tarmac. It had been a harrowing half-hour. He was frisked and taken away for questioning by unsympathetic uniformed men while an initial search of his aircraft was conducted. Cameras were removed, a film developed and his video watched. Nothing of a particularly sinister nature was found. The flour was in fact flour and not drugs. In the stark interview room with a cup of tea in his hand, our most recent illegal immigrant felt rather more relaxed. It was dawning on him that his presence was more of a problem for his hosts than it was for him. He was absolutely right.

The Military Commander informed His Excellency the Governor.

Neither of these worthies was observing the bank holiday, as they tended to keep the UK ones even though they were in the Falklands. As an employee of the Falkland Islands government I was keeping the Falklands one and had bent over backwards to stay out of touch with all evidence of human life since the early morning as I wanted to watch England versus Tunisia in its time-lagged form, without being aware of the result. This simulated reality can be worth the effort, but it rather detracts from being informed on vital issues, such as the one in hand. I heard my phone ring at about 4 p.m., but the answerphone was on and I sat captivated by the excitement of England actually being on top and winning.

After the match was over and all the commentators had had their fill of preening and showing a mini league table after one match, I flicked the answerphone switch. The Governor wanted to talk. Wouldn't you guess that when I rang back he was engaged? In fact, he was engaged for the next half-hour, but eventually I was told of the situation. No decisions had been made, but the military were handing Sr Barcella over to the civilian authorities for treatment as an illegal immigrant. He was on his accompanied way, along the bumpy thirty-five-mile road to Stanley. I was to inform the councillors and draft a brief statement for approval. This statement was read over the air at about 6.50 p.m.

Two councillors out of the four available already knew the news. The information had come from one of our own civilian pilots who had been listening in on the channel used by private aircraft. We only have three private aircraft in the Islands. Four, if one includes a death-trap gyrocopter, so I regarded this ability to detect information on the airwaves as close to miraculous.

The Argentine guest gazed at the primal scenery as he bumped along the MPA road, although technically he remained 'airside' and so was not there. A kind of bureaucratic bubble surrounded him. This artificial 'not here but here' situation was a helpful illusion while the issues were discussed and decisions made, though Hans Christian Andersen's little boy who couldn't see the King's new clothes might have blown the gaff.

He was placed in our Stanley prison, in the cell next to a young Chinese who had confessed to murder on the high seas and was thought to be awaiting some form of extradition. The actual form was not clear, as the vessel on which the offence was committed was Taiwanese and he was from the People's Republic – quite a diplomatic corker. I don't expect there was any communication by banging on the wall, as I doubt whether Sr Barcella was up to Mandarin in Morse.

Telegrams began to fly. Government House to London, London to the Embassy in Buenos Aires, Buenos Aires to Government House, Buenos Aires to the Argentine Ministry of Foreign Affairs, Government House to Buenos Aires; all combinations were tried. Our customs officers interviewed Sr Barcella, who was apparently showing signs of actually enjoying the predicament and probably anticipating the hero's welcome he would get if he managed to return to Argentina.

Legally there were quite a few options to consider, but confiscating his aircraft would be difficult. He could certainly be detained for a while, during which time we could put together a case, and a fine might ensue. What were we to do? Which comes first, legality, fairness, international relations, public relations, or the setting of an example? Is it best to show toughness or humanity?

Administrators and politicians in at least three locations thousands of miles apart spent Tuesday morning working on the problem. By the beginning of the afternoon (Brazil were playing Morocco), Sr Barcella was back at MPA watching the refuelling of his aircraft, and a group of senior civil servants and military men were meeting under the chairmanship of the Governor to reach some kind of consensus. The Argentine press had already got a hold of this bone and was not inclined to let go. They began to ring every contact they had in the Islands. As many of them had copies of the internal telephone directory, the task was not difficult. This barrage lasted for the next five days. The story was apparently headline news on two Argentine TV channels and on the front pages of virtually all newspapers. The misreporting and misunderstanding, when one multiplied journalistic licence by a language problem, understandable bias, and a cultural difference, was phenomenal.

At the Governor's meeting in the newly refurbished Government House (not even pictures on the walls yet, and a wonderful smell of new paint), the military men reported on the situation to date. The Customs Officer related his interviews and thoughts, photos of the plane were studied, and the video shot by Sr Barcella was pored over. All the available information tended to underline the opinion that he was not particularly malicious or canny, just offbeat and misguided. The options ranged from allowing him to fly home to incarcerating him and confiscating all his assets. Some of the Islanders had already made it clear that in their view he should have been shot on sight, but they were a small minority. They were also somewhat out of touch with the fact that the Falklands is part of the world community. The decision makers were painfully aware of the problems caused by wider public opinion, which already found it hard to sympathize with the general line taken within the Islands concerning Argentines.

It was concluded that the sooner our visitor left our shores, the sooner the whole incident would be forgotten. However, if that solution was seen as being lenient either within, or outside of, the Islands, it could have unfortunate repercussions. It was a matter of delicate balance. We certainly did not want to encourage the next joyrider by seeming easy meat, nor would Islanders put up with being seen to be soft towards Sr Barcella. The Governor ushered the executive councillors into his office and the door closed on their deliberations. The telegrams flew hither and thither once again, and, subject to the Argentine authorities taking action against him for his failure to file an accurate flight plan, it was decided that Sr Barcella could return from whence he came the following day.

Even in this rather neat solution there was complexity. As Argentina views the Falklands as part of Argentina anyway, there could be no way that this incident could be regarded as a flight to a foreign country. It was, in their view, internal, and the lack of a flight plan was the offence. Maybe not as tough as we would have liked, but better than nothing.

The solution was announced publicly but, life being as it is, Sr Barcella couldn't leave the next day. The weather closed in and the strange pilot from Bakersfield via his native Argentina spent another night within feet of a Chinese murderer in an admittedly crummy jail at the very bottom of the South Atlantic.

The next day, the Thursday, he did manage to get away and reached Comodoro without mishap. The ballyhoo of the Argentine media continued. We had an ongoing system to receive English translations of certain Argentine press articles, and Noticias, a weekly magazine, commented:

At 7 p.m. on Thursday 18th, Barcella got off his plane in Comodoro Rivadavia airport, where he had originally left for the Malvinas. He was received as a hero, with applause from ordinary citizens, officials (President Carlos Menem [67], immediately tried to contact him), and former soldiers, with whom he had shared something more than just belonging to the same generation. To them and those who will never come back from that sordid war, he dedicated his journey. He was practically unable to see any of the scenery of these islands he dreamt of for over a year, from California, where he lives. At all times he was detained and controlled by the British forces. Now, the Kelpers fear a wave of Argentine aeroplanes will land in these southern islands. And they are threatening to be harsher with the next ones.

Why do some articles insist on printing ages in brackets? President Menem, who was far older than he looked in spite of his somewhat exotic lifestyle, must have hated this kind of intrusion into the length of his existence. And they always refer to inhabitants in the Islands as 'Kelpers'. It isn't that anyone in the Falklands particularly objected, but I'm sure that the term in Argentina carries negative connotations. OK, there is a lot of kelp around the Islands, and great for the wildlife it is too, but nobody actually lives on it or from it.

Would the Argentines actually summons him over the matter of the licence as he was such a popular hero? While their press debated, we sat and watched, feeling that we had at least played the ball into their court and come out of the affair without seeming to be unreasonable thugs.

Another Argentine paper was persistent in wanting an article written from the Falklands explaining why Islanders were fearful of Argentines. The request was urgent and time bound and no councillor had the time to do it. The Governor was doubtful, so I penned four hundred rather whimsical words on the subject, that were a bit tongue in cheek. I insisted on it being non-attributable – after all, one couldn't have the Chief Executive issuing such stuff. The Argentines argued that they had to have a name to put on the article. They were so insistent, and I became so fed up with the whole thing, I tried the pseudonym of Albert Ross, a local high flyer (get it?) and to our immense amusement, they swallowed it!

On 17 July the *Penguin News* published the revelation that Barcella was not going to be punished in any way by the Argentines. As I was Acting Governor at the time, I ensured that we checked this out before firing off retaliatory press statements. The embassy in Buenos Aires believed the report to be untrue; the whole process of Argentine law had not rumbled that far yet. They confirmed that he was to be punished, but his licence was an American one and so the whole matter was highly complex and subject to indefinite delay. Maybe the Islanders would all forget about the incident. Two years later few spoke of it, so maybe they had. The Foreign Office was surprisingly vague as to what had actually happened to Ernesto. It had all been a bit of a storm in a tea-bag consignment.

Chapter 18

Fancy some outdoor sport? The wind can rise from dead calm to storm force in minutes. The world's most popular sporting surface, grass, finds it hard to grow. Sheep, upland geese and the entire resident animal kingdom regard any half-decent surface as a heaven-sent convenience. The sun, when it shines, can burn exposed flesh before you hear the sizzling and the climate, although cool, is never cold enough long enough for any winter sports. The sea temperature is far too near zero for swimming and the rivers are not large enough for rafting. So, you still want a game? Welcome to the Falklands.

Resourcefulness is a prime characteristic of Falkland folk. This is as true in sport and leisure as in everything else. The extreme nature of the natural environment is regarded as inconvenient at times, but hardly show-stopping. Take golf, for instance. Plenty of outdoor space is required. In the Islands space abounds. Indeed, it is claimed that there are more tracts of land purporting to be golf courses in the Falklands per head of population than in any other part of the world. The problems arise elsewhere. These courses do not have the lush greens, the neatly tailored fairways, the uniformly sanded bunkers and the predictable rough that any club golfer elsewhere might take for granted. The greens are not really green at all. They could well be termed 'blotchies'. A well-struck putt is likely to be deflected several degrees from its intended course by rock-hard pellets of sheep manure. Also likely to be lined up along the path of one's ball are the ubiquitous droppings of upland geese, which look for all the world like discarded cigar butts, and merely add additional textures to the hoof marks and range of assorted offerings from our dumb friends.

Considerable local knowledge is required even to find the fairways, as they can easily be mistaken for rough by the uninitiated. There are no bunkers as such, as all known types of sand will just blow away, but on the Stanley course there are some craters left by the war, which have a magnetic influence over any ball within thirty yards. If you fancy playing the long par five on that course when the wind is blowing from the west, it would be advisable to set aside the best part of a day. Never worry about the chap fifty yards behind playing through; he is unlikely to reach you with his next three shots. The rough is easy enough to find and so is the clubhouse, which has all the character that a portakabin can muster. (I mislead you – there's a portakabin at Mount Pleasant done up in a mock Tudor exterior.) But I digress. Many, locals and expatriates alike, love this strong man's golf. And what's more, they can achieve low scores. What an easy game it must seem when they holiday in Scotland, or the USA. Or, indeed, anywhere.

Farmers out in Camp build their own courses, hence the proliferation of playing opportunities. These are not sprinkled with dinky little par threes either; they are challenging, manly courses for those who can hit long and straight into a gale-force wind.

Even more unsuited to the environment than golf is a sport that provides one of the most unlikely events in the sporting calendar – the annual cricket match between the Governor's XI and the Military Commander's XI. On the occasion of that match in January 1998, I was facing a problem. Memories of the Bramhall Over Forties' Cricket Team came flooding back as I walked to the end of my run-up, polishing the ball aggressively on my trousers. There was one over left in the only cricket match of the year, and I had to bowl it. Deep within my subconscious I was lamenting the fact that there would be no more sound of leather on willow for another twelve months. But, far more to the point, and in the very forefront of my mind, the military opposition needed a mere three runs to win and two to tie off my six balls and they had several wickets in hand.

Many years before, in a different life on another continent, I had bowled a last over when the opposition needed nineteen. In your natural generosity of spirit you might imagine that to knock such a total even off a journeyman bowler such as myself would be an almost impossible feat. However, due to outrageous luck, abetted by some world-class batting ability that had been unsportingly hidden low down the order, they managed to get them. My teammates had taken a few weeks to talk to me again. In fact, on recollection, I believe that there were some that never spoke to me again. Such hard-won experience led me to the conclusion that the odds were heavily against me now. The South Atlantic Ashes were at stake. True, the Governor's XI, for whom I was playing, had been practising for weeks, but the CBFFI's XI consisted of men who had seemed throughout the match to have more familiarity with the game. Not only were these chaps combat trained, they hadn't bowled many wides and knew how to hold a bat the right way up. It had all been very discouraging.

This match is played on the only cricket pitch in the Islands, which doubles as a wind tunnel, known as the Mount Pleasant Oval. The east-west direction of the pitch is aligned to the prevailing wind and the bouncy matting surface generally means that, when bowling, one could be a demon at one end yet find it difficult to get the ball to reach the batsman from the other. When batting, it was a matter of getting one's head out of the way or hanging around chatting to the slips, while the ball looped in a gentle and ever-slowing arc in one's general direction. Unusually, this particular day had been ideal. Warmish sun and a zephyr-like wind, allied with tea in the Officers' Mess, had provided the backdrop to a most agreeable occasion. Now suddenly, having struggled for the whole match, we were within an over of getting a positive result. Our fielders had awoken from their zombie-like inertia and begun to actually take an interest in the match. I was certain I spotted movement from our Third Man. Even more surprisingly, the few spectators who had spent the afternoon lounging in luxurious canvas seats, exchanging civilian and military gossip and eating cream buns under a khaki awning, had divined the situation from the scorers and were behaving like hooligans. They began jeering and shouting encouragement and abuse, reminding me of a One-Day International at Old Trafford towards the end of the day's play, when the pubs had just run dry. A Crusader and an Infidel who had been fighting noisily on the boundary for most of the afternoon, actually rested on their swords and concentrated on the cricket – believe me, that is precisely what happened.

Modesty forbids me to bore you with detailed descriptions of the next six balls. The cynic, or anyone who has actually seen me play, would say that we just had a bit of luck. But with five balls gone they had lost a wicket and managed only one run. After the batsman swiped at, and missed, my last ball, our team erupted. They danced around the pitch like dervishes. Grown men noted for sobriety and dullness (some of them had, in fact, been selected for it) were whooping and waving their hands in the air. Chaps who in normal life would cross the street to avoid me scampered to slap me on the back. Even Jean ran on to the pitch and threw her arms around me. We had won by one run in what purports to be the southernmost cricket match in the world. The unique Penguin Egg Trophy was ours. For a brief moment of time I was a sporting hero. How the Over Forties back at Bramhall would have laughed. But at least we had a 100% record for the entire season, not something those men in white from leafy Cheshire had often experienced.

Any hard-pressed executive will tell you that the problem with most sports is that they take time. Time is not as rare a commodity in the Falklands as it might be in, say, Basingstoke, or any other place where the drudge of commuting consumes it. For the bulk of the Stanley population, work begins at 8 a.m., and ends at 4.30 p.m. Bear in mind that the lunch hour lasts for an hour and a quarter and is meticulously observed. The journey home might take as long as five minutes if the traffic is really bad. So, after that return home, what happens next? How are the long evening hours spent? What about the weekends?

A visitor from Mars, alighting in Stanley on a cool July evening, might just flick on the local radio and find an intensive commentary on the final session of the Governor's Cup darts tournament. Would this passing extra-terrestrial find this coverage exciting? The answer depends on how much the game has progressed on the red planet. It isn't yet that big in Nepal, as the lack of entries from the Resident Infantry Company demonstrates. However, the sheer enthusiasm of the coverage would awaken any stranger, whether Martian or Gurkha, to the fact that this is big time. So many people play the game in the local pub leagues that a high proportion of the population is able to relate to the atmosphere present in the town hall.

The air is pungent with alcohol and tobacco, the chatter is muted and reverent. Video cameras operated by admiring mothers whirr, occasional applause breaks out and the newly polished silverware sits on a table on the stage awaiting the winner. The combatants train for weeks to get their throwing actions into just the right groove. They prepare with studied professionalism so that under the pressure of competition they will be able to judge the optimum amount of alcohol required in their blood. This will ensure a delicate balance between the calming of nerves and any damage to physical co-ordination.

Do not be fooled into thinking the standard is mediocre, or that these Islander worthies can be challenged at this game to your advantage. Many a military missile firer has imagined he could do just that and has had to buy at least one round of drinks for his mistake. Quite a few of the talented locals beat Eric Bristow when he visited the Islands. Well, maybe he had had a few at the time, but even so, he had been world champion. And world champions should know all about that delicate balance.

The darts silverware is awarded as the evening draws to a close and the cumulative impact of relaxant is affecting competitors and spectators alike. A state best described as 'over refreshed' has been achieved by a majority. Thus, trying to make a brief speech of appreciation from the stage, as it has been my honour to attempt on a number of occasions, is doomed to failure. I have been left mouthing well-prepared witticisms to myself as the majority of people in the hall faced the other way and provided their own alternative entertainment.

This kind of atmosphere can prove embarrassing. I once apologized to a leading academic on a similar occasion as, being his host, I was rather taken aback by the drunken and loutish behaviour around us. To his great credit, he said that the Senate of the University of London was far worse. Obviously, he must remain anonymous, as the revealing of such truth could have a deleterious impact upon the future publication of papers.

On any Boxing Day in Stanley, the place to be is the racecourse. This is equivalent to 26 June in the Northern Hemisphere, so it can be warmish. Being the Falklands, it can also be numbingly cold. This racecourse is a much-loved venue. Although not exactly Ascot, it has two grandstands, white rails the length of the course, a finishing post, a steward's room, a tote room, adequate stabling for the performers and portakabins serving refreshments for the punters. It is way over the top for a settlement of only one thousand six hundred people. The uninformed may expect to see farmers' hacks galloping in a jolly manner redolent of a country fair. The informed will know that all matters equestrian are taken very seriously indeed. The breeding and training of racehorses is no exception. A distinguished local resident is Thyer, a son of Nijinsky, and with all due deference to His Excellency the Governor, Thyer is almost certainly the best-bred chap around. He takes his life's work as a stud very seriously (Thyer that is, not the Governor) and in time his offspring will encounter serious competition from locally bred horses and the Chilean bloodstock that has been imported over a number of years. The rivalry is fierce, the horsemanship of a high order and the racing genuinely fast.

The horse racing is part of the broader 'sports' concept that grew out of the Camp post-shearing festival. When shearing was over for another year, the communities met together to relax and celebrate, and the sports brought together old and young, visitor and local, in a series of events that nearly everyone could enter or simply enjoy watching. The tradition lives on in both East and West Falkland.

At my very first Camp sports meeting at Port Howard, I was informed that I had volunteered to enter the greasy pole competition. It sounded harmless enough. I imagined a bit of mild tomfoolery ending in a good laugh all round. As a guest I could hardly refuse to be involved. My never-ending naivety was exposed yet again. At the appointed time, I found myself astride a pole of about twelve inches in diameter, which had been covered in highly polished linoleum. The pole was suspended between two frames some enormous distance above the ground and, to cap it all, the pole rotated along its axis, so that if my weight shifted a bit, it immediately spun and deposited me on the hard earth after a free fall without a parachute. The sensitivity of the whole structure to my movement led me to believe that it had been specially prepared with high-performance lubricants. I was told that the rules forbade any touching of the pole with the hands to steady oneself, which seemed to me about the most natural thing on earth at the time. I was then handed a pillow with which to hit my opponent, who faced me about a yard away on the pole. The winner would progress to the next round by forcing the other one to fall off. Somewhere in the ether a voice said, 'Go.'

I looked at this rather slight man with grey hair and an intelligent face and pondered tactics. Unfortunately, it was His Excellency David Tatham, the Governor of the Falkland Islands. He looked so frail and vulnerable, and more to the point, he might just be asked to write a reference for me one day. Here was Her Majesty's representative, the man who must always begin every meal first and upon whom one could not turn one's back.

Debretts was full of protocol as to how to behave in his presence. We had studied every word carefully prior to arriving in the Islands and I could not recall any advice on how to deal with him in a greasy pole competition. Maybe I should strike him first.

I prodded him with my pillow, anticipating that he would fall off and that would be an end of it. He rode the innocuous but well-intentioned blow and swung his pillow against my side with some gusto. I only managed to stay upright with a supreme effort, involving a flailing of limbs and pillow. I heard the clicking of cameras as the Campers warmed to this incongruous spectacle.

I took a deep breath as I recovered my composure and looked at His Excellency. I could swear he was leering. This mild-mannered and immensely likeable diplomat had, in an instant, become a creature of the gutter. It was the nearest I am ever likely to come to seeing Dr Jekyll change into Mr Hyde. Surely the Foreign Office is there to ensure compromise and a meeting of minds? Not for David Tatham on the greasy pole it wasn't. He obviously had reserves of venom that none of us knew about. I could almost see the adrenalin pouring through his arteries as I tried to adjust to the fact that he really was going to belt me with his pillow till I fell from the pole. I remembered that he had been our ambassador in Beirut at the height of the fighting. Possibly some of the techniques or even the attitudes of mind of the combatants had rubbed off.

I prodded him again, and he merely grinned. It was then that I noticed his moleskin trousers and the vice-like grip on the pole that this afforded him. He had locked his ankles together under the pole and had formed a Velcro-like relationship with the device that I could not match without changing my trousers. Never before had I realized how important to a pair of trousers is their coefficient of friction. That look of impending victory on the Governor's face told me that pleading for a cease-fire while I changed into suede jeans would not be very fruitful. He struck me a solid blow as I tried to pin my ankles together and I retaliated by offering up a somewhat more substantial prod. I could hear my supporter, Jean, shouting, 'Hit him.' So I did. Or, more accurately, I tried to. My massive blow glanced from the diplomatic chest and the sheer momentum of the lunge carried me with it as my trousers slipped away from the lubricated lino and my shoulder smashed into the ground.

I arose sluggishly, realized that the massed onlookers were cheering my opponent and began to slink away to lick my wounds. The master of ceremonies, or whatever Camp sports have, said, 'Best of three – get back on the pole.' Thus I had to undergo the whole experience once more. I wish I could relate that I somehow got my act together, that the well-meaning chief executive triumphed at last over the leering governor, but alas he simply whacked me off the pole again as though he was swotting a fly. This time, I was allowed to retreat and it was only then I realized that all David had achieved was to get through to the next round, where he would be meeting some real Island opposition.

This was not a pansy expatriate exhibition match. His opponent really had a go at him in a manner that was almost embarrassing to watch. After all, he was the Governor. Even his moleskin trousers could not save him. He lost with good grace and picked himself up to applause. It was almost as though beating me so comprehensively had been his objective all along.

We evolved Falklands Tennis. Jean and I tried most of what the leisure centre had to offer in the never-ending search for an activity that was easy to play yet challenging. We wanted a sport that kept one fit, facilitated weight loss, was instantly enjoyable, could be played at any time, and didn't take too long. Everything on offer had a downside. Badminton was promising but meant commitment, and squash was feasible but I could never predict where the ball would end up. Table tennis was a mite too static and indoor soccer required youth and skill in significant quantities. The manager at the centre suggested we tried short tennis and provided us with plastic racquets, some yellow sponge balls and a badminton net at about half height. It all seemed a bit easy – mind you, it was designed with children in mind.

We patted the balls to each other and pretended we were grown up. It was pretty sterile stuff. Then we saw some racquetball racquets lying around and experimented with them. The fact that they were strung immediately changed the game. Now swerve and spin could be applied to the yellow sponges and a decent smash could be given velocity. We adopted badminton-type scoring, in which one can only get a point when serving, and began to enjoy the balance of movement and skill. The only thing spoiling it was the fact that I used to win with boring consistency. Jean accused me of playing too hard, of being particularly bigheaded in the way I moved around the court and having other grossly unfair or overstated characteristics. If I eased up a bit to encourage her, I was indicted for being patronizing.

Then Governor Richard Ralph arrived on the scene. Here was a man who played tennis to a reasonable standard – proper tennis, that is. He asked if tennis was played in the Islands and I explained that no outdoor court existed but that we had adapted short tennis, which provided a poor substitute. He was rather derisory but said he would try. So we arranged our first game. It must have been in January or February 1995. In a way it changed my life. I believe it also had an impact on his.

Richard was a good tennis player and highly competitive; shades of his predecessor on the greasy pole came to mind. The first game was a bit of a cakewalk for me as he hadn't adjusted to the speed of the ball, but as he improved rapidly the whole thing assumed an importance out of all proportion to the game itself. We were both striving and thinking as we played, trying to outwit the other by the unexpected nature of a shot or by getting the other man out of position. We hurtled about, we lunged, and occasionally we commented inwardly on our own ineptitude. Richard's comments were sometimes audible. From the gamesmanship angle I was pleased at any disturbance in his mental equilibrium, as it increased the psychological pressure. We played so much that we improved and became fitter. Others watched the two ageing colonial leaders elephanting around the leisure centre and began to want to play. Soon there were a dozen or more involved, and that spawned a league. Eventually that league kept over forty competitive players honing their game. It also occupied the courts at the leisure centre. Numerous non-league players formed doubles partnerships. It was a game for all seasons and for all skill levels. Even at the government-sponsored membership level of £2.20 per court per hour, takings rose. Falklands Tennis became not only a feature of our life, but established itself as an Island favourite. Serious players scoured Northern Hemisphere sports emporiums for better racquets and returned from leave passage with bags full of yellow sponge balls.

There is one soccer pitch in Stanley and the locals love the game. It is just like any UK town, with youngsters wearing the latest shirt of their team and football being a major topic of conversation. The difference, though, is that as there is no local allegiance, support is widespread. One can travel to the very furthest recesses of the Camp and find there a shepherd wearing a Southampton scarf and bemoaning his team's performance the previous Saturday. There is even a Grimsby Town supporter – yes, one travelled to the UK and back to see them play at Wembley – and of all the unlikely things – a current Spurs season ticket holder!

The local international team toured Chile. Well, a combination of some of the very best from the three teams in the local league played three matches in Punta Arenas. Three teams is all the league has and they all play on the same – the only – pitch. It rather negates home advantage. They won one match (on penalties, I think), drew one and lost one. They returned in triumph to a public reception as they stood on the top deck of an open-topped bus and received acclaim on the town hall balcony. No, I am getting carried away again; they actually had a reception organized by admirers (well, wives and girlfriends to be precise) in the Trough. The Trough is a facility for dances and social events lovingly put together from portakabin parts and placed at the edge of town. There were speeches, tales of heroism on and off the pitch, and a drop or two of alcohol. The point is that there was a genuine pride in having actually taken the Stanley game abroad and played reasonably well. After all, it would be akin to a village side from Hampshire visiting Punta Arenas. The lads had given their all and played against dark-haired men whose language was foreign, and who had the referee in their pockets.

A surprise to many visitors is the lack of water sports. True, noisy and irritating jet skis now buzz around Stanley harbour replacing the absent bees and serious sailors drop in on their way around the world, but windsurfing is rare and just mucking about in boats seldom attempted. The reason is to do with water temperature, which in turn is due to the lack of the Gulf Stream, which so warms the North Atlantic and thus influences the UK's climate. However, Falkland folk defy adversity and Neptune gets his share and so, on New Year's Day, there is the raft race.

The rafts must be made by the participants, cannot have an engine and are required to cover the distance between the government dockyard and the public jetty – about a third of a mile. Creative talent is displayed in the variety of approach to the rafts themselves, as there is no proven design that is always superior. Some have sails, some have rudders, some are painted in bright colours, others go for subdued functionality. At the firing of a loud shot by the Governor or the Military Commander, a dozen or so of these assorted craft heave their way through the cold water. Everyone gets soaked, the wind normally blows any craft with a sail way off course and the race itself is usually won by a team consisting of chaps who are both young and fit.

Entering water that is near to zero degrees is not a lot of fun and yet a great gathering of inhabitants does so to aid charity on the shortest day of the year – 21 June. Half of Stanley and a good proportion of MPA congregate on the white sands of Surf Bay and at the firing of a signal splash into the breakers and splash out again. Dolphins sometimes play almost within reach. One year about thirty Gurkhas marched straight in, aided by the swirl of the bagpipes and the commands of their officer. A huge bonfire provides a few calories of heat. Several thousands of pounds are raised for the Lighthouse Seaman's Centre and the worst that winter can do has been defied yet again.

Jean and I loved the innovative nature of sporting activity. We were never tempted into the distinctly expat world of the bridge party or the mah jong set. We felt a bit past our potential peaks at moto-cross and as for world-class sea trout and mullet fishing, not once did we try it, even though we should have done. We might have become hooked. The environment may be harsh, but sport is played hard and taken seriously. In that it is no different from virtually everything else about the place. Islanders may have been taken advantage of for a century or so, but they play to win now.

Chapter 19

It always began with restless pre-journey sleep and rising earlier than usual. A solemn breakfast preceded the familiar thirty-five-mile drive to Mount Pleasant Airport. The 'Great white bird' was drawing its clients magnetically. Inevitably, the ride was tinged with sadness unless Jean was flying as well. I hated leaving her alone on the Islands. Not because she couldn't cope – far from it, she had a whale of a time. It was more that I had come to rely utterly on the discussion of issues, the chewing of fat, the banter and the daily give and take that is the fabric of any marriage. The Chief Executive really needed that supportive wife if the job was to be done effectively. Now I was about to be launched into a solitary existence for a couple of weeks. My life would be crowded with people that I was not close to at all.

Jean would sit patiently in the passenger seat of the car, probably hating the process as much as I did, bearing in mind the thought of driving back along the infamously dangerous road.

The problems of the road were related to its surface and configuration. The British government built it after the war to link Stanley and the new garrison. It was conceived as a grand road, a road that any road designer could tell his grandchildren about, a road with huge ditches on either side. The reason for the ditches is shrouded in folklore, but the most believable story is that the annual rainfall on East Falkland was taken as the monthly figure. If so, it was a costly and crucial mistake, but nobody has ever owned up to making it. Thus, the ditches anticipated a volume of water some twelve times the actual level. This might be far sighted in these days of rapid climate change, global warming and El Ninos, but until the rainfall rises to such heights, the road remains for much of its length rather hopelessly perched above parallel ditches. These are visited by hapless vehicles from time to time, but the expense of barriers was always too high.

The pattern of marshalling civilians for a Tristar departure was conceived by a child of four during a vindictive game with Fisher Price play people. Although the flight does not depart until 11 a.m., all civilian passengers must check in by 9 a.m. This is in spite of the fact that military passengers checked in the previous day, that any errant passenger is easily contactable and there are seldom more than twenty-five civilians wanting to travel at any one time.

Another strange thing about the way that the RAF handle civilians (sorry to go on about this, Sir), is the lack of consistency. This is mainly due to the fact that the normal tour length for military personnel in the Falklands is four months. Thus, one rarely comes across the same folk twice if one is travelling, say, three times a year. New brooms at junior officer level make irritating minor changes in their attempt to sweep clean, and when this happens every few months, no real pattern becomes established. Take the matter of VIP status, for instance. There has been more argument over this single issue by people who have no more right than you or I to be considered a Very Important Person, than there has about whether Argentina has a legitimate claim to the Islands. Well, actually I did have a right to be a VIP, as there was a written agreement that states that my predecessor was an 'X category passenger'. OK, so there's a caveat stating that it was 'personal to holder', but the RAF had forgotten that, so I had inherited the status. Or had I? You see the problem. It all goes to prove my draft Theory of Social Relativity:

One does not mind being treated badly if one is being treated better than the chap next to one and if the chap next to one is being treated better than oneself, then one wants to know the reason why.

I have proved this theory empirically on numerous occasions. Grown men with PhDs have admitted to me that their salary calculations are absolutely correct and fairly judged, but that they will not accept them because someone in their peer group is being treated rather better. Differentials can be more important than absolutes. Giving in to this kind of pressure causes all wages to reach the top of every range.

The benefits conferred on the VIP passengers on the classless Tristar are several and varied. Firstly, there is the 'Commander's Lounge' at Mount Pleasant. Do not be impressed by the name. This is an airless, windowless rectangular room of about ten feet by twelve feet with adjoining loo. It has a few pictures of planes and penguins, three sofas and tea- and coffee-making gear. The good and the great of the UK have passed through this symbol of status. The memorable ones have included royalty, ex-prime ministers, ministers, numerous MPs, and peers of the realm, many, many generals, admirals, air marshals and other men with one, two, three, four and even five stars. There have been men from the MOD, men from the FCO, men from organizations too secret to even mention, wives, assistants, hangers on, local politicians, ex-local politicians (the RAF had forgotten to take their names off the list), people who know someone, and so forth. Even Jeff Banks – no, on second thoughts he wasn't considered 'important' enough, even though he'd come down to make a

Clothes Show that provided priceless positive PR and was far better known by society at large than almost all the others.

The room itself is possibly the most unimpressive room I have ever been in – excepting the cell for drunks in Stanley Jail. Not that I have actually been 'in' the cell for drunks, you understand – I saw it by way of an inspection. However, the point is that it is a room that provides a haven from all those who are excluded, the relative riffraff, the rank and file, ordinary folk. It is a room to sit and chat, to ponder the elevated concepts only grasped by the 'important' ones.

Secondly, travelling as a VIP, one is provided with a seat at the front of the aircraft. If there are not too many VIPs this will almost certainly be in the coveted front row. However, as so often happens in life, the enjoyment of this deal is mollified – by the draught from the forward door, the flow of well-intentioned but loo-bound folk passing one's elbow, the intermittent niff from the loo and the fact that the seats are just the same as everyone else's. Also, unless the aircraft is full, one can be sardined into the front row with no elbow room for all sixteen hours, whilst the squaddy has a stretch of five seats near the back of the aircraft upon which he can recline horizontally. In theory, one could make a dash down the gangway as soon as the seat-belt sign turns off, but it is a trifle non-U. In any event, the average serving soldier should be considerably fitter than oneself and it may not be a good idea to stimulate competition in anything that contains a physical challenge. If all VIPs were to do that, it would get the status a bad name. One has to bear with the disadvantages as well as the advantages.

The third benefit of being a VIP is the treatment one receives at Ascension Island. Normal folk enjoy sitting in the cage. The air is pleasantly warm and one can hear the whisper of breeze in the tops of the palm trees as it mingles with the *Blackadder* soundtrack. The VIP lounge is relaxing in a different kind of way – it has air conditioning and comfy chairs. It also, rather unnervingly, has a photograph on the wall of the view from our bedroom window at Sulivan House. However, the real benefit of the lounge is that the local RAF commander on the island normally comes to chat. This provides a welcome shift of conversation. Ascension is fundamental to the Tristar link and listening to snippets of how life is in a tropical paradise makes a change. There is also a visitor's book. The heads of African states call here on their way back from South America. Before scanning that visitor's book I had no idea that such visits took place, never mind the mid-Atlantic stopover.

Fourthly, the VIP benefits from the lounge at Brize Norton. This is in a different class altogether. It is well appointed and was well staffed until some new broom cut out personal service. It is also more difficult to get into – one has to be even more 'important'. This is due to the fact that the actual written agreement about VIPs and partial VIPs says that it remains at the discretion of the individual Station Commander. So, one may commence one's journey as a VIP in the small room at MPA, be entertained in air conditioning at Ascension, but find oneself back in the mainstream of life at Brize. So what? I can take a little downgrading now again, it is good for humility. But the problem was that sometimes my bags didn't understand the switch. They remained tagged VIP as designated eight thousand miles away. Thus, they could be taken uptown to the VIP lounge for collection whilst I was on the wrong side. It took a while for me to twig the problem when it first happened. All other bags had been collected, the carousel stopped, and I was alone. I collared a uniformed chap who adopted a true Brit shrugging posture. I then walked with a ready confidence fuelled by annoyance through several 'No Entry' signs to get along the airside front of the building to where I knew the VIP lounge to be. Outside the lounge was an estate car with a duty driver in uniform and my bags in the back! An Air Vice-Marshall had acquired them by courtesy of the system. I exchanged words with the duty driver as I recovered them.

On this current trip I was busy availing myself of the claustrophobic VIP lounge. I was chatting usefully to two councillors who were travelling to London for a conference when, with about thirty minutes to go to boarding, the door opened and a military whirlwind blew in. A 'one star' naval man gushed all over the room. He was charming, and we became very aware that he was there and that we were not military.

Once airborne, I watched a movie. Two years before, a visionary hidden in the recesses of RAF Movements had acquired a job lot of Sony personal video cartridge players with customer service in mind. The infiltration of this individual had obviously been masterminded by the same genius that placed Gorbachev in the Kremlin, and Pope John Paul I in the Vatican. Admittedly, there had been teething problems, patent rights on films, and the sheer weight of the original carrying trolleys that had fatigued the gangways, but as a way of passing time it was a welcome innovation. The lack of *Blackadder – The Movie* was puzzling.

At Ascension the commander dutifully came to chat to us in the air-conditioned lounge and offered a quick trip to see the giant turtles. The 'one star' was the reason for this treatment, but we all leapt at it. The beach was very dark. The Milky Way glittered like a silvery dust in the sky (the 'one star' showed no outward evidence of inadequacy) and the partial moon lay lazily on its back. I struggled with the 'low light' setting on my camcorder and stumbled into a turtle's hollow, spraying sand in all directions and not managing to capture a picture of anything at all. The sand was later to emerge from my turn-ups in my hotel bedroom

We did actually see a turtle, a large lumbering creature that took one look at the crazy mixture of humanity approaching and legged it for the sea. That was all we had time for.

The leg from Ascension to Brize heralded the opportunity for sleep. Of course, I had the whole thing taped by now: blow-up head pillow to stop the head slipping sideways; blow-up foot cushion to provide a soft resting place for ankles; ear plugs and the invaluable mask. To the casual observer I probably looked like a professional sleeper. I slept for about ten minutes out of an attempted five hours when the lights flashed on and the unsympathetic RAF voice bade us wake, I joined the scrum for the loo to get some aftershave on before the untempting breakfast. How can food that one assumes must have started out as being edible end up like that? As day dawned through the starboard windows we were descending through the West Country to a frosty Brize Norton.

The engines died and the steps were nudged alongside, so I stood to get my blazer from the overhead locker. Observant readers will notice that I'd done this sort of thing before on the Tristar. This was a try on – merely testing the system. Within seconds all the passengers noted my initiative and were on their feet, stretching thankfully and clicking the catches. 'Please be seated,' came the harsh cry over the PA system. I was amazed. Of course, I had expected the military men to obey – that merely proves Pavlov – but to see some hardened oil executives, whom I knew could give Red Adair lessons in masculinity, just sit down like obedient dogs was astonishing. I sat down, of course, not wishing to appear as a ringleader in case my VIP status might be brought into question. I was not offered the lounge, I had hardly deserved it, but the bags found the carousel. Maybe at last the act was coming together.

Chapter 20

HOME THOUGHTS FROM HOME

I emerged from the terminal and breathed English air. I was home and yet abroad. I stood on my native soil in the guise of a partial stranger.

The taxi was waiting and we set off towards London. It was a dry, fairly bright day; frost was on the grass. The trees were leafless and harsh against a Turner sky. I had not seen deciduous trees for at least nine months and it was immensely satisfying just to stare at them. However, my artistic reverie was short-lived. Fear gripped me as I realized that the driver was insane and intent on spectacular, passenger-involving, suicide. He was hurtling along at a breakneck pace and only my substantial natural reserve stopped me from asking him to slow down. Then I dared to look at the speedometer – sixty miles per hour. The months of Falklands pace had conditioned the mind to slowness. I used to be a thirty-thousand-miles-a-year man, year in, year out, yet now I had become a snivelling jelly at a mere sixty miles per hour. I resolved to ignore the speed. I assured myself that I was safe and, despite my vision contradicting such logic, I put up with it.

London was still there. Massive, complex and nothing like Stanley. Both are capitals, they both have cathedrals, but one medium-sized building in London could house the entire population of Stanley. The suburbs were taking a breather after a hectic week and the West End was surprisingly quiet as I checked in at the Goring Hotel.

The Goring has been called 'boring' by people with poetic aspirations. In a way that is one of the attractions of the place. It is simple but stylish, traditional but air conditioned. It is also reasonably quiet and very well located for our London office. The service was spectacular. I knew it fairly well, as I was an inhabitant for over six weeks during the Oil Licensing Round climax in the summer of 1996. Such an hotel is the best substitute for home, but it can never actually be home.

I managed to stop the receptionist, who had accompanied me to my room, telling me how to turn on a TV set, draw the curtains and switch on the heated towel rail. I then unpacked my half-empty cases. The space was to be filled with an array of acquisitions, all carefully listed, the kind of things that cannot be found in Stanley. I tried to be methodical as I sorted out items for every eventuality. My philosophy of being prepared had done the family proud over many years. Nevertheless, it was generally a subject of derision: 'Look how many bags he's got! He's got more than the rest of the family put together!' The ever-useful Swiss Army knife awaited fresh challenges – it had already been called into action at least three times over a thirty-year period. There were books for every mood that just might be read, a number of different aftershaves providing choice and variety, spare batteries that could help those in need of them and so forth. I took care to remember the location of each object. Someone could bleed to death while a patented easy-to-apply tourniquet lay listless in a forgotten drawer.

A stroll through the park seemed a good idea, if only to recover from the traumas of unpacking, and how right I was. Deprivation adds to the enjoyment of fulfilment. I had worked in London and never loved it, but on that sunny February morning, having been denied whatever London offers for many months, I appreciated it to the full. The atmosphere was so familiar, so evocative. I fondly imagine that children, as they mature, grow to appreciate their parents, and that is how I was feeling about London.

I wandered up the path that runs parallel to Park Lane. It wasn't so much a path as a designated routeway for a variety of forms of human motion. The Watford Gap on the M1 is famous because although it is a thoroughly inconsequential place, it contains the Grand Union Canal, the Euston line to the north, and the M1, within about four hundred yards of one another. That path through Hyde Park is a bit like that. There is a cycle track marked, but cyclists were not the only ones to improve on walking. Joggers chugged and wheezed past me, roller skaters swooshed by rather like skuas in semi-attacking mode, and prams were pushed by, containing sticky children. How complicated they had become (the prams, not the children) – so many springs and covers and funny-sized wheels. I expected that the *Sunday Times* Appointments Section would soon be on the lookout for Pram Engineering and Design Executives (PEDEs).

I saw the long-dead leaves crisp and rusty on the green grass, the handsomeness of the bare trees as they stretched across the pale blue sky, the planes slipping sideways as they turned for Heathrow, and I could smell and feel that this was London. Even the drone of the traffic seemed no worse than the sound of a bee in summer and I remembered that I once hated it. How familiar, and how comforting. I'm not given to homesickness, but I realized then how much I had been missing.

I arrived at Speaker's Corner and passed by, not wishing the embarrassment of listening, yet admiring the nerve and near lunacy of the speakers. Does this kind of concept selling work? Do people really listen to what is said? The style of the messenger seems to be more significant than the message. The handful of listeners appeared stolidly neutral. I turned into Oxford Street and made my way towards the shops. I saw the signs and thought my luck was in – it was the very last day of a sale. The doors would open in five minutes' time. A crowd was gathering and I was engulfed in an atmosphere of anticipation.

I surveyed the cross section of humanity squeezing against the doorway. This was a veritable United Nations retail shopping day. Every race was represented here. If a map of the world had been shown to us and we had to fill in our birthplaces, it would have been uniformly covered with dots. I looked passingly at the faces so as not to stare (especially objectionable from a foreigner); I listened to the languages; I pondered the variety of clothing. It felt so very different from my Stanley existence. Once more I tried to avoid the natural orgy of comparison.

A clock above us started to strike twelve and the doors began to revolve. Possibly, if all races really were here, there could be Basques in that exit and we could stage an enactment of one of my favourite old jokes. But I'm not sure I could distinguish a Basque anyway. I forced my way to the doors with a passive aggression, steely resolution hidden by a benign Euro smile. Then at last I was disgorged into a large shopping zone where myriads of items were on sale, choices were everywhere and prices were as low as they were going to get. This was bliss indeed.

That feeling didn't last for long as I soon discovered that on the wonderful last day of the sale there wasn't much left that was part of the sale. What there was turned out to be unbuyably awful, made for either giants or midgets, and had probably been tried on by one person every ten minutes for the past month. In effect we were being offered the opposite of bargains. The shelves contained everything that the retailer could not sell, things that nobody else wanted to buy; in short, I had clicked for 'Mug's Day'. Or possibly 'Giants and Midgets Day' – such folk, sometimes regarded as being unfortunate, enjoy a lower cost of living than those of us nearer the peak of the bell curve, as they can wait for such a day as this, and cash in. I gave up and decided to enjoy myself by having my eyes tested (great fun all that guessing of letters, and puffs of wind in your face) and then an hour's indulgence in HMV, lustfully scanning CDs. A few came to hand that were on my list, so I bought them.

I walked happily along on the hard pavements of Regent Street, rounding the hockey-stick curve at the end to arrive at Piccadilly Circus. I had visited this spot so often as a child. My paternal grandfather had worked in Jermyn Street, and sometimes, when on holiday from school, I would be taken up to London to have lunch with him and visit toyshops. 'Grandpa works where Eros is shooting,' I was told. Lunch was always at Lyons Corner House and would be fish and chips. I adored it. Not only was it my favourite meal, but pushing trays along a silvered track in order to get it was a great bonus. Come to think of it, all that joyous cavorting around the fleshpots of London as an impressionable child had probably led to this current feeling about the place. My grandfather may be to blame but I forgave him instantly. He was always kind and thoughtful, generous to a fault even though he couldn't really afford to be. Not a pushy man in any sense, he would accept the vagaries of life and just get on with it. I could never visit this part of London without remembering him fondly.

One of the ways of marking that emotion was to saunter along Jermyn Street buying a commemorative shirt or two. I then caught a cab back to the hotel, tired but in many ways fulfilled. The shirts found hanging space in the wardrobe, alongside previous memorials. By this time I was shattered, but determined to experience the restaurant before catching up on lost sleep. It felt mighty strange, sitting in solitary splendour at a linened table, toying with an impressive menu while a piano tinkled to entertain. I always felt sorry for the pianist on these occasions. Folk in restaurants appear to polarize where pianists are concerned. They either ignore them completely, which seems to me to be bad form, or they go over the top in clapping embarrassingly or proposing a string of forgettable requests. Some small appreciative glance seems an adequate compromise, but one does have to be careful in this day and age that it is not misunderstood. After all, being a pianist requires an artistic bent.

The urge for comparison returns right at the start of the day. As the curtains are drawn one sees chimneyed rooftops against the sky rather than rocky moorland, brickwork and aerials rather than gracious wrecks. The creaking sounds of the logger duck have been replaced by the shrieking of sirens. Maybe the Falklands is the best place to be in the morning and London the optimum location for the evening, or maybe I'm suffering from a kind of double homesickness. Worse still, the affliction may be perpetual, so that nowhere is home and I'm always longing to be somewhere else.

The business week began by speed-walking up Victoria Street. Not only had speed-reading and speed-writing caught on in England, but also most inhabitants of the office warrens in this area have advanced qualifications in speed-walking. The sheer exhilaration of it all meant that I arrived at the office breathless and in need of a good rest.

However, I set about the week's work. Normally the meetings are squashed as so many demands come to light when visiting London. There are governmental matters, so the FCO are always visited. It is very useful to view the Islands from Great George Street, the home of the Foreign Office – they seem very small and far away. But then, that is exactly what they are. There are commercial matters. Many business meetings are held. They may relate to oil, communications, purchasing, ideas, banking, the Seamen's Mission, consultancies – the list is longer than the time available. There are internal office matters. The Falkland Islands Government Office in London (FIGO) is a multi-faceted facility that requires management and reporting like any other part of government. It is very useful, providing advice and essential linkage for all the detailed work that goes on between mother country and emerging late teenage country. There are interviews, there are receptions, dinners, lunches and phone calls. There are the media, always seeking sensation, desperately trying to find it in unlikely situations. Taken as a whole, there is little time to surface.

I caught breath on the walk back to the Goring. The air conditioning in the FIGO basement had not been improved since my initial interview, my fault almost certainly, but it meant that I welcomed the apparent freshness of the Central London air. The twilight time in a big city is special. The pedestrians portray that communal feeling that work is over for the day, that humanity is free to scurry home, to relax and to enjoy the hours of darkness in recuperation and indulgence. Nearly everyone has somewhere to go; there is a purposeful atmosphere that matches the morning rush. The experience of life itself feels sharpened. Beggars remain restless in the subways, looking hopeless and helpless yet never far from alcohol. I was thankful that my rest for the night would not be a cardboard box – far from it – but nor would it be home. And where was home, by the way?

The most homesick moment that I experienced in all my five years in the Falklands was in London just before Christmas one year. This twilight homing period, when all the lights were twinkling in the shops, carols were playing from every doorway and even in the street, was really too much. Just then I felt that I had no home at all. Pigeons know where to go, and they cover vast distances to rest in a smelly coop. I had a house in Cheshire, but that was miles away and occupied by strangers. There was a house in Stanley, but that was at the other end of the world in another season and another time and it was not really home. I subdued the emotion of the moment, but it was always latent when the night drew in.

I can recall that the first working evening was spent with an executive search chap. They are always worth seeing, as they are personable and knowledgeable about quite a range of issues. In any case, you never know when you might need one and you can be pretty sure that when you do, they won't be inviting you out for dinner.

The weekend came rapidly out of the future and it was time to go and see Kathy in Leeds. Kathy, our daughter, was in her final year of Accountancy. She was great to bring up, bright, thoughtful and hard working. I had always been amazed that I had anything to do with her existence. I sat on the train reading and staring out of the window as the fields and semi-detached houses of middle England flashed by. Kathy met me at the station and we began a weekend of easy reunion. There was no difficulty in conversation, no edge, just father and daughter discussing the glorious trivia of life. Our relationship has always included irrational badinage, which somehow improved the quality of understanding between us. Such conversations were held in the streets of Leeds, and later on the Saturday, in York.

'Dad… that's a really interesting shop.'

'What's interesting about it?'

It actually looked singularly dull to me. It was full of rather shapeless feminine clothing.

'It has these really smart suits, just the kind of thing I need for work.'

Kathy's taste had changed over the past two years from 'student' to 'power'. This meant that a whole wardrobe of jeans, sloppy tops and boots was having to make way for pinstripe suits, plain blouses and smart shoes.

'They have obviously got their marketing right. It should be an interesting audit for you.'

'No, I'm not doing their audit, I'm a bit short on suitable office wear.'

'I'm sure something will turn up.'

I realized this was a weak answer, but refusing Kathy something outright was not one of my strongest attributes.

We entered the shop. Kathy tried on the suit, and then didn't like it enough to buy it even though I'd offered to pay. She did buy some other stuff that I paid for though, and maybe that was her intention all along. I came away feeling I'd won, as I might have spent more, but just possibly I'd lost. What Kathy had achieved was what the direct sales experts call 'Price Conditioning'. She takes after me in some ways, but that ability to get me feeling that I've come out of something as the victor then wondering if I may have actually been defeated undoubtedly comes from her mother.

Kathy had bought her first house and I inspected it with incredulity. The only house I could envisage her having had been a doll's house, yet here was a small but well-constructed three-bedroomed dwelling, well chosen and potentially very comfortable. It was sparsely furnished, but then I was easy meat for dragging into IKEA and Habitat. I slept on the sofa, and then tried the floor, but it was all in a good cause.

In York we wandered about the historical core, and it was like drinking history. I had already noticed, in walking the London streets, that people passing the other way don't look at you much. In Stanley they do. In the UK anonymity is the norm, yet there in York folk would, occasionally, cast an interested glance at us. Then I realized that it was mainly young men, and they were, in fact, looking at Kathy. As we walked across a bridge, three of them coming past said something to me that I didn't quite catch, and they passed on by. I asked Kathy whether she had heard what they said.

'Oh yes,' she replied: " 'I hope that's your daughter.'' '

It was a wonderful weekend. We had missed each other over the months that had passed and we both hated saying goodbye again. I arrived back at the Goring to a business dinner and a hard week's work.

That week included a re-run of life as I had once known it. I hired a car and drove to visit the British Geological Survey at Keyworth, beyond Loughborough. On that sunny morning, the way north out of London and the M1 itself became Memory Lane. It didn't take long for me to remember that a strange thing happens to the law of averages when I get behind the wheel of a car – it ceases to operate as it should. For instance, I always find myself in the wrong lane. I don't mean I end up in a 'right turn only' lane, I mean that I get behind the driver who lacks any positive brain cells. The one who always allows other drivers to push in, the one who loiters when a child could predict that the lights are going to turn red, the one who waits endlessly at roundabouts to make sure that there is no traffic between London and Scrabster before venturing forwards – that sort of driver.

I'm not complaining about the slings and arrows of outrageous fortune at traffic lights. That's bad enough, especially in Scotland, but fair's fair, they have a function and unless they have been badly set, I can wait in relative patience. However, joining the wrong queue is quite a different matter. It applies at supermarket checkouts as well. If someone is going to have to begin a hunt for a missing price tag then it happens in front of me. Credit card investigations invariably occur in my queue. I have waited patiently in queues while others have woken up, had breakfast, walked idly to the store, browsed around and then whisked through the checkout. Of course, I respond to the apologies of the flustered one in front with: 'It doesn't matter', 'No, don't mention it', 'I'd set aside a few days for shopping anyway', but I take issue with the law of averages for exposing me so consistently. You might imagine that after over three years in the Falklands I could start with a clean sheet, and at least 50% of my lane selections would move faster than adjacent lanes, but no. I made my way through North London less smoothly than I would have liked. Then, suddenly, Staples Corner, the delight of the once proudly clogged North Circular Road, appeared, and the M1 opened up before me with its promise of unfettered progress. No boggings and bumper jacks here today!

This initial motorway had been built when I was at school. The very first stretch had ended in the middle of nowhere. Well, almost nowhere, it was a place called Crick in Northamptonshire. For a while, Crick became one of the most visited places on the planet. It was more popular than Lourdes or Mecca. Anyone who could include the motorway in their journey did so, even if it meant effectively traversing two sides of a triangle. This was defended on the grounds that it was so much quicker. London to Norwich via Crick in record time was the kind of trendy claim that was being made at parties in the early Sixties.

My few years away hadn't heralded any change in driving patterns. Nobody leaves enough room between vehicles. The occasional short stretch of clean crash barrier provided evidence of the fact that very nasty things happen on motorways. Giant lorries thunder along with seemingly unstoppable momentum, hammering the road surface. I passed the timbered cottage just north of Toddington service area. It was still there, as puzzling as I had always found it, with leaded patio doors leading charmingly to a twenty-yard lawn and then the M1. I wondered if the occupiers ever held barbecues in that trembling garden, proudly proffering medium rare steak with just a hint of blackness on the outside caused not so much by singeing coals but by oil fumes. Still, they would have less lead in them now than in past years, so things are looking up.

The motorway bullies the countryside. It cuts a path unthinkingly through pasture and ditch, through copse and hillside, dividing whole communities. The once-charming and rather out-of-the-way Charnwood Forest was severed in the Sixties by this very road charging straight through it. The government built underpasses for cattle and there is at least one exit (22, I believe) where the great road can be entered, but the ability of an already relatively isolated community to communicate within itself was taken away. The thought of underpasses brought to mind that dank, dimly lit and slightly unhealthy atmosphere that characterizes them in London, and I wondered whether the less fortunate cows used their artificial routeway to beg from the others as they mooched past on their way to milking.

On the return journey I dropped in on my parents in Leicester. I was aware of growing old, they were aware of growing old; they had done a bit more of it than I had and were very conscious of that fact. It was another of those heart-rending moments for the expatriate visiting the mother country. How can one just leave aged parents with a wave of goodbye when eight thousand miles will separate us next week? And yet one must. It is part of the balance, a roundabout to go alongside a swing. There are high points, there are low points and part of the distinguishing character of those who voluntarily work abroad is that they learn to live through, if not cope with, such awful moments. I surged off into the night, revving the characterless Mondeo and listening to a new CD that I seemed to have acquired.

I managed to get back into my hotel room to find that the second half of a football international I had been pacing my journey for wasn't even on the TV. It must have been on some other channel that the hotel didn't subscribe to – what is Britain coming to?

If one opts for a Monday night flight to the Falklands, then there is an inevitable aura of farewell to the parks and shops during the last weekend. The undesirable nature of this was somewhat dissipated by the arrival of son Paul in London on Friday afternoon, joined by his wife-to-be Katie on the Saturday and Sunday. We lounged around the bazaars, enjoying some of the warmest February weather ever recorded. The old-town atmosphere of Covent Garden on a Friday evening was a worthy experience. Paul had recently changed his job, and now worked in the sanitary ware industry. Suddenly his conversation had become laced with facts pertaining to the siphonic action of flushing systems and the relevant EU regulations. He had an in-depth knowledge of the manufacture of plastic toilet seats that was most enlightening. It brought a whole new topic of conversation into our repertoire. Saturday lunch at the Savoy was of equal interest. Such extravagant lunching was not a regular habit, but the atmosphere was unique and, unfortunately, reminded me of one minor disappointment in my past.

I had just made my first big career move, to tackle the challenge of managing the growth of a national timber importer. I was in my early thirties, ambitious and, although with hindsight I can see no reason for it, confident. On my very first day in this new job the chairman invited me to lunch at the Savoy and we were shown to a table overlooking the river. The view was enchanting as one looked through the trees stretching upward from the small area of garden below. Over gin and tonic at the table, the gentlemanly chairman explained that although the advertisement for the job had indeed mentioned investment, growth and acquisition, there had been a slight change of plan. The new strategy was one of cutback, saving, and in general terms the exact opposite of what I, not unreasonably, had thought the job entailed. He was, of course, sorry to relay such news and that was why lunch at the Savoy had been selected as an appropriate gesture. A substantial blow was being cushioned in as civilized a manner as he could find. He was a good motivator. I spent the next six years struggling with the fallout from that strategic change. As for the chairman, he had been pushed into early retirement. So the River Room had memories for me.

On this occasion, being overwhelmed with the freedom and flexibility of the great city, I had quite forgotten the propriety of jackets and ties. I enquired of the head waiter what the Saturday ruling might be and was assured that being tieless was quite acceptable on a non-business day, although being jacketless was not. Fortunately, both Paul and I had jackets. Or did we? To my surprise, Paul's was revealed not to be a jacket at all, but something entirely different. It had pockets, a collar and was being worn on top of his shirt, so I had the temerity to challenge the head waiter to define precisely what he meant by the term 'jacket'. He obliged with precision as requested by saying, 'A blazer, sir.' The futility of argument was all too apparent, and the Savoy produced a dark red blazer, which Paul wore rather uncomfortably. He also took to spotting other male lunchers who had actually removed their jackets altogether as the day was so warm. Life is unfair, even in the Savoy.

After a classy lunch that will always be remembered for jackets rather than sustenance, we decided to become real tourists and visit the Tower of

London and Tower Bridge. I had not been inside the Tower since I was at school. I remembered that it had been pretty uninteresting then. Now it was even worse, the White Tower was having all its displays changed and thus notices everywhere merely described what one was missing. My relationship with the law of averages with respect to queuing is matched by the incredible number of refurbishments that I seem to catch. There is a disappointing incompleteness about visiting something that is being refurbished. Jean and I once visited a famous film set near Tucson where many Westerns had been shot. Most of the place had burnt down the month before, but that didn't discourage the Americans from offering tours of the trail of devastation, describing in detail what we would have seen, and selling little bottles of ashes from the fire as souvenirs.

Give me a castle that I can wander about, not one that plans my every move for me. I want castles that have nooks and crannies that are waiting to be discovered afresh by every visitor with an inquiring mind. I suppose it is the sheer volume of visitors that provides the rationale for this authoritarian behaviour with a national treasure. Related problems occurred at Tower Bridge. Here, a guided tour was the only way of getting to the top, and the whole thing was so over-blown that it was amusing. The little group moved from one room to another and in each room parts of the monumentally dull story of the construction of the bridge were conveyed by videos, speaking life-size puppets and other devices. However, the view from the top was well worth the tedium.

That evening, we continued in the tourist vein, sitting in the second row in a West End theatre. A strange feature of my tenure in the Falklands was that I had never attended so many London theatres. On every visit to London, I picked a play and greatly enjoyed watching it. Deprive me of something, and I want it.

The sun shone gloriously on the Kent and Sussex countryside on Sunday as we toured old haunts by car, although as we descended into the core of the Weald, the morning mist was reticent to let the sun through; it swirled and drifted stubbornly. During the afternoon we drove along the lane where we had once lived. It had been twelve years since we left that house, but I can still remember the pain of parting from a glorious location into which I had invested many hours' hard DIY. We gaped at the front of the property through the very driveway that Branston had rolled balls for the ramblers. Was all that wall panelling still in place? Did my sunken patio still exist? What about the wine rack in the dining room? Was it still the dining room? Paul noticed the absence of a huge Scots Pine tree — someone had clearly felt threatened by the fact that it towered over the main bedroom. We gazed and remembered and clambered back into the hire car and left it all behind again.

We visited Eastbourne and savoured the old-fashioned south-coast atmosphere before heading north to the metropolis. If only there had been some other way to get there. A traffic jam stretched all the way from Polgate, just north of Eastbourne, to the traffic lights in Brixton. Not everything about England was so enjoyable after all.

Monday came, the visit rushed to its end, and after a last hectic day in vital meetings, I found myself journeying back to Brize Norton. The cab was not going at such a breakneck speed this time, and yet it was the same driver. Actually, it was not a cab at all but a mini-bus. We had ordered it owing to the 'Could you just take this?' syndrome having reached ludicrous proportions. It is one of the dangers of leaving FIGO for the Falklands direct that numerous parcels and bits and pieces appear from the ether, demanding to be transported along with one to the Islands. Normally this is no particular hardship, as my bags are already so heavy with items that were once mere whims on my list that a few extra lumps of lead will not make any difference. On this occasion I was rather taken aback by the appearance of a twelve-foot-long cylinder about six inches in diameter that contained vital aerials for the Falkland Islands Defence Force. How on earth could I stuff that in my case? However, we managed to pre-warn the RAF, who were most helpful; hence the mini-van.

Brize Norton had something in common with the Tower of London – refurbishment. One fellow passenger commented that he hoped the plane wasn't being refurbished too. I rather hoped that it was, but it wasn't. The flight was again punctual and smooth and I arrived back in the bland little VIP lounge at Mount Pleasant tired but relieved to be home from my visit home.

Chapter 21

It is quite a challenge for a grown man to get into a thoroughly waterproof babygro-type garment. I felt like a butterfly getting back into its chrysalis. The bright yellow, rubbery, many-zipped suit was essential for the long helicopter journey over the South Atlantic to where the Borgny Dolphin rig was situated. This rig I knew to be a third-generation semi-submersible, although learning what that really meant would take a bit longer.

The Military Commander, who was travelling with us in the Bristows helicopter, had flown fast jets for many years. So he knew all about these suits. He informed us that we could survive for quite a long time in the open sea as long as the suit maintained its integrity. Maintaining integrity meant that we had to put it on properly, thus making sure that all the watertight seals were effective. Having achieved this, one sat in the helicopter feeling rather less comfortable than those African women who wear all those rings around their necks. The Commander thoughtfully used his experience to comfort us with the fact that dying of cold in the open ocean is really relatively painless – he compared it to a kind of gradual sleep coming on. We were glad he had found the time to accompany us.

These sombre considerations were balanced by the sight of the none-too-lean-Attorney General, looking for all the world like the first Falklands Teletubby. The *Penguin News* reporter was on hand to take helpful pictures of the leading figures of government looking utterly ridiculous.

The ride was virtually all above the sea as we headed northwards for nearly an hour and a half. Then we saw it, bright red in the afternoon sunlight. My first reaction was that it looked thoroughly artificial and somehow inappropriate. The sea was flat calm and a deep translucent blue. The rig was at once both impressive and incongruous. The standby vessel and a pale blue supply ship were busying themselves around it, but the rig dominated the ocean, its drill head towering above the structure. It reminded me of the kind of untidy contraption I would have built at the age of six on a bad Meccano day.

From the air everything looked open and functional and nothing had been finished for appearance. Red paint dominated and there was no sign of the ninety men that were supposed to be on it. Possibly this was the *Marie Celeste* of oil rigs. We would find the place deserted and lunch half eaten, a whirring drill whipping into the ocean floor out of control, the earth's crust about to be punctured...

We landed gently on the platform, kicking up a whirlwind yet descending as delicately as an autumn leaf on a still day. Various essential items were unloaded before we could de-helicopter. (No such word? If you can de-plane then you can de-helicopter, especially in the modern world of oil exploration.) We were handed bags with our names on them and ushered to a pitifully small cabin to de-babygro and assume rig-touring kit. This included boots, hard-hat, gloves and a company anorak.

Changing clothes in a very small area, especially when the garments themselves are totally unfamiliar, accompanied by three councillors and the Director of Mineral Resources, was an experience. One had to contort one's limbs in order to get the waterproof sleeve off and movements can be very sudden when the whole thing gives way in response to immense pressure. I ended up slapping female councillors, quite unintentionally.

After the required safety brief, which informed us that in an emergency we should follow any instructions that were shouted at us and was thus easily committed to memory, we began our tour of this unique self-contained world. We were shown the drill string – the long pipe that has the drill bit at the end. It looked very thin and fragile. Why this fundamentally important piece of kit should be called a 'string' was lost on me. We could see how the various lengths were added to it and began to understand how tedious it must be to have to retract the thing and undo the work of the previous day.

We visited the control room, where the drill operator manages the screwing motion, and we also viewed a TV screen where a camera on a remote submersible was able to relay the scene on the ocean bed where the drill entered terra firma. That particular picture was remarkable. I spotted squid swimming idly past the rotating column, wondering what on earth was happening in this hitherto unexplored Mesozoic basin that had effectively been all theirs for millions of years, until last week.

The atmosphere was one of intense functionality. It was like a highly compressed, production-orientated factory, only more so. Everywhere were pipes, wires and walkways. Trained men were going about their jobs with precision and apparent confidence. Every single fragment of the structure appeared to have some specific use. The focus and the concentration on what they were there for was overwhelming. I suppose if you are spending $200,000 per day on something, an hour saved here and there could pay for the odd evening's entertainment. In any case, these guys were on a twenty-eight-days-on, twenty-eight-days-off cycle.

187 / OIL — THE RIG

It provides long holidays but it also places enormous demands and I saw nothing to suggest that they were not able to cope with the round-the-clock working. Rumour had it that they could handle the twenty-eight days off with some panache as well.

The support vessel stood off, slowly circling the rig like the turkey vultures around Sulivan House – watching for disaster. It basked in the late afternoon sunlight. The lack of wind emphasized the sound of the generators and the occasional seabird. As the sun began to lower itself towards the western horizon, the colours became even more pronounced as orange light bathed the whole area. We were on an artificial island miles from any land at the southern apex of the South Atlantic.

Several vigorous movements jerked the rig. We visitors were faintly alarmed. It was explained that the drill had clogged and the drillers were freeing the bit by creating some surging movements. The operator did not want to have to bring the whole string back up – that would waste time and possibly bonus. The jerking worked. Within minutes the drill was twisting into the rock way beneath us once more.

After a cup of tea and the answering of questions, it was time to leave the fantasy environment and clamber back on the helicopter, but not before an arduous re-suiting procedure. It had been a trip well worth doing, but a rig is not a place to work unless you have a taste for the solitary life.

Chapter 22

THE DAY WE STRUCK OIL (13 MAY 1998)

That's today. This is diary format – real time (well, written in the evening, actually, but pretty close). Apart from the deadly secret oil news, it has been a pretty normal day. The weather has been sunny and calm, the streets of Stanley have seen the usual mixture of Islanders going about their business and strolling seamen and servicemen who stare at every feature for the very first time. They see everything through passing eyes, amending expectations. To the vast majority this was an average kind of day, a pot boiler, thoroughly normal. Yet, for the future of these islands it may well prove to have been the most momentous day of all.

Jean is in the UK at present, so I arose slightly earlier than when she is here. There is so much to do. Drawing curtains for one thing, feeding the chickens for another and, of course, the frugal breakfast. I arrived at the office early in order to prepare in some depth for a Union negotiation tomorrow. The councillors have been querying the necessity to award a pay rise that is strictly parallel to an index in the UK. They clearly have a good case, as the Falklands economy has many unique and distinctive elements about it. However, the argument is somewhat tarnished by the fact that the vast majority of civil servants, who represent getting on for half of the working population, believe that they were clearly promised that linkage when they agreed to a change of working hours and other employment details last year. Councillors had actually approved a form of linkage at that time. Legal action against the government is officially threatened and a strike has also been mentioned. These kind of things are absolutely unheard of in the Islands. Withdrawal of labour in the power station could bring Stanley to its knees quite quickly. However, the Union negotiators are reasonable men and I believe that a compromise is possible.

Once in the office I studied the 'in tray'. As the UK is five hours ahead of us at present, quite a lot of work can be generated by the UK before any of us reach the office. I selected those items that could be dealt with rapidly or I could pass on elsewhere. My PA had been granted a half day's leave to enable her to drive to Mount Pleasant with her daughter, who was having a haircut there. There is really only one hairdresser in Stanley and for the sake of variety the military option is sometimes preferred.

Thus I fumbled my way through some routine matters, with no wife to get my breakfast and no PA to sort out my office life! I answered the phone about twenty times and I had an exchange of views with the financial secretary on issues arising from the pay award before I was able to settle to the preparation work about halfway through the morning. I had just come off the phone when the junior clerk informed me that Wendy, the general manager in our London office, wanted me urgently. I rang back.

I knew very well that the oil rig, positioned about one hundred and fifty miles to the north of the Islands, was about to get to the interesting bit of the whole exercise. I had, after all, been on the rig only a few days ago and seen, by way of remote camera, the drill string actually screwing into the sea bed. But the Director of Mineral Resources had gone off to an exhibition in Salt Lake City reasonably sure that no news would emerge for a couple of weeks. In any case, this was now a 'Tight Hole'. The company drilling, Amerada Hess, wished to maintain strict secrecy for commercial reasons and although we, as government, would be party to the results, there was to be no excitement. We had prepared a carefully structured trail for the handling of any news.

The message was almost unbelievable: the story was emerging in London in a thoroughly unplanned manner. Wendy, who was not part of the carefully structured trail, told me that Amerada had told her that they had found hydrocarbons already, and that they feared the story would leak out rapidly. Clearly some quick positioning had to be done.

I phoned Amerada's London office and spoke to one of their PR staff who had been in the Islands only two weeks ago. She confirmed the information. The key word was 'trace'. Yes, there was a trace of hydrocarbon, but there was also good porosity and the regime was almost certainly lacustrine and not marine. I have been exposed to enough petroleum geology over the past three years to realize that, at one swoop, some of the biggest remaining imponderables had been resolved. The fact that the environment was non-marine could be regarded as good news and the presence of hydrocarbon means that the maturation process models that so many specialists have debated for so long have some reality in them. What's more, she confirmed that suitable reservoir rock seemed to be there – another positive indicator. The probabilities in all the financial models were about to change dramatically and a few share prices were going to rise rather quickly.

Amerada did not wish to issue anything to the media but they had prepared a defensive statement for those who would inevitably learn that something had happened. This skeletal paragraph ran as follows:

Amarada Hess can confirm that well 14/09-A in the North Falklands basin has encountered minor hydrocarbon indications. This does not constitute evidence of any substantial or commercial quantities of hydrocarbons, and further drilling and evaluation of the well will continue at least until the end of the month.

Understatement it may have been, but it was also a bombshell for the Islands, the UK government, the Argentine government and participating oil companies. It meant 'farm-ins' would become sought after as pressure was put on existing consortia partners to dilute their holdings. It meant more exploratory drilling, which, in turn, was good for the local economy. We could neither issue this information, nor should we comment on it. All queries, and there would be many in the near future, would be referred to Amerada. The PR manager said she would fax me the statement and the well log from the previous day that contained the geologist's report.

I set about building the fences, making sure that only those that really needed to know actually knew, and that no hint of such phenomenal news leaked out from our end. How monumental was this smidgen of fact? The answer must be that it was highly significant. For the last three years we had been working extremely hard, through legislation, licensing round, evaluations and the setting up of administrative and logistical frameworks, all in the unlikely event of the discovery of oil. This North Falkland Basin is one of the last great Mesozoic basins of the world that had never been drilled, and until today, all the evidence we had was secondary in nature – seismic for structure, oil seeps for hinting that there may be something, and interpolations from other places.

I sought out our London Representative, who happened to be visiting the Falklands and was in the next office, and briefed her. She was to brief the General Manager in London on the agreed line. Then I rang our PR agents in London to inform them and to get them, in turn, to brief the London office and to liaise with Amerada. I then phoned the Governor and made an appointment to see him within the next half an hour. I waited for the fax from Amerada, but it didn't come, so I ensured that the fax room was secure and went and told His Excellency. Then I had a normal lunch. I played Falklands Tennis and lost a league match. After lunch I picked up the fax, interpreted some of the geological terms, went and had a haircut, at the only one in Stanley (this was clearly a day for haircuts), and then went to the small Department of Mineral Resources to brief them. The PA to the absent Director seemed miffed that she hadn't been the first to hear. In fact, she should have been, but in any event she was now in the loop, and all who needed to know now knew.

Two unusual sensations had been with me since the first phone call from London: immense satisfaction at the success of the well and the promise of future prosperity for the Islands, and a strange smugness allied with fear, that I have possession of a fact that is really very valuable. The value would now diminish as the news got out.

The pattern of news breakage is of some significance to us as we much prefer to ensure that news relating to the Islands actually surfaces first in the Islands. The councillors get a bit hot under the collar if they hear this kind of thing on the radio first. There was a real risk that the news would break in London, but there was nothing I could do to overcome that problem. I would have to sit tight, just like that hole.

I gave a brief press conference on our privatization policy this afternoon and then held a preliminary meeting with the government negotiating team for tomorrow. A quick visit home to change was followed by a trip to the broadcasting studio to record my music programme. Later, in the evening, I played a tennis league match, and then watched Chelsea win the UEFA Cup against Stuttgart on our four-hours-delayed same-day TV.

A day to remember and a day to forget. I wonder whether these lonely islands will ever be the same again. They are set for changes that we cannot envisage. There is a sense of excitement in living through such events in real time.

Chapter 23

OIL – WHAT HAPPENED NEXT

It took until the nineteenth, a mere six days later, for the news to become totally public. That morning I had been involved in a tree-planting ceremony at the Estancia farm, some twenty-five miles from Stanley. This was a particularly worthy occasion, as trees currently mean so little to the Islands yet they could, and should, mean so much. Estancia was the home of my favourite de-boggers, the Heathmans. If anyone deserved plenty of trees, it was them. The Agriculture Department had organized the planting of a shelterbelt on a scale far grander than I had expected. A vast area had been transformed by trench ploughing into a striped and heavily rutted bog. We slogged and squelched our way through this peaty challenge to arrive at the carefully prepared furrow. Then we wedged our tiny saplings in the treacle toffee soil and they looked ridiculous – thoroughly inadequate for the task ahead. But then Hercules' mother must have felt the same at the beginning. This great event was witnessed by three of the media, who insisted on interviewing us with inventive questions such as: 'What does it feel like to plant a tree?' and 'Do you hope it will grow?'

Back in the office that afternoon I learned to my horror from a councillor (my fear of brickbats from that quarter bearing fruit) that the lunchtime news on the local radio station had trumpeted to the world that evidence of hydrocarbons had been found in the well currently being drilled by Amerada Hess. Apparently, the share price of one of the participating oil companies had risen above the point at which a Stock Exchange statement had to be made. Thus, some cautious words emerged in London and the hounds of the press immediately assumed that a bonanza was imminent. The *Daily Mail* carried the following on 20 May:

Falklanders to get £5m each in oil bonanza

The 2,100 people of the Falklands were last night set to become multi-millionaires after oil was found off their shores. A huge rig, 200 miles out at sea in British territorial waters, brought up a trace of oil after only two weeks of exploratory drilling. Experts said the speed at which it had been found indicated that vast reserves were there – it took years of exploration in the North Sea before the first rig began producing crude.

This was the thin end of a massive wedge of hyperbolic journalism. The newspapers competed with each other in the sensationalism stakes. Folk began phoning our London office wishing to emigrate to the Islands. One lady, born an Islander but living in the UK for the past thirty-four years, demanded payment of her £5 million. She cited the *Daily Mail* as proving the veracity of her claim.

The *Financial Times* carried the story, indicating that the shares in Desire Petroleum had already risen by 46%. Desire was the company that had been set up with the Falklands specifically in mind. The chairman was Dr Colin Phipps, ex-chairman of Clyde Petroleum and an ex-Labour MP. Also on the board was our old favourite Sir Rex Hunt. Many Falkland Islanders had bought shares in the company and became hourly watchers of the stock market. *The Times*, also on 21 May, carried an accurate but misleadingly headlined article from the sophisticated pen of Michael Binyon:

Falklands oil strike after two-week search
After only two weeks of drilling, an international oil company has discovered oil in the waters off the Falklands, raising the prospect of an oil bonanza in the South Atlantic...

Locally, the Desire shareholders were counting up their paper profits and the debate as to how all our money was to be spent gathered momentum just as councillors began to leave the Islands for their annual holidays. I knew some of those who had bought shares and calculated, as they did, that if they sold now, they might never have to work again. A referendum was requested by some, although there was never any clarity as to what the question might be. Others wanted the infrastructure sorted out right away. The prospects of a ferry across Falkland Sound and faster road building were openly discussed. The business community was not frightened of onshore development, but just about everyone else was.

The reports coming from the rig that remained secret, contained such gems as: 'Micropalaeontological analyses carried out over the interval have yielded no foramenifera.' My knowledge of such matters meant that I was no wiser than anyone else was when confronted with such classified information. However, it was obvious to those who understood the meaning of probabilities and life itself that all the excitement in London and the expectation in Stanley would soon get a dose of cold water. It happened. The well yielded no further good news at all. In fact, on the twenty-seventh of the month Amerada announced that it was dry and they abandoned it. Their statement was particularly low key: 'The well encountered traces of hydrocarbons. Appraisal showed that these were not present in commercial quantities.'

The national press in the UK who were more or less up to date, cottoned on to the negative message but the earlier positive news was just beginning to gain momentum around the world. This Mexican wave effect on news coverage was staggering. Reporters were phoning from Japan and Scandinavia. Far more importantly, in a way, the politicians in Argentina were becoming particularly fraught.

On the negative side, a wonderfully insulting piece of journalism appeared in the *Sun* on 1 June. William Langley's thesis was that the Islands should be handed back to Argentina and in making his case he wrote that the Islands were: '... bleak, cold, wet, and populated by the most dislikeable, greedy, miserable and ungrateful people on earth'. He went on: 'Now it turns out there may not be much oil anyway. Good. Another reason to get shot of the place.' In reacting to this kind of assault, one is always on the defensive; nevertheless, it was agreed that we would contact Langley and try to 'educate' him. We did so and he was, as I anticipated, rather relaxed about the whole thing. It had, after all, only been a few column inches in the *Sun*, and it would be forgotten by the following morning, if not before.

The wave was just reaching the provincial papers in the UK. Apparently they were behind both Japan and Scandinavia. In Aberdeen, the two-week-old news was hot. I suspected that we were going to have to get used to this kind of switchback ride. It was 7 July, a whole fifty-five days later, that I saw the last reference to oil riches being found in our waters, and by that time the scene had shifted several times.

LASMO were drilling the next well and they opted for a total news blackout. Lessons had been learned from Amerada's experience. Well, this well began well. The drill bit was biting through sediment at a fair old rate, and all seemed set fair for some significant additions to our awareness of what exactly was out there in the basin. Larry Smith, a wonderfully laid-back drilling manager from Utah, provided a competence and a drawl that made us feel the US oil industry had come to town.

However, all was not well with this well. Each well has an estimated depth to TD (I spy something beginning with 'a' – acronym), which is where they expect to encounter the 'basement'. This basement is the boundary between the older, mainly metamorphic rocks, and the newer sedimentary ones. Oil is far more likely to be encountered in the sediments, and so reaching TD (Total Depth) signals the effective end of drilling. This time the drill bit came across very hard rock far earlier than TD had been anticipated, so it kept on drilling, hoping to break through into softer structures below. Drill bits began to break. The sediments began to cave in above the whirring bit, and the lubricant used in the process, called 'mud', was in great demand. Bits kept on breaking, the strata kept absorbing mud, and this was proving to be an expensive and not particularly successful operation.

The information coming from a well is particularly useful to both driller and government. This was especially true as the first one had been at best inconclusive and the location of the second had been agreed because we all felt it would provide the most useful data. LASMO were convinced that they were at the basement and could go no further. They also were unable to provide us with complete information, as the well itself was collapsing. Yet they had undertaken contractually to provide information to a certain depth. Our advisers recommended a firm line for quite a while, but in the end the situation became obvious. We were not going to be bullied, but nor could we be unreasonable. We concurred that they had arrived at the TD some time before anyone expected. There was a licking of wounds and we looked forward to Shell/Agip and our third pull on the massive fruit machine handle.

The share market responded as hints of gloom descended. The chairman of Desire Petroleum was reminding punters that everything was really quite rosy and he had never promised a rose garden anyway; meanwhile Desire shares spiralled downwards towards their point of origin. As a government, although we had tended to discount the whole oil issue in our forward planning, just for good measure we discounted it again.

The rig took a deep breath and was towed towards the north-east and the Shell tranche. Shell's approach to the whole exploration had been individualistic right from the beginning. A massive company; they had their own way of doing things and their own culture – a kind of corporate mini global village. They were extremely polite, very public spirited and quietly confident of their own methods. The whole circus revved into motion once again, but this time with new performers. The local media pushed for information, the London share market fluttered, and the oilmen busied themselves on rig and on shore.

The middle managers of the oil world wear jeans and tartan shirts, making them almost lumberjacky in appearance. They are always on the phone or staring at a computer screen and many of them have Scottish accents. The example that they set the locals in terms of focus and work ethic was superb, but the Islanders were well able to accommodate the pace, whether on the wharf or in the pubs of Stanley. The Shell boys beavered away. This costly hole was quite a distance from the previous two wells and the seismic revealed them to be attacking a separate structure. The weather was bad and they were cautious. By the third week of July they were approaching the really interesting depth, and said as much to the local media. Even this innocent comment had an impact on the share prices of three of the smaller companies involved. Middle managers get told off for breathing in such an environment, in spite of their macho appearance.

On 22 July I was informed by the Director of Mineral Resources that she had heard that Shell had encountered evidence of oil. Only in small quantities, but, just as with the Amerada hole, at least something to investigate and set the blood racing. The stifled euphoria was rather short-lived. No sooner had the London stock market got a sniff, than denials of any significant find emerged from Shell and an air of gloom descended on the few who knew anything at all. It just wasn't that different from the Amerada hole. There was evidence that the oil could have formed, source rock was there in abundance, but the quality of sandstone needed for a good reservoir was missing. I had a meeting with Shell in The Hague and then one with Amerada in London. The two interpretations were very similar, and the prognosis for an oil boom was not good. We were about to enter the grey area, where future prospects are at best uncertain. That had always been the most likely outcome, but the realization that riches could be somewhat less forthcoming than originally thought might have a negative impact on our tiny economy.

The last half of the exploration seemed to rush by. Before Christmas 1998, three more wells had been drilled and the rig was gone. The managers had overseen the bits and pieces being placed back on the northward-bound vessel, and we were left with a few empty offices and vacant houses. Ironically, one of the targets we set ourselves was to paint the surface of our floating pontoon port (FIPASS) with non-slip paint by February 1998, in order to comply with the Health & Safety requirements. We managed to complete this just in time for the last oil executive to see it before he left. It was, of course, the weather's fault.

There were postscripts galore. We were not going to know the full geological truth even after years' analysis of the results, so almost any conclusion was valid. Some locals, who had been pushing for a referendum when the first well looked a winner, had commissioned a proper survey to see how the population was reacting to oil riches. It was published around 15 January 1999, contained no surprises, and was a good example of how perspectives change. The Islanders had already adapted to the lack of oilmen in town and the lack of a bonanza on the horizon.

A couple of months later I was in London for meetings and a man acting for the government of Dagestan approached me to find out how an oil licensing round could be organized. I described to him a process that had almost become second nature to me. He took notes and seemed satisfied, and I was able to discover where Dagestan is.

We had lived through the full cycle. The promise had been enormous, the hype had been over the top and the excitement of potential riches had been real at the time. Some speculators had made money and some had lost, but the oilmen had spent money in Stanley; the economy had experienced a fillip.

Some one hundred and fifty miles north of Cape Dolphin, the plugged wells lay silent on the dark seabed. Their secrets were being examined in Dallas, London, The Hague and Edinburgh. Morsels of promising information seeped through the strata of communication as the world oil price discouraged any further adventures.

Our strategy was to keep the ball in the air. We attended conferences and discussed findings in academic and commercial contexts. BGS briefed me in June 1999, over a year since the first traces of oil had been found. They were not despondent, but then they were consultants. The necessary conditions for the formation of oil were present in the basin – good source rock, adequate maturation and decent capping. However, the anticipated reservoirs just hadn't been in the most obvious places. Possibly different 'plays' should be generated, a 'play' being a guess made by an exploration geologist. Maybe there would be substantial reserves further to the south, or the north, or on the Argentine border, or in fact almost anywhere that an unsuccessful well hadn't been drilled. The final story will unfold with the passage of time.

Chapter 24

People come from miles around to shop in Stanley. In fact, before the war, many Argentines flew in simply to enjoy the pseudo-British atmosphere and fly home laden with whisky and Cadbury's chocolate. Even today the good folk of West Falkland and the outer islands wing their way to the capital and the military men and women from MPA bounce down the gravel road for thirty-five miles, just to saunter around the centre of town. Some twenty thousand cruise ship passengers a year scramble off their tenders at the public jetty, eyes wide and wallets and credit cards at the ready. They come not because this is the Arndale of the South Atlantic or the mall to end all malls, but simply because it is where it is, and it is all that there is.

The primary consideration in marketing is to know your market. However, that knowledge is hardly required if you are the only available retail outlet within several thousand miles. Those who expect smart shop fronts and snappy customer service are soon forced to admit the naivety of such assumptions. Do you remember playing 'shops' when you were very young? I do. We used to collect all the stuff that we could readily do without, assemble it in a simplistic way on some old tea chests, then cajole passers-by to show an interest by parting with hard-earned cash for the tasteless offerings we had laid before them. I developed enormous respect for innocent neighbours who actually spared some coppers in response to our pitiful innovation. I have an equally high regard for the hardy shopkeepers of Stanley, but my early impressions of consumer merchandising in the capital were that a similar process was taking place. The difference was that it was not spare change that was changing hands and a large proportion of it seemed to come from my pocket.

Technically, the fierce winds militate against picture-type shop windows. Thus, sauntering around window-shopping on a warm summer's evening is impossible on two counts. Some outlets are heavily shuttered, others you would need to pole vault past the window to see in, and the most common feature is simply a lack of display. In some cases, you would be hard pushed to know what is a shop and what isn't. Retailers are found in such surprising circumstances that a newcomer has to receive very detailed instructions merely to have the opportunity of spending money. Some are in Portakabins, some in warehouses, some in houses and some in sheds. The previous secondary school has become a shopping area and there are very few purpose-built shops. The Standard Chartered Bank building, opened in 1995, is possibly the only one, and it shows. Just walking into that bank is like transferring continents. Moreover, there are few warm summer evenings.

The lack of advertising is an interesting aspect of Falklands life. It is true that the private-sector satellite television does have advertising, although it is normally in Spanish and hardly ever for any goods that are available. Such interruptions to programmes are merely irritants. There are no billboards, nobody receives junk mail, direct sales canvassers are unknown and advertising in the *Penguin News* could best be described as functional. The radio station does provide the daily 'notices', but these are not psychologically constructed to tempt one into retail submission.

The military TV channel has a problem with advertising slots in that they can't fill them with the adverts that would normally appear. It must be to do with the agreement when they buy the programmes. They have concocted a number of alternatives to fill these natural breaks, the most entertaining of which is real British soldiers, located almost anywhere in the world, sending messages to their loved ones. These follow a predictable pattern: 'Hello Doreen, Bob here. I hope you are well. Young Brendan must have grown a bit. I love you to bits. Looking forward to my next R&R.' It is not riveting stuff, but may well be better than adverts.

Most locals know exactly where to shop for what item, even though at first glance it is hard to classify the retail fraternity. The mix of goods in the shops lacks clear differentiation and in many cases also lacks variety of choice. Until fairly recently you could have chosen as your new vehicle a Land Rover or another Land Rover. There is only one filling station, so it is wise to remember opening times. The ability to select between brands is almost non existent – lip salve is exactly that, the fact that in a small town in the USA you can find twenty-six flavours on one display is irrelevant. The size of the market dictates the level of stock and hence the variety.

People have allegiances to various shops for various items. It may be to do with perceived attitudes, something that might have happened in a previous generation, or even family relationships. There are no genuinely specialist shops. Once again, it is size – the potential turnover in, say, men's clothes or shoe repairing is just too small. For such requirements people either wait for a holiday or business trip abroad, or they use the time-honoured mail-order systems that have served well for many years.

All Islanders have long learned the distinction between a 'sell by' date and a 'best before' date. Back in the UK, I had hardly noticed this vital consumer information so sensibly displayed on most packets. In the Falklands, there is a cry of unrestrained delight if one locates an item that

Prince Charles meets the famous Falkland Island penguins.

Above: The author being interviewed by Ken Lukoviak. Ken was a paratrooper at Goose Green and wrote *A Soldier's Song*. He came back to the Falklands in 1995 to write for the *Mail on Sunday*.

Below: A view of the Two Sisters, with a reminder of the war.

Above: Saddle Island, viewed from New Island.

Below: The coastal scenery on New Island.

Views of the *Jhelum*, the wreck in front of Sulivan House.

King Penguins.

Above: A King Cormorant colony on Carcass Island.

Below: A Black Browed Albatross with its chick.

Carcass Island: a view over the settlement, and Jean, pictured outside the small cottage where we stayed.

Above: The New Year's Day raft race in Stanley Harbour.

Below: The cathedral in Stanley, with the whalebone arch on the right.

is on sale well before its 'sell by' date has arrived. It is generally news that is hard to keep to oneself – once, of course, one's own bag has been filled. The word would buzz around the bazaars, only there are no bazaars – the market is not large enough to justify their existence. The network employed is the diddle-dee telegraph.

Information processing of this type is superior to e-mail, optical fibres or even thought transference. It is brought into use in a big way when shortages are threatened. With long lead times on bulk shipping and the imperfection in the forecasting of demand, not to mention human error, certain items will run out. I can well remember it being sugar, but it could equally well be tinned asparagus, lard, or ice cream. On one occasion, it was rubber gloves. Whatever the item, the word goes round. Then the rush begins and is over almost before the far end of town gets the news. All the shelves at all the shops selling that particular item are bare.

Stanley is a community where the shoppers still drive from shop to shop. There are no multi-storey car parks, no precincts and there isn't really a concentration of shops into a defined area. Thus, each likely shelf area for the missing product can be scanned by half a dozen park-and-search exercises. Anyone on foot or waiting patiently for the Senior Citizens' Blue Bus might as well give up.

Imagine life without being able to actually buy the fundamentals for a recipe you want to try. Imagine not being able to buy a slide film, or a newspaper less than four days out of date, or decent cooking chocolate, or a clothes brush, or even cream. One either puts up with the situations or improvises and substitutes. Strange concoctions can emerge when recipes are fiddled, repairs to rubber gloves are hard to make waterproof and hairbrushes used as clothes brushes can have an interesting short-term impact upon your hairstyle. Your black jacket might not look the same for a while either!

Of course, a rumour can produce a shortage when there wasn't one in the first place. Such situations may arise through genuine error or a mischievous suggestion. What fun it must be for the initiator of the false shortage story to achieve the remarkable effect of empty shelves at all the shops and know that larders all over town have been needlessly stuffed with violet creams or some other essential item. I mention violet creams because by one of those strange twists of Falklands fate, the Coop happened to carry a stock of the most delicious violet creams, for which we provided a steady market.

Deprivation can inflame desire. One can be overtaken by a compelling urge to partake of a particular food. Pregnant women are known for this kind of yen and I once found myself longing for a sausage. Images of toad in the hole and sausage and chips welled up from my subconscious. There was not a sausage to be had in any of the shops. I hadn't even noticed that

I hadn't had one for some time, then the desire grew with each meal. I whinged to anyone who would listen and at a reception happened to mention my longing to a sympathetic military wife. She joyfully announced that they had a huge surplus of sausages at MPA that nobody wanted because they were approaching their 'sell by' date! Yes, she actually said, 'approaching'. I smiled as sweetly as I knew how to and before long we had the most wonderful coils of Cumberland sausage in our freezer. The surfeit of sausages I enjoyed quite put me off them for a while.

Visitors from South America often remark on the fact that the cross section of wares is so British. To be fair, the produce can sometimes seem a bit tired. Neither observation is surprising, as what we are seeing almost certainly began a long sea journey in Southampton and has had at least four weeks lurching around the Atlantic. It can make a difference if the product actually wallows in the company of another. On one occasion some creosoted wood happened to be allocated a stateroom adjacent to foodstuffs. There was an outcry even from the long-suffering Stanley consumers − everything tasted of creosote. 'It is good for you,' said the company confidently. 'It won't harm you,' said the chief medical officer with equal conviction. Hard to believe when beer inside a can is flavoured with wood preservative known for its ability to kill everything and produce warts all over the place.

The exception to the Britishness are the products that come from Chile; either by airfreight or by way of the Islands' own coastal shipping vessel, the Tamar, nipping across to Punta Arenas. Thus, on some packaging, Spanish is the only language. Certain expats who may be linguistically disadvantaged have been known to buy entirely the wrong product as a result. That too can upset the balance of a recipe. Unexpected differences emerge − they use a different type of mayonnaise in Latin America. It is the same make, but it has a deeper colour and tastes unusual. Chilean beer has many admirers and some excellent Chilean wines rest on the shelves, which knock spots off those transported across the oven of the equator. Obviously, fresh fruit and vegetables arrive on the weekly flight from Chile. They are expensive, but at least they are available, and often of excellent quality.

Not all the surprises are from the Southern Cone. The wonderfully innovative hydroponic vegetable-growing in Stanley produces brilliant lettuce, small tomatoes and succulent peppers. Occasionally, some exquisite local crab appears in the freezers. Local produce comes wrapped in a homespun manner, but it is probably the tastiest and the cheapest in the store. In all the shopping, knowledge is the key − know where to look and when.

Traditionalists buy their beef and mutton directly from Camp. There are endless debates as to which particular farm rears the most tasty meat, or the tenderest. The fact is that although the lamb and mutton is universally delicious, the Falklands cannot yet produce a consistent standard in beef and thus a whole hindquarters may be as tender as could be, or as tough as old boots.

However, shopping in Stanley is not just a matter of knowing where to go; it is also a social experience. Most people know most other people, so a trip to the supermarket is also a chance to have a chat with friends. The post office is a social centre and a wonderful con. There is a large red pillar box outside and lots of individual boxes inside. The highly skilled post office workers move the mail from the outside one to those inside. There is no hapless postman to fight his way past your harmless dog – you have to go to the post office to collect it from your box. It is a cracking deal for the post office. It is quite common to post a letter then walk inside to collect one's mail, only to find that the intended recipient of one's letter is standing next to you! Actually, my attention generally focused on the fact that I always forgot to take the key to the box, so I ended up pleading with the skilled staff, who would obligingly open number 519.

The overseas airmail arrives on the Tristar twice a week. Well, it arrives if the Tristar itself arrives and if it has not been left off due to some military priority. It is unloaded at Mount Pleasant and bumped down the road by the returning customs officers or the passengers' coach. Then it is sorted. If the Tristar is on time the post office re-opens in the early evening, or whenever is appropriate, so that homesick expatriates can get their long-awaited correspondence. There is a tangible air of expectancy as the doors open and a sizeable proportion of the population surges towards the boxes, keys at the ready. A polite scramble ensues and the faces of those emerging from the double doors reveal the expectancy due to either bills or letters from loved ones.

In the UK, science has proved shopping to be a social exercise. However, that is because of the breadth of ambience and selection. Who can doubt the appeal of pondering the multifarious choice on a supermarket shelf? In the Falklands, the social dimension is altogether different, yet equally enjoyable. One can gossip and chat and find out where the government went wrong yesterday. One can put the micro world to rights while buying something that has just arrived off the ship and is in date. Of course, you may also buy the last item on the shelf knowing that the boat doesn't come for another two weeks. In fact, you may be the last person in Stanley to enjoy the taste of tinned soft roes for quite a while.

Chapter 25

SHEARING SHEEP

Isuppose that 29 December 1997 will always have a place in my memory. Out there in the whitegrass pasture lands of West Falkland there is a sheep without a name, yet he too may, brainpower permitting, remember that day as well, and for exactly the same reason.

During my first three years in the Islands I had pontificated at farmers' meetings in an appropriately woolly and broad manner on subjects relating to sheep: the international wool market, the influence of micron size on market price, the importance of quality control, the value of selling the benefits of organic wool, the management of the National Stud Flock and the significance of coastal proximity to lambing percentages, among others. For all those words that felt fine to me at the time, I had never handled a sheep and, most spinelessly of all, I had never dared to shear one. It had been mooted rather obliquely by Campers on several occasions, but the more shearing that I witnessed, the more certain I became that it is both a skill and an art form that is best approached early in life, when the limbs are bursting with energy and bending over double while working is done without a thought.

However, some weeks prior to visiting the Ram & Fleece Show at Fox Bay on West Falkland in order to fulfil the ever-pleasant duty of presenting the awards, I had felt constrained to offer to have a go at easing the fleece off one of these cuddly animals. It had seemed like a good idea at the time. On the day in question, Bobby Maddox, a fit-looking chap exuding an air of rustic skill, was appointed as my mentor, and he proved to be an instructor of considerable merit. Teaching on the job while a raging beast is hurling itself wildly in all directions is not ideal.

I watched as the shearing mechanism was prepared, a sort of giant electric hair clipper that hung from above, with a string pull for on and off. The vibration of the handpiece was more than I expected; it had a mind of its own, rather like a hosepipe when the water pressure is high. I was happily fiddling with the device, confident that the local shepherds would find some small docile lamb for me to begin on, when I heard a scuffling and men's voices shouting urgent instructions to each other like 'Grab him there', 'Don't let him do that' and 'Watch out!' Staggering erratically into the shed came a solid cluster of four men and my sheep client. They were all intertwined in a mobile wrestling pose that made the errant sheep look like a giant mutation with mortals clinging to it helplessly. This was the first ever supersheep, a brutish King Kong of a specimen; but there was no nuclear power station nearby and I realized to my horror that it was just a big sheep making a bit of a fuss. I suppose it had had a premonition, or had possibly been warned in a dream of what lay ahead, as it was kicking and carrying on in a thoroughly unruly fashion.

This was not at all what I had expected. I had thought that it would anticipate that I was intent on removing its coat in a gentle manner. True, it might have raised a token objection by prodding me a bit with its hoof as I started to apply the clippers, but to hammer into these sheep-wise chaps of West Falkland indicated the kind of strength of character that I would rather avoid tackling. Surely passivity is something a sheep inherits; it should be meek and entirely lacking in assertiveness. But this was obviously the only sheep on offer, and for all I knew it might have been specially prepared for this moment by the anarchist underground in Fox Bay. There was no exit path, no fall back position; I had volunteered for this and the sudden appearance of a significant number of spectators clutching cameras rather underscored my fear that possibly Campers really had been serious about all the roads being built in one year and this was their way of ensuring that I was serious too.

Bobby managed to assert a kind of control over the beast by turning it on to its back, I failed to see exactly how he did it, and then he offered to start the process by removing the belly part of the fleece. This he achieved in about one and a half seconds, then he showed me where to put my feet and how to lock one of the front legs of the sheep behind my right knee. This took a bit of manoeuvring on the part of both King Kong and myself, but eventually the position satisfied Bobby and he told me to start on the rear right leg. I had already had cartilage problems with my left leg; this pressure was going to cause problems.

Although I have often eaten leg of mutton and thoroughly enjoyed it, and in spite of the fact that I generally do the carving on Sunday lunchtime, I had no idea how awkward a shape leg of mutton really is. One just cannot begin to get a clean sweep of the shears as it curves and bends in every direction and the head of the shears is flat. In addition to this rather technical problem, Bobby warned me not to cut the sheep along the sinewy part of the leg, as that would make it lame. I think King Kong actually heard that instruction and reacted by flexing the sinewy part of his leg rather rapidly. I realized as the sweat began to surface that there was no vet at this show, and I don't believe the sheep suffered the same remorse on realizing the lack of a doctor. I gingerly tackled the task, concentrating on making a clean cut of the wool, but not cutting the animal. It seemed impossible to achieve. Not only did the shears feel unacceptably blunt when tackling wool and like Macbeth's dagger when faced with a bit of sheep flesh, but the creature itself was still trying to spin rapidly in an anti-clockwise direction from where I was standing (or rather bending) in order to get back on its feet and get the hell out of it. My right leg could sense the cramp coming on.

The fleece is supposed to come off in one large piece so that it can be properly graded as an entity. I had already provided about twenty mini fleeces before the leg in question looked suitably bare. The attempted sweeping motion across the underside rear of the animal met with little success and, once again, small chunks of wool were produced. This kind of thing could probably be made into jumpers for Cindy dolls, but it was not going to impress the folk from Pringle. Bobby then suggested that I could try some more of the attempted sweeps along King Kong's right-hand side. Here at last was something akin to the open road of shearing – no nasty angles, no bumps, and not even any twisting contortions as he built up his reserves of strength for another attempt.

It really wasn't that easy. There is an optimum height that the cutting head must be above the flesh: too low and blood runs, too high and wool is left, slightly higher and the shears just become entangled in a greasy mesh. Even the realization of these facts is not all that helpful, as you cannot actually see where the flesh is in relation to the dense white fibres that you are trying to cut. It all comes down to experience and feel for the complicated body shape of the sheep. I tried several different approaches, slightly different angles for the cutter head. Some seemed to work better than others, but in the tension and excitement I couldn't remember which ones were best.

Nevertheless, a kind of rhythm was emerging. Nobody watching the spectacle would have noticed, of course – all they were delighting in was this hapless expat from Stanley being entirely lost in the world that was real. But I felt that the sheep was beginning to understand who was master, and when Bobby told me to roll it over some more in order to get at the wool along the centre of the back, I realized that I had almost removed half of the fleece and for the past few minutes it had remained in one piece. Rolling it over was not one of those things that comes naturally; in fact, the energy my ovine friend had been saving was suddenly expended in an explosive attempt to gain freedom. The creature leapt free as I partially moved my leg (cramp had made the movement inevitable) and stood, momentarily, half naked with its coat hanging awry, as it began to launch itself from the height of the shearing level to the floor of the shed (a distance of about three feet). That slight hesitation gave Bobby the chance to recapture it, and we succeeded in pinning it down once again in a more rolled-over position as I scraped away at more back.

A competent shearer will remove over two hundred and fifty fleeces in one day, well over thirty an hour, or one every two minutes. So far I had taken about twenty, and it had seemed much longer. As I neared the end, and the rather scruffy fleece hung ever larger on the wooden floor, I began to experience a sense of partial achievement. It must have been similar to that experienced by the Boutros Galis on finding a Christian name for their newborn son.

When the end came and Bobby told me to let my victim stand up, I could see that I had reduced the poor creature to a laughing stock among his mates. What self-respecting sheep would settle for nakedness in strips along his back, allied with an extremely woolly rear right leg, bits of wool hanging randomly from all angles of his body and some fairly raw-looking cuts in key places?

I had noticed throughout that it is very difficult to establish eye contact with a sheep. A dog will look at you in a way that reveals a deep awareness of the human condition; even a cat might occasionally stoop to share a glance. But a sheep just seems to want to mind its own business, and thus no real rapport can be established. I had meant him no harm, and now look at him; life as he knew it had come to an end. He had, after all, been a good-looking sheep and rather proud of his appearance. When he was penned up I tried to sympathize. I told him that his handsome coat would grow again very quickly, especially if he chewed all his greens; but he considered the middle distance impassively in an air of deep sadness. He had become inconsolable. I just hope that time will heal all the scars, both mental and physical, and he may one day regard 29 December 1997 as a worthwhile experience. I certainly do.

Chapter 26

LEO

'I know Leo is my name because it has been sprayed on my side by Italian scientists using hair lacquer. I can't read it, but they tend to say "Leo did this" and "Leo did that" when they discuss how I manage my harem. As a name I like it well enough. An elephant seal needs a name with a bit of class to it. Luigi further up the beach is not too happy with his.

'My home is really the South Atlantic Ocean but my base is Sea Lion Island, about fifty miles south of East Falkland. I use my base for mating, resting and moulting. Most humans seem to think they have a weight problem – you should see me! I have been described as "enormous". When I take a nap on the beach my body tends to sag all over the sand. However, in the world I live in, size is an asset. At over eighteen feet long I am one of the very biggest of elephant seals. Without being in any way racist, I am bigger and more successful than my South American cousins. When I come ashore for the mating season around late August I am at my heaviest – just short of four tons.

'I don't actually weigh in, of course. The Italians tried to lure me on to a portable weighbridge by dragging a blow-up female seal in front of me. I was so insulted. Why on earth should they imagine that I, of all the bulls around, wouldn't be able to tell the difference! Luigi fell for it though, but then he's after anything he can get. In any case, he weighed under three tons!

'Body weight is there to be used. It is no good just building up the fat and not exploiting it. It certainly tends to put off the other bulls who try to steal from my harem. In 1995 I had a harem of one hundred and twenty-nine females. That was the highest recorded number of wives for any bull elephant seal in the Falklands and I am proud of such an achievement. It may also be an international record; I believe the Italians are going to find out. You may imagine that being responsible for such a large family would be a problem, but actually I was able to manage them fairly well. It is hard work, though – the other males are so persistent and one can only stay alert for so many hours in a day. The wretches tend to sneak up and try and poach some of the less faithful cows at the edge of my territory. If I see them coming, and I normally do, then I warn them off with a sort of protracted growl that I have perfected over the years. Nine times out of ten they get the message and swim back to sea or lumber off down the beach.

'Occasionally, they become bold enough to challenge my authority and come spoiling for a fight. I have been a fighter all of my life. Even as a young pup I thrilled to the thumping of bodies and the challenge of scraping my opponent's neck with my fast-developing teeth. As I matured, I realized that the fact nature had made me rather weightier than my contemporaries gave me a real advantage if a fight became serious.

'Fighting is all about timing and judgement. The technique is to face the opponent head on while ensuring that tail and flippers are firmly grounded. Then, rising upward and backward by arching one's body and rising on one's flippers, you surge towards the opponent. The distance between combatants is also critical, as once the lunge towards the enemy has started there is no going back. Momentum at impact is all important, as the idea is to unbalance the other bull and leave him vulnerable to a bite around the neck. The meeting of two massive bodies creates a wet thudding sound and a reverberation of the layers of fat as they absorb the impact. Over the years the fights became more and more serious and I have acquired scars around my neck, which in our society are regarded as status symbols.

'What with my scars, my bulk and my large bulbous snout, most tourists think I am really ugly. I seriously doubt whether any of them have had one hundred and twenty-nine wives. Certainly not in one year, anyway. If being ugly brings that kind of success, who cares?

'When I was about nine years old and keen to prove myself, I was able to persuade a small group of females to desert their ageing bull. They followed me off down the beach with some fetching wiggles as we looked for somewhere far enough away from their ex's sphere of influence. He saw us, of course, and came at me bellowing with his mouth gaping wide and his eyes flashing red in hatred. I was able to use my weight and my more youthful dexterity to parry his predictable blows. I also inflicted some fairly deep cuts around his chin as I counterattacked. Eventually he let me take the cows, as I think he had become tired out by trying to protect too large a harem. While he was fighting me another bull also made off with some of his wives.

'I generally select my part of the beach during September. I know the beaches of Sea Lion Island like the back of my flipper and I normally go for the same location. I need broad, shallow sand so that the females will come ashore easily with good vision in all directions to facilitate defence. The females heave themselves out of the ocean to give birth to their pups. I use all my innate charm to persuade them that I am their best bet as a mate. Frankly, they don't require much persuasion and over half of them return to me from the previous year. The growing pups from the previous season also come back to the Island, but they don't really form part of the family once they have broken away to fish at sea. The cows are usually grateful for my protection around this period, but are not particularly interested in me as a husband. It is only as their pups are approaching the end of weaning that they suddenly come over all feminine and actually seek me out. I was fortunate in 1997 that they didn't all do so at the same time!

'When first born the pups are covered in black velvet. They are less than a metre in length and spend their early days suckling from their mother at every waking moment. Humans find them cute, but from my point of view they just get in the way. They sleep a lot and grow a lot. Then they become large enough to move around and bark just like dogs. I don't much care for all the maternal bit that goes on at this time, but then it is tradition for me to protect and bide my time. After a few weeks, the youngsters begin to swim and play in the shallow water. It is really important that they master all the skills required for rapid change of direction under the surface and work at developing their lungs, which will give them the ability to dive to great depths.

'Once the mating season begins, the whole beach is in a kind of tension as bulls seek territorial advantage. If there are going to be proper fights, this is the time. I take up a position in the middle of my females, rather nearer to the sea than the landward side. The wives form a huge semi-circle around me and anyone watching might be tempted to think that we are all asleep. However, I generally stay alert. Even when I doze I can sense the movement of a fellow bull many yards away, as his weight will create vibration along the beach.

'I am a great one for growling. The Italians have recorded my voice many times. Dr Fillipo has a cassette recorder that he carries around. He comes right up to me and virtually shoves the microphone in my open mouth. I don't really mind, but it is a bit off-putting when one is trying hard to be macho and see off genuine competitive suitors! The Italians have managed to prove that when we growl, we do so with a different accent from our cousins on South Georgia or those on the Valdez Peninsula in Argentina. If they could interpret my growls I could have told them that and saved them the trouble. The Italians spend hours just watching us and making notes; it must be awfully boring for them. At least I have scores of wives to look after. Dr Fillipo only brings about three females – poor chap.

'Humans consider us to be very tame and as far as they are concerned I suppose that is true. I'm not at all interested in wasting energy chasing or even biting humans. I heard a story from Franco (the Italians tend to give us names they are familiar with), one of the oldest bulls, that a human was bitten on Sea Lion Island some years ago. He was taking a photograph, which is obligatory for all humans who visit us. The seals were quite close together on the beach and he was adjusting his lens while he walked backwards to get one of us totally in view. He stepped on a young male and had his behind quite badly bitten. The story goes that he didn't taste at all fishy.

'I stay on shore throughout the three months of the harem building and mating. There is no food on land for a grown elephant seal, so I have to build up my body fat during the fishing season and then live off it. I make sure that I eat rather well at sea both before and after all that fighting and fathering. When the pups and females have gone, I swim off to stock up. The first few minutes back at sea can be quite tricky. I may have to run the gauntlet of the killer whales. These evil creatures tend to swim around the coast as though they owned it. They glide in and out of the kelp at some speed and can mount a vicious attack on a rather less streamlined seal.

'When the layers of fat have returned and I am happy with my size I return to the Island to moult. I might simply sprawl on the beach where the tiny tussock birds will pick at my peeling skin, but sometimes I crawl into the tussock grass. It is pleasantly warm and sheltered there. This can be unnerving for the occasional tourist who stumbles across me while stomping through the fronds of grass – they are far more frightened of me than I am of them. I can move even further inland if I want, but it takes time and effort. All that heaving about on flippers is very tiring. The sea lions, who inhabit another part of the island, can actually lift themselves up on their flippers and use them like men use their legs. They can move really quickly like that, fast enough to frighten humans and catch penguins if they fancy a snack. I've tried moving in that way, but it doesn't work for us.

'The number of elephant seals that use Sea Lion Island has remained stable for some years now. It is a relatively threat-free existence. We can get on with our cyclical way of life as we have for centuries. It is also much more exclusive than South Georgia, where there are thousands of our cousins. The beaches there are too crowded. There is nowhere to settle properly and harem control is far more challenging.

'Sea Lion Island is ideal for me. I intend to slow down a bit soon and go into a kind of semi-retirement. I've earned my easy life and I intend to enjoy it.'

At the beginning of the 1998/99 summer, Dr Fillipo Galimberti, the leader of the elephant seals research group on Sea Lion Island, was disappointed that Leo did not arrive for the season. In view of Leo's age it has been assumed that he died at sea during the southern winter. His huge carcass has presumably sunk to the ocean bed to lie at rest.

Chapter 27

A CHIMNEY STORY

One day early in 1998, I was working away at my desk when I heard a familiar noise moving from the corridor into the outer office. Councillor Norma Edwards was in town from the wilds of Fox Bay West and seeking a few moments of my time. I never thought it a particularly career-enhancing action to refuse to see councillors, and in any case Norma was usually excellent value, especially if she was in her crusading mood; and she was.

The story she wove was one of Foreign Office intrigue, of an unhealthy disregard by powerful men of the clearly expressed wishes of the deserving Islanders, of philistinic and arbitrary actions by hordes of heartless monsters trampling across the Falkland Islands with rape and pillage in their eyes. Well, it was almost that bad; and it was all about a chimney.

I was Acting Governor at the time, His Excellency being away for the usual mix of holiday and business that is the familiar pattern for most expats. The problem involved Government House, which is the Governor's residence and by far the most prestigious and historical building in the Islands. At the time it was being renovated. This was more than just a 'Fill the cracks and paint' job. It was a major £1.5-million refurbishment involving a considerable amount of destruction and reconstruction, preferably in that order. The main part of the work had already been completed and the contractor, brought expensively all the way from the UK, was working under the direct supervision of the Foreign and Commonwealth Office in the person of Ian Jack, a temporarily resident clerk of works. The cost for all this was being shared between the Islands government and the Foreign Office. His Excellency had been understandably browned off with having to relocate for the past few months while his living quarters had been torn apart and reconstructed. He had mused that the whole episode had been made more galling by the fact that exactly the same thing had happened to him in his previous posting in Latvia. It can be tough at the very top.

Norma said that the magnificent west chimney was about to be demolished even though the original plans for reconstruction had shown that all the existing chimneys rising skywards from the main part of the building would be left intact. The preservation of the status quo decision to leave chimneys in place had been approved by the Historic Buildings Committee, the Planning Committee and virtually everyone in sight or out of it who had even a remote interest. After all had been refurbished it was to look exactly the same as it had before. Yesterday evening the Boadicean Councillor Edwards had chaired a meeting of the Historic Buildings Committee and had uncovered the fact that we were only hours away from the west chimney being demolished in an act of sacrilege that could never be atoned for. 'It appears on our £10 notes,' she spluttered. Although I believed her implicitly, I immediately began a search for such a note in my wallet. Norma, being competitive by nature, rummaged in her handbag, and she won. Sure enough, there, small but clear, was the representation of the chimney stack in question on the green note.

What could I say? I sympathized; I empathized; I may have indicated that it was a shame people could be allowed to get away with such obvious vandalism. 'We were promised nothing like this would happen,' she intoned as she stopped just short of sobbing. She was evidently deeply saddened by the issue. I had an overwhelming urge to console her. Short of actually putting my arm around her, I made sympathetic noises. But I should have realized that Norma does not need consoling. She is built of strong stuff and she had an Exocet up her sleeve that had been programmed to explode my smug equilibrium. 'You can stop it. You are Acting Governor. You can issue a prohibition order now.' I was astonished at such power that I never knew I had. I felt that I needed to know some more facts as well as ensuring that the chimney wasn't knocked down before the issue had been considered. I asked Norma to wait while I rang Ian Jack.

I believe it fair to say that Ian was not overly pleased with the questions about the chimney. I had judged him to be a mild-mannered FCO employee, who possessed the usual overabundance of social graces necessary in a career that has diplomatic connotations. Now I could tell right away that his real background had been in the construction industry. It had been his plan to tear the wretched chimney down yesterday, but the rain had held him up. He was already behind schedule, and time costs money. Every available expert had condemned the chimney anyway as being totally unsafe – it was incapable of proper renovation without rebuilding from the foundations upwards, and that was out of the question. He had consulted throughout with the local planning officer, who had approved every action and breath he had taken and to stop now was not an option. It would be unsafe, unbelievably costly and plain impossible. It was, after all, only a chimney, and a useless eyesore at that.

One of the delights of being Chief Executive of the Falkland Islands is that this sort of challenge can appear as quickly as the west wind gathers strength. You never know when you tumble out of bed in the morning what the day will bring forth. In fact, I have been known by Jean to break into melodious song on such occasions using the words of that well-known screen nun, Julie Andrews. I always get the tune wrong, but the sentiment is the same. However, musing about the challenge of unexpected problems, and even admiring their complexity, doesn't help to solve them. I promised Norma that I would investigate the whole matter with some urgency, and with that she departed through the outer office. I could still hear her muttering as she moved away along the corridor and down the stairs.

I then rang the local source of all knowledge and advice, the Attorney General. He felt that I hadn't actually got the power to stop the destruction of the chimney in the manner that Norma had suggested. He also advised that the legal ramifications surrounding the issue were, as legal matters invariably tend to be, far more complicated and intractable than could be dealt with adequately within the proposed time frame, and so forth. I realized that the easy option was to ignore the situation and let events take their course: the chimney would come down; Ian Jack would be restored to happiness; the Historic Buildings Committee would feel cheated, but they would recover in time. We could even use that well-worn but ever useful civil service device of appointing someone to investigate what had gone wrong, after the event, to ensure that it never happened again.

However, there was only one west chimney. The committee had been given a promise that it wouldn't come down and the preservation lobby in the Islands was particularly strong. Understandably, the time span of heritage is short, historical buildings are few and the loss of even one part of one significant building is proportionally relevant. Also, the preservationists carried substantial scars about their persons from earlier contests, the tearing down of the old gymnasium and subsequent building of the new bank being an example. These experiences had produced battle-hardened warriors who, under the capable generalship of Jane Cameron, the Government Archivist, were formidable.

Not only does news within the Islands travel faster than the speed of light, but if folk should come to believe that something is being done without the fullest consultation, a widespread sullen mayhem breaks out. Although yesterday nobody had even noticed that this chimney existed, tomorrow it would be at the forefront of everyone's mind.

I decided to go and see the offending chimney for myself – nothing like 'eyeballing' a problem. Ian Jack and I were joined by Russ Jarvis, the First Secretary at Government House. The chimney rose with ageing elegance from the green tin roof at the western end of the main two-storey part of the building. It consisted, for some reason, of yellowy bricks for about two-thirds of its height; then the bricks became red to the top, which was just below the level of the apex of the main roof. I had never really noticed it before and it looked rather thin and spindly to me, although there was no evidence of leaning or even undue spalling of the brickwork. It was supported by a couple of braces, which Ian assured me had rotted through. Below the roofline the chimney was encased in the main wall of the building and I could see at once why any rebuilding of the lower part would need to be done from the inside. The house itself was constructed of stone and mucking about with that could influence the structural integrity. It was suggested that we take a look inside to determine precisely how inconvenient rebuilding might be.

In terms of potential inconvenience this was in a class of its own. It could not have been worse. The area that would have to be torn apart to get at the chimney was His Excellency's brand new super dooper luxury bathroom and dressing room. These abutted his equally wonderful bedroom. No man, having sacrificed comfort for the sake of his successor in Latvia, and having given up months of normal living for the sake of refurbishment here, having ensured that the intricacies of design of this area were exactly to his taste and believing that at last he would have somewhere appropriate to sleep, would appreciate being turfed out of these quarters for the sake of an unused and hitherto unknown chimney. Also, I knew well enough that I would not have selected this particular Governor as most likely to come top of my 'People to upset with enforced inconvenience' league.

Russ remembered some discussion with His Excellency with regard to the chimney before he had flown away. At that time the view had been that, although it was regrettable, the cost of keeping the unused chimney merely to remain an unnoticed feature of the skyline could not be justified. It had to be the right thing for the chimney to come down. I could not really fault the common sense of this position.

It seemed I would upset someone, so who should it be? Or, from a more ethical standpoint, what is the right thing to do in a situation like this? Should I do nothing and irritate the councillors, or should I try and stop the demolition and incur cost and potential inconvenience to the Governor? Was this rather unappealing chimney worthy of being spared for another century or more because of its undoubted architectural or aesthetic contribution to Island life? Maybe playing for time would be a sensible option. I decided to phone Jane Cameron, the knowledgeable inspirer of preservation, to get a clear view of her perspective.

She began by assuring me that I did have the power to stop the desecration instantly and she read me the relevant part of the law to prove it. She admitted that the Attorney General had drafted the law, but felt it not impossible that the complexity of his own work had misled him. She went on to indicate that removing the chimney would be about as unpopular as Murray Walker at a 'Ban Motor Sports' convention, and she felt that although the rules had been obeyed by Ian Jack, the feelings of local people should have been taken into account when any change to the original plan was made. She hinted darkly that the councillors were of one mind with her on this important issue, and going against their united will was something that even the Governor would think twice about. I could not really fault the common sense of this position either.

I chatted again with Russ. He had to agree that if all eight elected councillors were opposed to the chimney coming down then His Excellency might take some notice. He also agreed that Jane was quite capable, with the powerful co-operation of Councillor Edwards, of ensuring that she had that degree of support from the politicians. Helpfully, he did what most deputies must dread doing – he phoned the Governor on holiday. His Excellency played the twisting ball with elegance, indicating that he would be happy to deal with the matter on his return the following week and it would be best if the chimney were left in place until then at least. Phew!

Time can be a great ally to a civil servant. In the Falklands in particular, one's perspective on a problem can change dramatically in a relatively short period of time. It is merely a question of knowing when to wait and see. My caution was rewarded.

When the next day dawned, a slightly different aspect of the situation emerged. It seemed that the horrors of the structural integrity of the lower part of the chimney had been somewhat exaggerated and the Environmental and Planning Officer assured me that it was his view that the only problem was damp and that an airbrick in the right place might do the trick. Even if the airbrick were in the Governor's bedroom, this seemed a far more manageable affair than tearing the place to bits. Proof that the tide really had turned came when the Public Works Department Structural Engineer suggested that not only was the airbrick going to guarantee success but a metal tube could be inserted in the chimney stack, concrete could then be poured around it, and the safety and aesthetic appeal of the whole thing would be assured.

On return His Excellency went on the local radio station and indicated in a very FCO way that 'There was never any serious danger that it was going to come down... we wouldn't make any changes to the appearance of Government House without the fullest possible consultation with all the relevant bodies...' Being a diplomat must be hard sometimes.

Chapter 28

Most of humanity lives in the Northern Hemisphere. Therefore, the chances are that for you Christmas is not about bright sunny evenings and warm breezes. It is about twinkling lights, turkey and mulled claret being quaffed by cheery carol singers as they demand figgy pudding. It is about snuggling into a huge armchair in front of a roaring log fire or perching a numb behind on an under-sized seat in the perishing cold watching your football team lose. All the teams I have ever supported seem to make sure they acquire players who simply can't resist eating and drinking too much at Christmas. This over-victualing is invariably reflected in their Boxing Day speed and effectiveness. The thought has occurred to me that they must have a similar attitude to Friday evenings. It would explain so much.

We approached our very first Christmas in the Islands with some trepidation – could we engender some atmosphere? We spread coloured lights all over the place. But they couldn't twinkle in broad daylight and looked impotent. At least, we reasoned, turkey would be on the menu. Not so – the traditional Island meat at Christmas was (wait for it…) lamb. Carol singing in broad daylight just wasn't the same and not one troupe of wassailing waifs yelled for their pudding in five years. The chances of finding a Yule log, never mind somewhere to burn it, are many millions to one in the Falklands, and horse racing has usurped soccer. In a word, Christmas is totally un-Christmassy.

This line of thought might lead one to anticipate that the normal frosty delights could be replaced by the certainty of sunbathing. A few attempt it and get used to putting a brave goose-pimpled face on any disappointment. Snow can drift down on Stanley at any time of the year. It can come totally without warning. I have experienced the delight of sunbathing in the collapsing lean-to garage by the side of the slatted peat shed one moment, only to find snowflakes slowly melting on my chest the next.

Christmas is therefore the time of the attempted barbecue. The invitations to such events prudently indicate the 'poor weather alternative'. The super-prudent should change the wording to 'average weather alternative'. It is also the time for family camping in the Camp.

Rugged adventurers set out in wide-wheeled vehicles to explore the further recesses of the rural expanse. The isolated 'outhouses' stand alone all year, left only with the wind and echoes of shepherds long forgotten. Suddenly it is Christmas and folk with sleeping bags and blow-up mattresses appear. The gently decaying walls can again absorb casual conversation.

In spite of the insuperable problems, many expatriates from the UK attempt to create their own Christmas atmosphere. It is like setting up an ice cream stall on the sunny side of the planet Mercury. The demand is there, but the ability to provide is limited by the environment. Santa's sleigh just won't run on a carpet of diddle-dee against a background of sun-drenched hillsides. As for the sun itself – to my conditioned mind it is a yellow orb that saunters around the southern horizon throughout December. Not so in the Falklands: there it glares out of the northern sky at a high angle. It even starts to shine in through the back of the house in the early morning and late evening. No matter how we drew the curtains to see the lights twinkle, as soon as they were drawn back the illusion was seen to be worthless.

Compromise is inevitable in these circumstances, and human beings begin to adapt. I found myself cladding the artificial Christmas tree longing for the pine smell of the genuine article. The aroma of a real tree is magnificent, but it isn't until you sniff the artificial one that you realize what you are missing. Not that the artificial one is in any way offensive; it possesses all the neutrality of a stationery cupboard.

Admittedly, there is hearty carol singing to be done on Christmas Eve under the Whalebone Arch by the cathedral (poor weather alternative – the parish hall). Christmas Day is as indulgent as anywhere else and then the town wakes up on Boxing Day determined to go to the races. The three days of varying amounts of fun that make up the Stanley Sports Association Annual Meeting culminate with the award of the trophies by the Governor, or his hapless stand in, at the town hall. But that is not the end of the Christmas season.

Yet to be enjoyed are the shearing competition at Estancia and the Ram & Fleece Show at Fox Bay. The celebrations continue right up to the raft race on New Year's Day. In order to pander to all these attractions, the activities of government grind to a halt. Pressing problems just seem to dry up. So do we really need a government at all? If we can all be happy at Christmas without one, is the answer not obvious? Possibly a New Year Resolution for the Chief Executive should be to turn anarchist and overthrow the whole machine. But then there were those in the community who imagined that that was happening anyway.

Chapter 29

Stumbling ashore from a tender at the public jetty the average cruise ship tourist must wonder why on earth they didn't tarry in their expensive bunks, or finish that book in the ship's library. Was that lecture last night from that man with a beard really so lyrical about the 'Stanley Experience'? What do these folk expect to see? In other far-flung ports they are usually surrounded by local traders trying to press worthless items into their hands and pockets – not so in Stanley. In fact, persuading a local vendor to even open his shop for them if there is some unusual timing involved is a near impossibility. Nor is Stanley awash with tourist essentials such as signposts, public toilets, teashops, souvenir emporiums, burger bars or litterbins. There are no cable cars to take sightseers to the top of the nearest vantage point and there is hardly anything that could be classified as quaint or folksy – most is functional. There are few locally produced souvenirs and as for dancing girls wearing colourful national costumes – forget it. In short, the Falklands is not geared to the influx of over twenty-five thousand well-meaning sightseers who walk the main streets ever year.

Then again, they don't actually walk. As the locals are not particularly good at telling them where to go, they respond by being inept at getting there. They drift as though they were inhabitants of another dimension, like giants observing a model village. They have no concept that the roads carry traffic and real people are doing real work in real offices while they shamble around gazing at everything through virgin eyes.

They are instantly recognizable to all the local residents. Strangers stand out like chapel hat pegs. Locals do not dawdle in the wind, nor would they gaze in awe at an architectural abortion like the West Store. The clincher is that the tourists nearly always wear red anoraks. The story goes that they are forced to do so by the cruise ship officers so that they can be recognized for rounding-up purposes. And what a palaver that can turn out to be.

One day in December 1998, a particularly vicious storm hit East Falkland. The minders from the huge *Royal Princess*, realizing that time was of the essence, began to trawl the town for red-anorak wearers. They found them in batches, innocently sampling the delights of terra firma, and chivvied them towards the pitching tenders for the short, but rather scary, journey into the outer harbour. They reached the *Royal Princess* but realized, in the very middle of passenger transfer, that the operation was already too dangerous. The tiny tenders bobbed around like corks, giving thrills to the occupants far in excess of anything promised in the guidebooks. The captain of the ship didn't want to leave fare-paying passengers, but he could not find a way of getting them on board safely, so the tenders pitched through the surging waves all the way back to the public jetty.

Thus, a group of holiday makers, having been bounced around in a phenomenally rough sea in a small boat, were separated from the comforts of their large floating home and, in some cases, from their loved ones. Twenty-four of these unfortunates were parked in hotel lounges until someone could decide what to do. The weather forecast was not good and all day the wind raged with a ferocity we had not seen in four years.

In the early evening Jean and I braved the howling wind to drive to a hillside vantage point from which the outer harbour could be seen. Other worthy locals had the same idea. We had armed ourselves with binoculars to watch what the *Royal Princess* was up to. We were immediately riveted by the fact that she was trying to turn around and leave for the open sea. In order to do so she had to reverse towards the Narrows. The wind was gusting at well over eighty knots and the harbour was a welter of foam and spray. A giant tug, normally employed for oil rig support, was assisting by means of a long line. We watched the process in fascination as the huge liner, looking more vulnerable than its owners would appreciate, managed to negotiate the problem with skill and safety. It steamed off to the east, leaving two dozen passengers marooned and the captain's career intact.

The problem was not too bad at first. Morale was high. There was novelty in the situation. Photographs of local bars would have a scarcity value back in the USA. The hostelries had enough spare beds and all was well. The West Store sold out of toothbrushes and most of our unexpected overnight tourists enjoyed broken sleep as the wind continued to whistle around the gutterings. The next day the weather was even worse and to add to the problem, tenure of hotel rooms could not be extended. This was due to a combination of factors happily coinciding to make the town of Stanley more crammed with humanity than was ever planned. The crew from the oil rig was changing over, there was a passenger exchange for a cruise ship where the passengers had arrived by air but the ship was delayed and (wait for it)... there were the Tristar passengers. When the Tristar comes in one day and goes out the next it doubles the pressure on hotel beds for that one night – that was the coming night. There was nothing for it but to broadcast emergency requests over the local radio for beds for the stranded tourists. The brochure had said nothing about spending the night in cardboard boxes along Ross Road. The prospect of such un-neighbourly behaviour and damage to our international public relations was too horrible to contemplate. We offered our five spare beds.

We clicked for five simply wonderful Americans. How can these people be so positive in adverse conditions? They arrived full of apologies and thanks, as if the situation was somehow their fault. They continued to insist that they were trespassing upon our goodwill and that they were having a wonderful time. We drove them to see the local penguin colony at Gypsy Cove in the howling gale. Jean created a tasty meal. I used the bottle decorker a few times. The conversation was fascinating and the evening passed quickly. We thoroughly enjoyed ourselves and they contended that being marooned was far more exciting than the mundane existence on the *Royal Princess*, which by now was stooging around off the coast in severely unpleasant weather.

The next day the captain cautiously brought her in to sit in the outermost reaches of the harbour and managed to get the adventurers on board by hoisting the boats up with the passengers still inside. Our new-found friends were in contact again at a later date; they said they had been the envy of all the other passengers.

The cruise ship passengers, welcome though they may be, are not as economically satisfying for the Islands as the tourist who comes to stay and enjoy the unique experience of getting to know the Islands in more depth. There is a finite limit to the numbers that can be transported and accommodated and that is probably less than five hundred per year. Thus, the stay in a cosy lodge, the dining on slow-cooked mutton, and the strolling on pristine silver-sanded beaches, is open to only a few privileged persons each year. Those who make the effort find that many in the Islands will help with the details and the getting around. For anyone who wants to see nature at its best and to experience a unique community that is developing rapidly, there can be few better options.

Chapter 30

The glitterati of Stanley became Chileophiles fairly quickly after the weekly jet from Punta Arenas had been going for a few months. 'You really must go there, the scenery is magnificent, the food is wonderful, it is all so clean, so cheap, and so near. Would you believe it, we travelled all the way from the Atacama Desert to Cape Horn on a shoe string, living only in a cardboard box with wheels, all eight of us...' We listened, trying hard to look impressed, wondering if it could be true.

To resolve the matter we decided to go to Chile to see what it was really like. We also had a feeling of 'If we don't do it now...', and we wanted to see people in ponchos playing flutes. Or was that Peru?

It is a very strange thing about living in the Falklands, you know for a fact that South America is there, but when evidence of its proximity arises, it is somehow out of place. Chile is miles from Britain, hours and hours of tortuous travel; yet the Falklands is the very essence of Britain in atmosphere and you can jump on a plane and be wandering about the terminal at Punta in ninety minutes.

Actually, the truth was rather less appealing. By early 1998 the weekly flight run by Lan Chile had become so popular that the first few rows of passenger seats on the inbound leg were often occupied by cardboard boxes. These boxes would jostle at the check-in to ensure the best seats with views of the stewardesses and of West Falkland. They were not, of course, the same boxes used for incredible journeys along the Andes. These were full of fresh fruit, destined for the deserving digestive systems of the good citizens of Stanley and MPA, and the wealthy cruising fraternity. The cruising fraternity I'm implicating here were the temporary inhabitants of giant cruise ships. These luxurious vessels enable experience seekers to claim that they sailed around Cape Horn and visited Antarctica. The fact that they do so surrounded by stabilizers, champagne, smoked salmon, air conditioning, zimmers, nurses specializing in geriatric conditions, videos, tax advisers and credit cards does not appear to devalue the experience for them.

The RAF was unloading these self-same boxes that had arrived on the inward leg of our flight. The RAF is justifiably proud of the fact that they are fastidious in ensuring that everything is done correctly. This attention to detail enables them to get a Tornado airborne in an incredibly short space of time, but it is this same attention to detail that means that it takes them aeons to ground handle a passenger aircraft. In the normal run of things that's fine, everyone accommodates it. Books get read, letters get written and beards grow to knee length. However, on this occasion, the steady approach meant that it took them an inordinate amount of time to unload all those individual cardboard boxes occupying passenger seats.

Nevertheless, as the gateway to another world, this link with Chile had a great deal to offer. The passenger terminal at Punta Arenas was pretty much the opposite – nothing at all to offer. We just hung about waiting for our connection, which was the same plane anyway, with nowhere to sit, nothing to watch and nothing to drink. We stared idly at the other transit orphans as they peered through cloudy, sightless eyes in return. The delay multiplied inexorably, but nobody seemed the least bit concerned. Mount Pleasant had been the territory of the RAF; this was the land of 'mañana'. Everything gets done, the timing of it is only for those with an eye for detail and in Chile such details sometimes lose their edge. No reason was proffered, or if it was, it was garbled in Spanish and we missed it.

Full marks, though, to Chilean hospitality and friendliness. The late plane was met, and the driver taking us into the town of Puerto Montt was keen to speak in English. Neither of us could remember what we had learned from the phrasebook, so it suited us well. He expounded on the subject of the improving nature of the national economy and his considerable personal role in it. The hotel was on the front, our room faced the sea, and the bed was both hard and comfortable. I had thoughtfully provided Jean with a cheap giveaway sewing kit to accommodate all eventualities, just before we left Stanley. Being of insignificant quality, it had come apart in her case and pins, needles and all manner of sewing things were mingling happily with clothes. Extracting them was not easy. As luck would have it, a similar thing had happened in my case, where of all things, my breath pills (who knows when you might need one – always a good thing to give to a friend) had emerged from their inadequate plastic container. These tiny round pellets had found their way into every available space, my shoes, my shirts, my socks and other, less mentionable garments. I found them, of course; but not all during the initial search. We crashed into bed, dogs barked, the people behind paper-thin walls in the room next door shouted until they were hoarse, but we slept soundly.

Our first full day in South America was a Sunday, and we appeared for breakfast, Jean clutching the phrasebook. The first question from the waitress I almost understood, but by the time my brain had translated the most likely meaning, Jean had ordered apple juice for us both, even though I would have preferred orange. It would have been ungracious to complain, so I merely mentioned that orange would have been my choice. Jean ignored the comment as she studied the phrasebook, at which point I began to wish that we had brought two phrasebooks. During that day we also began to wish that our phrasebook had been geared to Chile and not just Spain and Mexico. And why did it contain so many useless phrases? Why not produce a phrasebook with the things one actually wants to say? 'Is there a beauty salon in this hotel?' was not only inappropriate, but also extremely unlikely. I, for one, did not want to stay in an hotel with a beauty salon. As we struggled for fragments of intelligible words, a couple of slices of cake appeared and it seemed as though that was that – cake or nothing. I began to eat the cake, and as soon as I'd started, some cheese and toast appeared, but then the supply chain stopped. In many countries of the world, 'Continental Breakfast' has become a euphemism for 'No real breakfast at all'. Chile, in its efforts to internationalize its economy, so well exemplified by the efforts of the taxi driver, had apparently joined that club.

We ventured forth to tackle the town, but there seemed to be nothing to grab the interest, and being a Sunday, few shops were open. We wandered along the front, rather disappointed in the Puerto Montt atmosphere. It was neither as quaint, nor as clean, as we had anticipated from the guidebooks. The sun refused to shine through an autumnal mist, and our ability to appreciate our surroundings was similarly dimmed. It is always useful to study postcards of local scenes in order to see what a place looks like at its tourist best. In the few shops open, such pictures revealed snow-capped volcanic peaks in the distance in every view, yet on that Sunday the greyness had swallowed them all. I sensed a mid-European spirit to the place. But then Germans had founded it.

There were fascinating wooden buildings, finished with timber shingles that had an alpine appearance. However, the proliferation of prominent busts of military-looking chaps with enormous epaulets as well as the multiple occurrence of the names of Bernardo O'Higgins (an unlikely national hero) and Arturo Pratt (an unfortunately named one) meant that it just couldn't be Europe. Clearly, the English language was not in common use. That fact was emphasized by the existence of hotels named O'Grimm and Colon. Imagine saying to one's PA: 'Reserve me a room in the Colon for the night of the twenty-fourth.' At least if there were a fire a few sennapods would soon evacuate the place!

About every fifth shop was open, and five shops out of six that were open sold boots and bags. Everywhere were boots and bags. Is the market in Chile really so big in boots and bags? It was like T-shirts in the USA. Speaking of the USA, there was a small shopping mall that was a rather gruesome attempt to copy everything American. Fast food vendors sold Kentucky Fried Chicken lookalikes and there were sports shoe shops, greeting card shops and jeans shops. It is all very well the USA being the leader of the free world, but I wasn't so sure that I wanted every country to come up with poor simulations. There's no point macheting one's way through steaming jungle to find a clearing with a McDonald's. It just seems wrong.

We decided that we ought to have some local cash, so we searched for a bank. We had been told that there were cash-dispensing machines everywhere and I had even gone to the trouble (and it is a trouble) of finding out yet again what my PIN number was, so that I could use it. Heavy advice on the risk of writing down PIN numbers means I always forget them, the same way that I forget people's names one minute after I've been introduced, or a phrase I've just memorized from the inadequate phrasebook.

If you are in Puerto Montt on a Sunday soon and need a cash dispenser, don't look in the external walls of banks, because there aren't any there. It may be a hangover from Butch Cassidy and the Sundance Kid, who, as legend would have it, made it to South America. Although they were rumoured to be a bit north of Puerto Montt, the security implications of not having external automatic till machines could just be a throw back. Or even a safeguard against copycat crime. It was, after all, a very popular film. There were banks-a-plenty, but no dispensers. Could the advice we had received be that wrong? It was, after all, from the same person that advised shorts and short sleeves for all occasions in Chile. If we had followed that recommendation to the letter we would have been hospitalized suffering from exposure by lunchtime. However, logic insisted that there must be a fragment of truth in the information, so maybe the dispensers were inside the banks, and all we had to do was to get to them. None of them seemed to have the swipe-activated door-opening facility that one finds in the UK, so we had virtually given up when we noticed a couple actually going into a bank.

We scurried across the road and sure enough, there was a dispenser behind a door with a swipe-card entrance mechanism. I tried my card in the device. I used every combination of angle and aspect without any confidence in its success. My feeling was entirely justified. Of course it wouldn't work. However, the couple inside took pity and opened it for us, so we entered expectantly. I doubted whether the machine would accept my type of card, as there was no indication that it would, and it hadn't opened the door. I noticed that the sign had logos from every other card but mine. I sought the help of the man, who was by now counting his own dispensed cash. He appeared to understand some English and said that the machine would work for me. He and his wife then opened the door once more, and they were gone. Could I risk my precious card in this unknown machine?

I was once asked in a job interview whether I was a risk taker. I replied in the negative at the time, although subsequently I believe a better

229 / A HOLIDAY IN CHILE

answer would have been that I was a risk minimizer; but how could I minimize this risk? Would the machine gobble and confiscate my card? Did I need this risk at this stage of the holiday? Why not wait until Monday? Taking a deep breath, I shoved the card in the slot and it asked for a PIN number, which I gave. Then a list of options in Spanish appeared, none of which I could decipher. I reached for the phrasebook and started desperate flicking through useless pages of ridiculous and irrelevant questions. The machine lost patience and started to bleep. In panic I selected one option at random. Immediately I realized my mistake. All kinds of further, completely unintelligible questions appeared. I felt that the machine was convinced I was a fraudster. Bolts would shoot across the door and the carabineros would arrive in a cacophony of sirens to clap me in irons. But I managed to guess a cancel option and my card was returned. I decided that I was a risk taker after all and tried again.

This time I was prepared for the options and I selected one that had a friendlier feel to it. Then, and only then, it asked, in Spanish, if I wanted to carry out the transaction in English. I felt that the easy option was to be respected, and suddenly it became plain sailing. Cash emerged from the machine and I felt a glow of achievement at having persuaded this alien mechanism to provide me with what was, after all, my own cash. I know people who will play foreign exchange experience capping, and cross London to achieve 0.01% advantage on an exchange rate deal. I had no idea of any rate; I was just pleased to get my hands on some pesos. I may not have known the language, but my pockets contained some local currency, and that speaks loudest.

We found a supermarket. Supermarkets are a great indicator of lifestyle and the state of consumer marketing. In any case, I love staring at the neatly stacked shelves. I also have a great urge to fill a trolley or two with things that catch one's eye, but that wasn't a practical proposition on this occasion. We bought some water and a few items for lunch and pushed the near-empty trolley to the checkout. Would you believe that even here, on our very first purchase on this whole continent, we had selected the queue that had just come to a halt due to an administrative problem? We waited while those around rolled their eyes in the internationally accepted manner and then, after all that time, I managed to get in a mess over the millions of pesos that seemed to be necessary for our modest acquisitions.

The day drifted past; dogs lounged around the streets. There was a dachshund in charge of a parked hatchback that was barking at every human within fifty yards. Typical of the breed; why do they believe they have the right to lay down the law in such an aggressive manner?

The sight of any sausage dog brought back the memories of Branston. I was beginning to realize how he must have felt – being a dog, that is. He had an obvious need to communicate with us, but had to use his eyes, his demeanour, the occasional wimpish sound, and any sign language he could muster. He didn't even have the benefit of being able to use an inadequate phrasebook. The way things were, we might well end up eating Pedigree Chum for dinner, simply because we couldn't speak or understand the lingo.

It nearly turned out that way. We located an attractive-looking restaurant that was recommended in the guidebook. An ethnic kind of music was playing gently in the background, not unlike the bazuki music in Monty Python's cheese shop sketch. The atmosphere was most acceptable, and we began to order from the menu. I knew that what I had ordered was steak, and I thought it should turn out to be a peppered steak for no better reason than the word alongside had begun with a 'p'. After ordering, Jean helpfully found the word in the phrasebook – it actually meant 'poor'. Now, what on earth was a 'poor steak'? It could be dog food after all, or, even worse, it could be raw. I could remember vividly an experience in Germany many years before on a business trip. My colleague and I had got back to the hotel from an exhibition, absolutely exhausted. We thought the waiter had offered us a cold beer, as he had certainly used the word 'cold'. German lager beer brewed locally, frothing enticingly in a huge stein was what we wanted most of all. What we got was a ghastly steak tatare. We didn't have the courage to admit we'd been misled, so we ate it for Britain. I can still remember the limpid lukewarmness of the meat, which had a floppy texture. We swore we heard all the waiters laughing with the chef in the kitchen. Was that experience about to be repeated?

When the plate arrived, it turned out to be a straightforward steak and chips with a couple of fried eggs and some onion. There was a problem during the meal, though. I had ordered a good bottle of red wine and was enjoying it thoroughly when the only bluebottle in the entire restaurant flew right in to it. It flew in so fast and with such precision, it was as though Luke Skywalker himself was at the controls. Why does that kind of thing always happen to me? There were other tables, with equally deserving diners. The necks on their bottles were the same size, some had more wine in (most had, actually), but there were no signs of insects infesting their vino. Normally, I would seek another bottle, but had we got the guts to do it with a phrasebook that we knew was unlikely to contain a selection of well-chosen sentences to cope with this eventuality? No, we chickened out and walked back to our hotel, the wretched bazuki-like music ringing in our ears.

The Monday dawned cloudy and there was rain in the air. We were coach driven towards the mountains and ushered on to a largish catamaran that cruised for one and a half hours along the Lago Todos Los Santos to the isolated settlement of Peulla. This was heralded in broken English as the most scenic short cruise in the world. Unfortunately, the view was obscured by thick cloud, but all was well because we were able to watch a video showing us what we were missing! The only problem was we could have bought the video and stayed at home and seen as much. However, the mountains swirled in the Wagnerian mist and the hotel at Peulla had a high waterfall behind it, which was worth watching and listening to.

The hotel room was interesting in that it was all timber. The walls were bare wood, the floor was bare wood and the ceiling was constructed of the same material. There was wood throughout the bathroom. Admittedly, the sanitary ware was ceramic, but the whole edifice seemed entirely tree dependent. It creaked, it groaned, and it had incredible sound-transmission characteristics. We could hear what was happening in the next room at Puerto Montt, but this was of a quite different order. In the black stillness in the middle of the night it seemed as though we were entombed in a small wooden box that in turn was encased on all sides by similar boxes. Noises assailed us from all directions: breathing sounds, wheezing sounds, coughing, snoring, grunting and most spectacular of all, the plumbing. Irregular whooshing occurred at random above, beneath, beside, and at times seemingly within our little room.

We had half a day to kill before catching the catamaran back to the west. It nearly killed us with boredom. The scenery was grand and the weather just might have been improving. We sauntered, we read, we loitered and we were getting restless.

The mountaintops remained stubbornly encased in their grey fluffy blanket as we ploughed across the lake. I marvelled at the steepness of the slopes on which the trees were growing, and the intense lushness of the vegetation. This was a far cry from the barren appearance of most of the Falklands. The water of the lake was a deep emerald colour, as are so many snow melt-sourced lakes throughout the world. The very virulence of that shade of green contrasted with the darker trees and in some way made nature seem unnatural.

Back in Puerto Montt, the boredom of Sunday paid off, in that in wandering the streets we had located a likely-looking restaurant that was not in the guidebook. The guidebook was turning out to be about as useful as the phrasebook. The food was magnificent, the waiter spoke English, the atmosphere was great, the bluebottles stayed clear of wine bottles and we felt as though we had struck gold.

The next morning the rain came sheeting down. This was wet rain, the sort of rain that hates the defiance of waterproofs; this was seam-seeking rain. We stayed put in the hotel lounge until a hire car was delivered for us. Have you ever picked up a clean – I mean a really clean – hire car? To do so would be an unusual event anywhere in the world, and this was not an exception. There was a used drink can in the space for tapes between the front seats. It is also rare for there to be a handbook with the car, and when one first picks up a hire car is the time when one actually needs this mine of information. They always seem to print the wretched thing in so many languages that it assumes a fatness unsuitable for any glove compartment, but when the call came in a foreign land, this particular one was found wanting. A car with air conditioning and a pretty sophisticated CD player should have had inside adjustable wing mirrors, but could I find the toggle? I had already pulled out into the aggressive lane-shifting traffic of Puerto Montt when I discovered the problem. There I was, with no real idea of where I should be going, in a strange town, on a strange continent, driving on the wrong side of the road and my wing mirror was reflecting the surface of the road beside the door.

At first it was Jean's fault for not finding the handbook, but then it became the hire company's fault for not providing one. Later, after I had adjusted the mirror manually, it ceased to matter at all. Although, in fact, it was my fault for not checking before we pulled out of the hotel.

Don't try to find a decent sign indicating the options for main routes out of Puerto Montt, because there aren't any. If you follow our example you will simply bomb around the town, selecting random options, until the road feels right. We got to know one or two little one-way systems and individual pedestrians quite well in the process.

Our plan was to peruse the shops of Puerto Varas as the rain was still bucketing and no scenery was emerging from the dire, drab mist. However, the good burghers of Puerto Varas had not been profligate with the provision of parking facilities. In fact, we went round the town about six times and no opportunity for depositing the car presented itself. True, we could have parked at the edge of town, but we would have won the drowned rat competition on returning to it, so we settled to the serious business of going somewhere else of equal excitement. The wipers stayed on their fastest sweeping for the entire journey.

The small settlement of Frutillar, on the Lake Llanquique was both interesting and appealing. As we arrived the sun came out and life suddenly became positive and colourful. We parked the car and discovered the second good reason for needing a handbook. This car had an alarm. It was obviously linked to some mechanism on the key fob, but it was far too clever for me. Even after driving the thing for a whole week I had no idea when I had set it, or whether just touching the car, even when we were in it, would set it off. It had a very piercing sound, too. It made leaving the car, and returning to it, a bit of nightmare. It would have been fine for a couple of extrovert attention seekers, or even a couple that had a phrasebook geared to erratic car alarms.

Frutillar was founded by early German settlers and there was a superb folk museum there, with reconstructed buildings all furnished in the original manner. Much of the information was in German, the guides spoke German, and one did bear a striking resemblance to Martin

Bormann. I spent some time wondering if he could be a son and, if so, how I might make a name for myself by somehow smuggling him out of the country. I could even get a free trip to Tel Aviv out of it. I concluded that the hassle, when on holiday, outweighed the slim chance of success.

As we walked along the front, enjoying the occasional shop and the waves gently breaking on the dark grey volcanic sand, I was befriended by a particularly perky and ugly little dog. He had one of those faces that was half black and half white, small ears and a particularly prissy way of walking, whereby he levitated over the ground while his legs whirred. I hardly spoke to him, but he followed me everywhere for about half an hour, finally settling down outside the cafe where we had a snack lunch. The sun soon went back behind the clouds, my canine buddy found a more promising companion, and we tackled the drive to Termas de Puyehue, passing through scenery that would be described in England as 'parkland'. But this was a giant's parkland. The deciduous trees were of enormous variety and profusion. They also grew to great height. The range of greens would have been even more impressive with a smidgen of sunlight. As we neared the Andean foothills the scenery became even grander, and the by now familiar steep tree-lined slopes dominated.

The hotel was absolutely remarkable. To describe it by simile would require a rummage through world-class barns exhibiting decaying grandeur on an unprecedented scale. I have no idea when it was built, or by whom. To ask would have only re-awakened our over-developed feelings of linguistic inadequacy. However, the public rooms were huge; they were reminiscent of the nave of Durham Cathedral. Several indoor cricket schools would have looked lost in the lounge, and five-a-side football could have been played with considerable ease in the secondary lobby area.

There were several gigantic hot thermal swimming pools. I had little experience of such pleasures, but the delight of wallowing in really warm water both in and out of doors is so relaxing that the pressures of everyday life just float away. However, these naturally heated pools carried alongside all the guff that thinks itself appropriate – massage, aromatherapy, beauty treatment and such like. Hang about – that phrase about beauty treatment in the useless phrasebook might just come in handy after all!

The evidence of aromatherapy was the pervasive presence of the ghastly whiff of Body Shop. If I am walking along a street and know that I am about to pass a Body Shop, I invariably cross the road to avoid the insult to my nostrils. Here one had to go outside in the rain to avoid that over-done pot-pourri odour. I put up with it, and hoped that it wouldn't turn out to be one of those smells that get into one's clothes.

The most astonishing aspect of all was the lack of people. It was only just March, I knew the northern equivalent to be September, where were they all? All those massive rooms were hollow and echoing with emptiness, and we explored this incredible place with delight. The slightly worn feel of the hotel was hardly surprising in view of the overheads and the lack of clientele, although the guidebook said that it was always full. Maybe the economic progress made by Chile had brought about a more even distribution of wealth and thus the market for a place like this has diminished, or maybe we just hit it in between the summer and skiing seasons.

In any event, the trusty Swiss Army knife was put to good use within the first hour. Jean's bedside table and drawer were sagging drunkenly. The screws were gaping out of the wall. Being founder members of the BAKIHL – Ban All Kids In Hotels League – we reckoned that some child had sat on the thing, not realizing in childish ignorance that the design criteria for wall-mounted bedside tables did not include such behaviour. It became apparent early on that simply screwing the thing back on with the screwdriver attachment would not do, as the screws had no purchase. Fortunately, a small bamboo table in the room had some wicker hanging from it. I cut this into small strips with the knife option, and by stuffing the strips into the existing holes, made an effective rawlplug. The bedside drawer in room 203 was more solidly fixed to the wall when we left than it ever had been; all thanks to the Swiss Army and British ingenuity.

There was another problem that was probably related to the encroaching decadence of the place. The bath tap refused to run hot. Having visited the thermal pools, I had believed that this was the one thing that would not cause a problem. The product was there all right, flowing out of the hillside for goodness sake, absolutely free of charge, the heat coming from the volcanic nature of the terrain. Surely it could have been channelled into our bath? I suggested to Jean that it may be because we were at the end of a long corridor and that by leaving it to run for a while we might receive hot water at last. That was exactly what did happen, but it took at least twenty minutes to run warm, and then we realized to our horror that the rate of flow was such that the bath took another twenty minutes to fill up. By now the water was unbearably hot and Jean announced that the cold tap wouldn't work at all. I managed to help a bit by getting some ice cubes from the ice-making machine along the corridor and chucking them into her bath, but that was as slow a process as the running of the hot tap! The cold tap actually did work the following day. We had misunderstood some of the finer points of Chilean plumbing systems.

Dinner was served late, beginning at half-past eight. When we arrived, the dining room, which was the size of the main concourse at Euston station, was empty. Tables were set, waiters were hovering; surely we couldn't have mistaken the venue? We hardly dared go in, but we were hungry, and it was undoubtedly the appointed place. We went through the now-familiar struggle with waiter, phrasebook, and our pride, and then waited patiently for the surprise dishes that could have been almost anything. After about an hour, other folk began to arrive in ones and twos. A bit late for dinner, we thought, but then we remembered the struggle with the hot water, and felt that these good people may also have found the plumbing had retarding impact upon their evening. For all I knew, they too could have been screwing things back on to the walls.

The next day the clouds persisted in hiding the peaks, but we set off to tour the National Park nearby. Antillanca is a ski resort at the end of an eighteen-kilometre track, and the drive to it was magical. We still couldn't see the snow-capped volcanoes, but the forested slopes plunging down to the lakes provided immense visual impact. There were large water lilies on tranquil lakes (that excited Jean), huge ferns, human-sized rhubarb-like leaves, and some pale green moss hanging from branches in places that gave certain trees the appearance of being dressed in old rags. The ski resort itself had a predictably deserted air, as though it was unsure whether it was lamenting the melting of the last snow or awaiting the coming winter. The nearby volcanic slope rose gently upward, smooth and dark grey, until the ubiquitous cloud consumed it.

The weather was a bit kinder in the afternoon. In fact, the sun shone for at least half an hour, during which time we sat in a glorious meadow gazing over a sylvan scene of memorable charm. Then it started to rain, so we found the hotel's generously scaled games room and played table tennis.

Our room itself in this leviathan of an hotel was actually rather small, but it was quiet and cosy. We wondered whether the proximity of Argentina, and the fact that our check-in document revealed our Falklands residence, had something to do with the size of the room, but that may have been an unworthy thought. There were, however, two aspects of the room that were unique. There was a leaflet instructing us what to do in the event of fire that had some well-chosen phrases in that little-used language – English. Such useful tips as 'To know the distribution allows to act quicker and to remain in the dark if is it cut the electricity' and 'If it is not possible to leave your room, fill the bath with water to humidify the room', should be memorized by all hotel users. Filling the bath with water might take a bit of time, though. The other incredible feature was the size of the radiator in the bathroom. It was no bigger than one foot high by six inches wide. It was located, particularly handily, just below the loo roll holder, thus fulfilling the role of keeping the tissue warm. Such luxury can only be marvelled at in a developing country. If I had been asked a week before to describe the rural Chilean scene, I would have floundered in unspecific phraseology. After all, I had had some involvement in politics, and I could have managed something that sounded adequate without having much research or thought in it.

'Pleasantly pastoral, verdant trees, with clear evidence of Mediterranean-type climate' and such like. But that would have done the place a grave injustice. The drive from Termas de Puyehue to Pucon on Lake Villarrica served to enlighten me, in fact to convert me, to the overwhelming beauty of the place. It was glorious from the moment we struck off the main highway. It seems to be possible to define off-road driving in Chile as everything below motorway standard, and this was a track. It was stony, winding, rough, and engendered slow progress, but there were curving fields, huge shapely trees, copses, hillsides, fences, wooden houses, lakes that reflected the mood of the sky and spectacular vistas as gaps in the hedgerows occurred.

We still failed to glimpse the elusive snow-capped volcanoes of the postcards, as clouds hugged them, but the sheer variety of trees was impressive, as was the balance of scale and configuration. Every conceivable combination of green and brown flowed before us as the early autumn fields revealed the dryness of a summer that had passed. The precipitation over the last few days had not been able to undo the golden hues, although the clouds scored ten out of ten for effort. The majesty of the countryside was something I could have looked at all day, and the next, and several after that. In spite of the occasional ox-cart with wooden wheels, the impression was one of pretty intensive agricultural activity and seemingly abundant productivity. The soil was fertile, the natural vegetation was lush, and the farmers had set about cultivation and animal husbandry with a concerted will. As you may gather, I was impressed. Jean was impressed too, but only after about thirty miles, when we managed to find a tarmacked road again, and weave our sinuous route around yet another rain-swept lake into Pucon.

There are some events in one's life that are few and far between. For most of us, getting married is one. Being shown into an hotel room and being taken breathless by the view is another. It happened in Pucon; the view, that is. A huge picture window provided a stunning aspect of lake and hillside. The belting rain only served to amplify what a truly great image this was. When the sun finally came out late in the afternoon, it was like the start of colour TV. Black and white had been great when we were kids, but colour added a new dimension and meant that snooker players could earn fat cheques.

We hardly dared to hope that our meteorological fortune had changed. We wandered in the hotel gardens, sauntered along stone paths that tumbled down to a black volcanic beach, with varieties of bright flowers displaying their all to squawking and colourful birds. The increasingly uncovered sun sparkled on wet leaves and grass. The freshness of the air was intoxicating. Chile was getting better by the minute.

The hotel seemed almost too good to be true; was it a dream? I felt it could be, as there were autographed pictures on the walls from visiting dignitaries such as King Baudoin of Belgium, his dad Leopold, Adlai Stevenson (fancy remembering him), James Stewart, and even Queen Elizabeth and the Duke of Edinburgh, looking incredibly young. They hadn't signed theirs at all. Protocol I suppose, but a quickly scribbled word of appreciation would have been appropriate I'm sure. Something like 'Loved the view, food was a wow, great to get away from the kids, Pucon much better than the name suggests in English, Liz and Phil.'

The pictures also contained particularly dramatic scenes of volcanic activity. There were huge flows of lava, glowing eerily in the night as they licked their way down the hillside towards, yes you guessed it – this great hotel. That was back in 1971, but there was activity in 1984 and regular seismic disturbances occur all the time. No wonder the guidebook had helpfully suggested that we check our insurance before buying a house here.

However, the purpose of our visit was not to acquire property, merely to enjoy the experience of seeing things for the very first time. We wandered around the town for a bit. Apart from some interesting woodcarvings displayed in every other shop, it was initially disappointing.

The dogs of the place had a kind of organized gang warfare going. There appeared to be clear packs, each with their own territorial ascendancy. All breeds roamed freely, taking no notice whatsoever of the less-than-thronging crowds and even less of the traffic that picked its way circumspectly through the grid-ironed streets. There were short-lived scuffles involving barking, snapping, wiry legs scraping on pavements and the eyeing of all the others. Dogs have a wonderful way of recovering their poise moments after being humiliated. We watched a very small dog frighten a Doberman (the small dog was clearly Mr Big in the canine underworld). The huge Doberman slid away, but when twenty yards or so separated him from the yapping mobster, he resumed his air of invulnerability with amazing panache. As Jean often says, and probably thinks all the time, we have a great deal to learn from dogs.

We dined, watching the sun setting over the lake and longing for a clear day on the morrow. At last we awoke to see our desires fulfilled. We watched fascinated through our wall-sized window as the sun rose, catching the opposite hillside. This was bliss at last, but only one day remained before we were to jet off to Easter Island. As we drove out of the gate of the hotel intent on a day's productive exploration, there it was, plumb in our line of sight. Rising above the tree tops into the blue sky – the snow-crowned head of Volcano Villarrica. We turned off the main road and on to a track that led towards the cone. The road wound upwards and there at the end of a long, straight stretch were two hitchhikers.

I seldom pick up hitchhikers. In fact, I can only ever remember picking up two, and one of those later became an MP, but that's another story.

The girl pleaded as we passed and we took pity and stopped. They were semi-back-packers from Boston – Sam and Kristen. 'Semi' because they were using Bariloche in Argentina as a base and making forays to various points of the compass. They were good company as we bumped and climbed. In fact, they were essential company, as I was just about to drive past a mandatory stop at the National Park warden's hut. They were fluent in Spanish, not a phrasebook between them – impressive.

We parked when we could drive no further. The view ahead was dominated by the sharply rising cone of the volcano, which increased in steepness towards the crater. The last thousand feet or so were white with snow, within which were lateral crevasse-type cracks. Through binoculars the blackening around the vent at the very top showed like soot around an exhaust pipe, and all the time the wisping exhalation of sulphurous fumes revealed the wind direction. Below us the lake was basking in sun; beyond were tree-laden hills and the golden fields.

The volcano possessed an ominous authority. Everywhere underfoot the dark grey pumice-type rock dominated. Where it had obviously been aerated it seemed crisp and hard to the shoe, like walking on clinker or coke. Remember coke? A corporate dream – extract all the goodness from coal, then sell what is left at a higher price. Where this friable stuff was not compacted, or held together by scrubby vegetation, even a slight angle of slope could prove difficult to ascend. There were denser bits of rock too, probably basalt and obsidian. Stationary ski lifts echoed the tale of sporting heroes defying Vulcan by tickling his pistes in the winter. Sam and Kristen left us as they attempted a partial ascent. Their thanks were profuse, as were ours.

We wandered laterally, skirting the slope to see if the terrain provided any interest and we were rewarded as we suddenly encountered a steep mini canyon-like valley, in the bottom of which was a lava flow. At first it was hard to make out exactly what it was. It looked as if some giant digger had been conducting major earthworks. It was rough, very rough, and the colour was uniformly dark grey. In the stillness we could hear bits breaking off it and falling to the sides. It came to a raspingly rounded end about a hundred yards downhill. We filled our minds with the views, the atmosphere, the whole spirit of this unusual place, and then jostled the uncomplaining hire car back down the road.

That afternoon we stooged around, flitting from stony tracks to sun-drenched lakeside, where an hour in the sun on the dark grey beach was supposed to prepare our pallor for the harshness of the sub-tropical sun on Easter Island. We visited waterfalls and returned to the wondrous hotel in time for Jean to have a swim in a delightfully sited pool. I did not join in; I do not swim. Not without armbands, that is, although I can make a fist of the activity with the armbands. They are an embarrassingly fluorescent red. Jean believes that my age in some way impacts upon the appropriateness of these flotation aids. I think I can trace this natural lack of fundamental belief in buoyancy to being chased by a jellyfish at Hastings when I was six or so. The recollection of the incident is far too disturbing for me to even begin to recall it.

The airport at Santiago was where we spent most of the next day of the holiday. The international terminal is well designed and, although not our first choice as a holiday venue, that is where we were. It pulses with people. Most of them are friendly, smiling, tactile Chilean folk, saying 'goodbye' or 'hello' to others. We had hours to kill, so we read and watched. At one point, in the departure lounge, I arose out of my reverie as I realized we were surrounded by Klingons. They were swarthy, ruthless in appearance and harsh in manner. The gate we were near was hosting the next flight to Buenos Aires. Had we been living in the Falklands for too long?

We left Chile to visit another part of Chile. An island community that in many ways was just as isolated and unique as the Falklands – Rapa Nui, or Easter Island. On returning to the mainland a week later, we had a hectic compressed night in the capital, Santiago. It appeared as a bustling, humming, vibrant place. Our hotel room reflected two aspects of Chilean life that had struck us throughout the entire two weeks: the incredible thinness of the walls and the erratic behaviour of the plumbing. Wall thinness in hotels may be cheap to construct but, as had already been evident on this trip, has obvious drawbacks for the sleeping customer. On this particular night, the man next door enjoyed a sonorous snoring session for about fifteen minutes in every thirty. There are echoes of refined torture in this experience, as one is just drifting into glorious deserved sleep and then hauled out of it again by pig-like noises.

However, it is the plumbing that must receive our rosette for providing a consistent standard of entertainment. I cannot remember one bathroom in any hotel that actually worked properly. The shower/bath relationship was the one that caused the most surprises. It was never possible to run the bath without the shower running as well. True, we could reduce or increase the volume of shower from substantial drip to torrent, but the drip was impossible to erase. The most popular mechanism had the ability to change its mind in the middle of the process. Thus, one could be sitting soaking reflectively in a gently filling bath when suddenly the shower burst into action. This was particularly unnerving if one was trying to heat the bath water at the time, as the result was a cascade of scalding water, through which one had to reach with a naked arm, to turn the thing off in order to stave off the oncoming visit to the local severe burns unit, followed by a session of plastic surgery. In one hotel, the substantial drip was all we had to fill the bath. Moreover, there seemed to be a national shortage of bath plugs. So marked was this absence that I began to believe in a national water shortage and that this withdrawal of plugs was an incentive, indeed an enforcement, to take only showers. However, there were no notices in any language forbidding anything, so we overcame the problem by placing a glass or plastic cup over the plughole. British ingenuity triumphed yet again.

Another aspect of the jet-set life was borne in upon us on our last day as we flew back to our island home at the end of the world. The pilot says something over the PA system, which may have some importance. At least it might tell you when you are to arrive and what the weather is like there. It is always a problem to grasp the meaning even of the version that purports to be in English. This seems to be an international problem on all flights where the host airline is foreign to oneself. The first time the message is relayed, it sounds long and colourful, with bags of expression, and the vast majority of passengers listen in silence. As soon as it is over the English version begins. This is generally much shorter, enough to make one feel that either one's native tongue is minimalist in nature, or that the message has been dramatically truncated. Most of the passengers begin to babble among themselves, creating a solid background noise, and the informant is speaking hesitantly, with misleading inflection and lousy pronunciation. We struggle to hear that the journey between Puerto Montt and Punta Arenas, a distance of some one thousand three hundred miles, will take two minutes. A few isolated laughs identify those who managed to hear this startling revelation. I recall being told that the international language for air traffic control is English; a bit worrying.

In the dreadedly unimpressive terminal at Punta Arenas we played 'Spot the Bishop'. It is seldom that this entertaining and competitive game can be played for real, but we knew that the Anglican bishop of Chile would be on our flight, so we spent time analysing our fellow passengers as to which one might be the said bishop. We were able to discount several for starters. All those wearing baseball caps, those showing tell-tale signs of a hard last night in Chile, those with earrings, and any wearing 'Hell's Angel'-type T-shirts. A New Zealand couple who joined in the game felt that we were being pre-emptive, as bishops these days were a lot more flexible than they used to be. However, we were sure that we were looking for someone without his wife, as we knew he would be visiting the Falklands alone.

It was Jean who won the game, mainly using the flawed technique outlined above. She approached a short and rather pleasant-looking gentleman in his late fifties or so whom we had been eyeing for some time. He held a long, thin object in his right hand that was wrapped in blue material. I had thought it might be a collapsible crook; it turned out to be a fishing rod, but he agreed with Jean that he was indeed the Bishop of Chile.

On the last leg of the journey we were accompanied, predictably, by boxes of fruit on the front rows. A horde of Falkland farmers had been for a week's fact-finding tour of Southern Chile and the exchange of agricultural expertise was much appreciated. It provided a good example of the way a regular air service could begin to benefit the community, and the economy.

Our time in the long, thin country had swung from disappointment to delight. Our glitterati friends who had sung its praises so loudly had been right. We had not found it as cheap as some had suggested, but then our tastes may have been more extravagant. It was a country with immense natural variety and beauty. The people had been gracious and welcoming. We were convinced that the Falklands was fortunate to have ready access to such an interesting neighbour.

Chapter 31

Let us assume, for the sake of argument, that you live in Polynesia. The year is about AD 400, give or take a few decades, and you are pretty good at fishing and mucking about in boats. You assemble together a band of people of like mind, including some adventurous women, a few animals and some fishing gear. Then you construct the very best boat, or boats, that you and your mates can build – state of the art Polynesia c. AD 400, reeds and bits of wood and such like. No oil drums, no polystyrene, no life belts, just natural products that come easily to hand.

After a few goodbyes you set out on a voyage towards the south or south-east. You venture upon the vast Pacific Ocean, the largest in the world. You can only drink the water that you derive from rainfall, and after a while all you have to eat are the fish that you can catch as they swim beneath or around your flimsy craft. There are storms, adventures, and mutinous talk, but you keep going. There is no logical reason at all to think that you will ever find land again. Nobody else has ever done this journey. There are no Fodors, no Michelin Guides; there is just ignorance and a total lack of information. Yet you row, and you sail and you struggle with the inadequate craft. Turning back may not be an option, due to currents and prevailing winds.

After many days, you sight land. The fact that this particular land is only fifteen miles across and there is no other land within one thousand two hundred miles of it and you had no idea it was there is immaterial. The probability of missing it altogether, as radar will not be invented for another one thousand five hundred and fifty years and satellite-positioning systems would take a bit longer, was pretty high. Yet you had faith, you always knew that there was something there and you would be the one to find it. You have arrived. You are the very first settler on Easter Island. Congratulations – it will prove to be a great place to live and to bring up the kids without all the problems of life in Polynesia. In fact, in the coming centuries your descendants will become so numerous that the island you have discovered will not be capable of sustaining them.

Now, all this speculation is based on the best available theories as I write. It all seems pretty unlikely. Would you have behaved like this? Was this kind of risk at all worthy? Yet, as I mentioned before, when we have discarded the impossible, what we have left, no matter how improbable, is probably the truth.

In 1947, Thor Heyerdahl risked his life and that of his crew in his craft the *Kon-Tiki*, in order to establish an alternative view that the first settlers came from Peru or thereabouts. Many thought that he had proved the case at the time, yet now the evidence points to Polynesia, in fact the Marquises, as being the starting point. Does it matter where they came from? Probably not to you or me, although surely any advance in human knowledge is worthwhile being specific about. In any case, there are even more impossible probabilities in store for the student of Easter Island, alias Rapa Nui, alias Isla de Pascua. The British tried to call it Davis's Land, but somehow it lacked the romance of the other names, so it never stuck.

Easter Island has many selling points: isolation, compactness, climate, seafood and friendly people to name but a few, but the dominant attraction is the ubiquitous presence of giant carved heads, or moai. Previous generations of Islanders somehow managed to deposit these on many strategic sites around their coast, only to knock them down sometime later. Surrounding these incredible statues is the largely unsolved mystery of why they were constructed in the first place. There is the almost equally fascinating question of how they were made and erected.

Some of the answers are not too difficult to find. The actual source of the moai is self-evident in that the quarry where they were carved is easily visited. The geology of the island is totally volcanic and the quarry itself is spread over about one-eighth of the exterior of the cone of an extinct volcano. The rock is a granular and light grey but it weathers browny, and sometimes has a yellow hue. The height of the cone is about five hundred feet above sea level and it is an easy walk from the car park to the quarry.

This is not like visiting some world-class tourist site in the USA. There is no tourist centre and there are no cassette recorders for hire. It is not possible to walk around a prescribed route and hear a trite explanation in your own tongue. There are no tickets to buy, no forbidden or roped-off areas and not one sign informing or warning of anything at all. In short, it is genuinely unspoilt. There is a wonderful freedom to explore, to ponder and to absorb the astonishing atmosphere.

The big surprise is that this is a fossilized production line. In the quarry, the moai themselves appear in all stages of manufacture. There are the fully finished ones that for some reason are actually standing, some of them at crazy angles. There is no logic apparent in their distribution. They are neither in rows nor clusters, they seem to be scattered randomly over the hillside. Although they are the colour of the rock above them, they stand out against the grain of the countryside like chessmen on a green velvet board. They generally face downhill, and it looks for all the world as though this was the shop front showroom, attached to the moai factory.

'Look at the lines of the latest model, sir, all the best families are buying these now for ancestor worship. They have the seal of approval of the local religious supremo, and if you buy two before Saturday you get the first half mile of transportation free.'

There are those that nobody has bothered to stand upright, or that have fallen over, those that have evidently been rolled or fallen from the slopes above, and those that have fractured and lie crazily at rest. They somehow serve to emphasize the eeriness of the standing statues. It is not so much that one imagines that they are alive, but it is weird to see huge faces everywhere.

So where were they actually carved? The answer, once more, is obvious. Looking upwards, the hillside steepens towards the top of the cone, and there, in the greyness of cliff and massive boulders, are partly finished faces at all angles of rest. They were obviously carved in situ. It is said in Italy that Michelangelo visited Carrara to select the marble that he would use and then it was transported to his studio. That is not the methodology applied by the moai makers on Easter Island. These sculptors (I assume they were male but I suppose there is no reason why coffee-coloured ladies in grass skirts shouldn't have been sculptresses) carved the forms while the rock was actually part of the hill – rather like Mount Rushmore and the huge presidential faces, only there the faces remained where they were carved. Here, once the creation was nearly complete, the area all around was hacked out until the whole structure was separated from the mother rock. Hacking seems the word for it. They used basalt lumps to scratch, clobber and beat the daylights out of the in situ rock until the required shape appeared. Imagine the foreman (or forewoman) having to ensure that each blow of the basalt weapon was correctly directed and weighted. Even those that had NVQs in moai carving must have made expensive mistakes.

Then, when the great structure had been cut away from its birthplace, the ludicrously laborious matter of moving it began. Still partly embedded in that cliff face are larger moai than have ever been found elsewhere. The largest one is about twenty-three yards long, longer than a cricket pitch! They lie on their backs, sides, or at an angle in between. They can lie flat across the hill or sloping downwards, either feetfirst or headfirst. Spotting them is quite a task. Remember that visual game that appeared in comics many years ago in which various items or shapes were hidden in a picture and the idea was to see if one could identify them? You could see a garden roller in a tree upside down. The moai factory is just like that. As the sun moves round, fresh shadows appear, noses and mouths spring out of what seemed like just another rock face. It is astonishing to witness, and worthy of time and consideration.

The experts are convinced that the statues were something to do with ancestor worship. Imagine the effort, the sheer hard work and organization required to move an eighty-two-ton moai without a crane. The average distance that each one was moved was about five miles. Then visualize lifting it into place on a huge platform, and then – as if all this wasn't hard enough – to put on the top of it a rather ridiculous-looking red scoria hat of enormous weight and zero aesthetic value. These hats came from another quarry some eight miles from the moai's birthplace. Would you really do all this in veneration of your much-loved parents? If you would, I hope you are a qualified engineer with public liability insurance.

Even more astonishingly, in carrying out these phenomenal constructions, the people were ignoring the ripening crops. They also appeared to take no notice that the trees were being used up at an alarming rate and that no time could now be given to fishing for food. Surely, even the most demanding of forebears would not wish their progeny to behave in this way? Yet this is what the archaeologists tell us happened. Are we arrogant in assuming that these folk were that simple?

As the stresses in the society appeared due to intense overwork to meet the moai production targets, the various tribal and family differences began to be exaggerated and real rivalry took the place of the odd tiff. They actually began to attack those things they all prized the most – yes, you've got it – the moai. They indulged in a programme of spoiling other tribes' moai by toppling them over. No doubt it was great fun to steal up on a huge platform in the Pacific moonlight with a few mates, carrying a telegraph pole as a lever. Then with a mighty communal heave, push came to shove and a multi-ton moai crashed down on to its front, sending its topknot rolling yards away. The fact that the only moai standing today are those that have been restored to that position is a measure of the success of the vandalism, but it is disappointing for the tourist.

Hundreds of these things just lie as they fell, looking dead and helpless after their adventurous and world-class existence. They were once important and even dominant in the lives of the inhabitants and now they are little more than a passing curiosity. Putting them back into place presents some interesting problems. It has been lovingly achieved by those who know about such matters, but it is never quite the same as seeing the original. Such is the bane of all reconstruction work.

So what, if anything, is to be made of all this? Are there fundamental lessons here, or is it all just an interesting aberration? Maybe William Golding was right in *Lord of the Flies*: living on an isolated island does drive you into a kind of madness. Is there evidence of it on the Falklands? There have been days when it seemed to me that it abounded, when all my dealings were with rank idiots, and when ungrateful wretches seemed to dominate the population. If I had been feeling vindictive I might have been pushing moai myself. On other days the evidence was scarce; folk were humane and considerate of each other. I wouldn't have toppled a moai for the world. Possibly I was the one going mad.

However, living closely together, generation after generation, can easily lead to feuding and the development of a focused bitterness that would be diluted in a larger society, where effective anonymity can be obtained. Easter Island has lessons for everyone.

Chapter 32

LEE THE SNIFFER DOG

The Falklands is workmanlike in its attitude to dogs, sensitive about drugs and along with many others, shares a concern and fascination over the unexplained disappearance of Marine Alan Addis in 1981. The strange history of Lancon Lee, the professional sniffer dog, combines all three elements.

Lee had been trained in the UK as a multi-purpose sniffer dog. Not only could he detect drugs of various kinds, but he had also been specifically encouraged in the unusual skill of sniffing for buried human bodies. Dogs, after all, bury their bones and find them again. This one could locate bones that he most certainly had not buried and he had proved it in action in Britain.

The Royal Falkland Islands Police, under the neatly pressed, white-shirted leadership of Superintendent Ken Greenland, had already made many attempts to clear up the mystery. There is no certainty as to whether Alan Addis had some kind of personal accident, or whether a more sinister event had taken place. The marine was last seen at a party at North Arm, which, in spite of its name, is the most southerly settlement on East Falkland. When a healthy human being just disappears from a relatively small group without any logical explanation, people talk, especially in a small island community. People can't just vaporize. North Arm has been likened to the edge of the world, but theories arising from that premise are not taken seriously. Surely something untoward had happened? Was there a reason? Was there a motive? Was there still any evidence?

Ken was not a man to give up on a problem. Only two years before, the Devon and Cornwall Police had come down to the South Atlantic in force and carried out a thorough and painstaking investigation. They succeeded in creating a mass of files and in upsetting those they detained for questioning, as well as having a good time. But they were no nearer to solving the mystery when they departed. This new initiative had TV behind it. *Equinox* was going to screen a film to be made in the Islands. This film was to demonstrate the effectiveness of underground radar when used in conjunction with the nasal brilliance of Lee. These techniques had brought serial killer Fred West to conviction and there was optimism that they could span the seventeen-year gap since Addis's disappearance. So far, so good.

The impending arrival of Lee and his vaunted range of talents was trumpeted by the local media. One of the unusual features of Lee's visit was that he was emigrating. We needed more professionals and he had apparently been unable to make plans to return to the UK after starring in the film. This was probably more to do with quarantine or age than taxable earnings, but I understand that Lee himself was not consulted over this decision. This gave Ken a good idea. He sought approval for the use of the highly trained Lee in his drug-sniffing mode once the body search was over. He would be here anyway, we were getting him for free, and we had occasionally voiced concern over the drugs issue.

To those who don't understand the Falklands it would seem a snip. But the decision had political connotations, as there was no specific policy on drug searches. To councillors, the matter was far from simple.

The debate generated entrenched positions on both sides. To the pro-sniffer lobby the case was self-evident. Here was a weapon in the fight against drugs that would be free. Although there wasn't any tangible evidence of a drug problem yet, there had been hints recently of some cannabis being smoked near the port and the issue was a worldwide one. We would be wrong in imagining that we would remain protected in some way from the problem. Lee could be used at the airport, on visiting ships, around the pubs and anywhere else that took a uniformed man's fancy. He was going to be a very busy dog and would be loved by all.

The anti-sniffers felt very differently. They resented any intrusion into what was considered sacrosanct privacy. There were no drugs in the Islands and the arrival of this dog would make it appear to outsiders that we were concerned when in fact we were proud. The advent of a nosey sniffer dog would make the Islands like the UK, where the freedom of individuals was constantly being eroded by petty officialdom. The police were far too bossy anyway and this additional device would cause them to annoy the population even more. The dog would have nothing to do and, as a symbol of bureaucracy, would be very unpopular.

The pro-sniffers argued that as parents they would sleep better at night in the knowledge that Lee would be protecting their offspring. The anti-sniffers felt that as parents they did not want their children to be insulted by being sniffed at by the canine detective. Clearly something had to be done to ensure that Lee had a worthwhile future, as he had sacrificed retirement in his homeland to help out with our mystery.

There was an impasse. Eventually the Militay Commander came to the rescue. He sat, trying hard to look interested during the debate at Executive Council (yes, matters like this reach such heights), then suggested that possibly his dog handlers at MPA would be able to look after Lee and, who knows, he might be able to help the forces in their own fight against drugs! This was widely welcomed, but the anti-sniffers insisted on the caveat that under no circumstances could Lee ever return to civilian duties. In fact, a detailed plan of action showing how Lee was to be housed and kept at Mount Pleasant was presented to the following Council for approval.

Lee went nosing around the settlement of North Arm, the film crew monitoring every nasal nuance, with his future in Her Majesty's four-legged forces assured. After several days of intensive olfactory activity at all the favoured or rumoured spots, after being interviewed while sniffing by inquisitive TV presenters and after being made a fuss of by all, he still could not get any fix on bones, human or otherwise. The search drew a blank. To add to his feeling of frustration, the request from a local shepherd to allow him to mate with his Welsh collie bitch was turned down by the political heavyweights in Stanley. The ageing canine TV star was escorted off to a military life.

A few weeks passed and rumours began to filter through to Stanley that Lee didn't much care for the rather proscribed kennel life at MPA, the whole thing being far too brash for his taste. He was, after all, a film star. He began to complain. He didn't write letters or even pout; he merely whined, frothed and refused to show even passing interest in any commands he was given. A tendency to ignore commands is a sure sign of a limited time span in a military environment. The professional handlers reasoned that his time on civvy street had ruined him as a working dog and a clear choice arose: either Lee could be put down, or he could be taken in by a family as a pet.

Lee opted for the latter. And so the highly trained, multi-purpose Lancon Lee, ended up as a family pet in the Falkland Islands and seemed to love every minute of his new existence. Lee had the last laugh. Or was it a knowing sniff?

Chapter 33

ALONE

The expatriate husband is sometimes left to fend for himself. The long-suffering wife may feel that it is about time to visit children, parents, luscious verdant scenery or, even more compellingly, shops. So I found myself alone in the vast recesses of Sulivan House for a whole month. Bachelor parties were on the agenda, CDs could be played at ear-splitting volume, and I could stay up late and watch *Match of the Day*.

The best-laid plans sometimes suffer setbacks. My list of tasks was rather comprehensive. Take ironing, for instance. It looks easy when Jean does it. A mere flick of the female wrist and the iron runs smoothly over the surface of the wrinkled garment, doing its flattening and improving job. When I tried it, the first shirt looked decidedly less wearable after my efforts. This problem just had to be like any other, so I adopted the logical approach – apply method, think before you flatten. I checked the iron temperature, the water reservoir, the height of the ironing board (not an easy thing to erect) and had another go. This time it was a smidgen better, the shirt looked no worse overall and in places seemed almost acceptable. It was the angles and curves that caused the problem; if only one had a framework over which to drape the garment it would be easy. Then I noticed that the ironing board itself was tapered at one end in a manner that might be conducive to this kind of approach. There was another giant leap for mankind as the quality of finish improved by a quantum or two. After a couple of hours on a few items of clothing, I felt I was getting the hang of it. I also noticed that the ironing board cover tended to catch the shirt as I moved it around. I checked the underneath of this metal monstrosity to discover that the clutching mechanism for the cover was rather worn. I bought a new one on my next visit to the shops, and this improved the stability of the ironing surface yet further.

In addition to learning the rudiments of ironing, I decided that this was the moment to get really fit. With Jean away I could increase the exercise regime. I would visit the Leisure Centre every day at least once, eat only wholesome non-fattening foods, drink only water, eat no chocolate and restore my body to the kind of glory it had never really had in the first place. I booked half an hour on the rowing machine. I had done the odd five minutes on it before and felt that this kind of rhythmic movement was well within my compass for a whole half-hour.

I jogged happily and puffingly to the Leisure Centre, paid my £1, and entered a smallish room full of machines, designed to cater for those who wish to appear sylph-like and are prepared to torture themselves in order to achieve the transformation. I was relieved that I was alone, and I settled down to the easy movements on the rower, having set the automatic counter so that I could enjoy seeing the calories wither away. After only a few minutes, just as I was beginning to feel that maybe half an hour could be a trifle ambitious for the first real exposure to this rather tiring experience, a couple of ladies in tracksuits came in and began to utilize the stepper and the static cycle. They were not yet sylphs, indeed they had a fair way to go towards that goal, but they seemed to cope with the arduous tasks they had set themselves with consummate ease. They chatted about this and that while I began to get annoyed by the sweat running into my eyes. To wipe my face would be the work of a trice, but I was afraid that by letting go of the hand grip I would stop the counting machine and thus my tally of calories gone would disappear. Not that it really would have, but I felt that there would be some kind of authority to it if I could reach the thirty minutes with a significant whole number on the dial. I tried to row with one hand while I ferreted for a handkerchief – not a great success. My brow got a rapid wipe, the regular whirring of the flywheel was disturbed, and the whole 'let's pretend' boat seemed to protest at my lack of concentration. The ladies paused momentarily in their gossip to give me a withering stare. I resumed the slog, chastened and sweating even more, but the total calories lost remained in sight, and a small number it seemed, considering the content of a Mars Bar.

I don't know if you've ever done this kind of thing, but the worst period is the second quarter. There is a bit of a lift at the beginning – after all, one is fresh and the challenge is there to be tackled. Once the halfway mark is passed there is a psychological downhill feeling, but the effort begins to hurt a quarter way into the piece, and all the questions as to why one needs to bother with such lunacy spring to mind. I amused myself by trying to work out my average calories per minute at each minute mark and then project the final estimated achievement. As all the oxygen in my blood began to drain away to vital organs, my mental ability reduced. Dividing by thirteen had never been my strong point, even before calculators were invented. By the time fifteen minutes had passed I had settled into a zombie-like monotony that was knocking off calories and although I was managing to achieve something on the machine, I doubted whether this kind of thing would move a rowing boat any distance at all. I spurted to the finish for the last minute, just to impress the ladies, who were still chatting happily. They ignored the whole episode as I finally fell off the machine, my legs unable to recognize the simplest instructions from the ineffective brain.

The homeward jog was far less rushed than the outward journey and for some days afterwards the stiffness in my calves hampered my movement to the extent that I tried not to wander about the office if I could help it.

I had to feed the chickens. They were absolutely beside themselves with fear the first time I took their daily feed into their run. They belted to the four corners as though I was intent on wringing necks, rather than bringing their staple diet. After about three days they got to know me and would rush to greet me at their gate as I chatted amiably to them, explaining where Jean was. They found the concept of a land eight thousand miles away across the sea hard to grasp. Throughout the whole time that Jean was away they seemed to spend their entire day digging escape tunnels by the perimeter fence. I kept a close watch on their progress, as the last thing I wanted to do was to be touring Stanley on a cold winter's night, searching for an escaped chicken.

The cooking thing is easy if one is prepared to sacrifice self-respect. Oven-ready this, heat and serve that, a rapidly scraped-together salad and so forth. Somehow I always felt that this kind of ease was cheating. Surely I was capable of creating a culinary delight to tempt my own spoiled palate? I love cassoulet – that subtle French peasant dish of beans and everything else besides that seems to have the essence of Gallic provincial feasting about it. Jean dislikes beans, and so it is a dish I generally forego in normal times. Well, to be frank, I just don't get offered it. However, I thought it worth having a go. The first time that Jean was absent I made a gigantic cassoulet from which I got two meals and managed to freeze another seventeen portions. It wasn't particularly pleasant to eat and I had to finish it all up over the next few months. The second time I was determined to get it right.

I think that the recipe book was wrong. It was one of those French cookery books that must have lost some vital instructions in the translation, as the beans turned to a kind of paste during the last hour and the anticipated fulsome flavour was lost in the wedges of garlic sausage that dominated the unbalanced mush.

While merrily cooking away one day I reached for the salt. It was kept in a specially shaped salt container near to the cooker, for just such moments. I noticed that for some reason the salt was soaking wet. I searched for an explanation. I couldn't remember spilling any water in this area of the kitchen. No other liquids had been hurled about. I was certain that the salt hadn't even been damp a few days before. Nothing could have spurted or bombed this particular container, and if it had, why had it been so selective? Someone must have entered the kitchen when I wasn't around and wetted the salt. It may have been the beginning of a personal campaign to disorientate me, devised by the councillors in order to gain total control over the government machine. But they wouldn't have needed to stoop to this kind of thing to achieve that end. Mind you, one of them had infiltrated our hen house once and placed a hard-boiled egg in it. But I digress.

I wasn't particularly worried. I didn't think that Anthony Perkins was going to stab me in the shower. But I was genuinely puzzled. The following Saturday I was watering the plants in the kitchen as Jean had instructed on her activity list, when I discovered that even though a plant pot may be standing in a shallow bowl, it doesn't take much water poured in on top of the plant to run right through the thirsty soil, flood the bowl, and overflow on to the surface. You've guessed I'm sure – the surface in question was strategically above the wretched salt container. Mystery solved, and plants probably overwatered for the second week running.

Shopping by oneself for food was also an experience. At the local sell-it-all food store known as 'Kelpers', the manager, Dennis, had been well briefed by Jean. I cautiously entered, aware that this kind of environment, where females hold sway, is not really my natural habitat. Dennis spied me straight away: 'Run out of chocolate, then?' I felt like an alcoholic who has reached for one more swig. Oliver Twist himself must have felt blasé about asking for more compared with this. The problem was that actually I was a bit low on the chocolate, and had to admit that it was a component on the scruffy list that I clutched secretly to my bosom. I browsed around the shelves, enchanted by the packaging and admiring the variety in such a small area. I grabbed some chocolate as the last item and blustered through the till routine, exiting the emporium with as much artificial dignity as I could muster.

As the month of bachelorhood drew to a close, I began the preparations for Jean's much-sought-after return. The shelves were replenished and well stocked, the surfaces were clean as a whistle and I even ensured that every single item that needed washing and ironing had been through the system. The chickens were well fed, the peat shed was as tidy as I could make it, and to cap it all I ordered a bouquet of flowers.

I was mightily relieved to welcome Jean back, and I felt that I too deserved my popularity. For a few days I admired her skill and resource in the household tasks. The temptation to take things for granted had gone – for a while.

John Humphrys smiled at me across the table and spoke. His voice came out of the ether – a disturbingly familiar sound. I was listening to the *Today* programme and for a moment thought that I must be in my car driving along the M6 to work. But a higher echelon of consciousness told me that I was actually in a studio at the BBC and he was waiting for an answer to his question. My brain sought first gear and my voice said something banal. I waited for the nail-prising to begin in earnest. But this man, who has been known to savage hapless interviewees at will, beamed at me in a friendly fashion. He even seemed interested in the subject and passably well informed. I warmed towards the unexpected comfort of the questions and his apparent sympathy. Had I been lulled into a dangerous sense of false security in the space of two minutes? Was I now about to make a career-ending gaffe? The thought flashed through my mind, which was by now stuck in second gear. The interview ended as starkly as it had begun and with whispered thanks I retraced my steps, through the amazing waiting room and back along the curving corridors of the BBC. Yes, the corridors do curve – you know what the building looks like from the outside!

That waiting room is the place to be. As a room it is nothing special – it would rank with the VIP lounge at Mount Pleasant Airport in the decor stakes – but there is a significant difference in the clientele. When you think about it, anyone who is in the news at that time is likely to pass through it on his or her coffee-soaked way to the live torture chamber. I have encountered some very newsworthy people there, nearly all bleary eyed with the early wake up, and all adopting that over-casual air characteristic of one about to be interrogated by a Doberman with a few million listening. The morning papers are strewn around and there is a high correlation between those in the room and those on the front pages.

The programme itself is a kind of patchwork quilt cobbled together by professionals who are busy professionaling all over the place. Some have headphones on, some sit in rooms behind glass screens, some just carry plastic cups of coffee around the offices. They all seem to have their sleeves half rolled-up. But there is a buzz and a feeling of being genuinely alive and relatively important. You could sense that it was a kind of drug.

These are the *Today* junkies and I doubt if there is a cure.

Being interviewed on TV turned out to be the same but different. The brain still has the gear lever problem, but physical appearance suddenly assumes an importance in that you really do have to wear sober socks and learn how to cope with that ghastly thing, the camera.

I had actually looked forward to being on breakfast television. I would sit on a comfy sofa, drink fresh coffee and be surrounded by perky people with happy, clean-teeth smiles. Unfortunately, although I was taken to Broadcasting House, the programme was happening elsewhere. I was offered one of those automatic studio rooms. No sofa and not a perky person in sight, but the idea was to have a chat with the clean-teeth people who were apparently drinking coffee in Shepherds' Bush, or somewhere miles away.

If you have ever had the misfortune to visit one of these rooms you will appreciate the problems. The room itself is like a broom cupboard with a huge camera in it. I was squeezed into it by a disinterested security man and told to sit on the chair and wait. That was all. The denizens of Death Row would have dreaded this, and quite rightly. I realized in that instant that it had been a terrible mistake to ever agree to do the whole thing. But the door of the cupboard had closed, the disinterested one had gone, there was only the chair, the camera, total silence and me. I could hear dust settling on the floor.

Behind the chair and facing the camera was a large photographic mural of the outside of Broadcasting House. So that's how they do it! I sat stolidly in front of this familiar scene with all the liveliness of a tired pudding and faced the hugely threatening camera. I may have looked at the underground map in the back of my diary merely to ensure that my mind was functioning.

Suddenly there was crackling and a disembodied voice said, 'Are you there?' I searched skywards in imitation of the Muppet's Veterinarian's Hospital, but could not trace the source of the sound. With hindsight, I now realize that I should have crouched behind the camera and kept quiet, but being naive and relatively well brought up, I admitted to existing. There was further chattering and then the camera made warming-up noises as it turned on. 'We can see you,' said the disembodied voice. I felt I had just lost the hide-and-seek challenge. 'I can't see you,' I retorted as I scoured the room for a screen or some evidence that this was actually a television programme and there really was a sofa. 'You can listen to the programme and then they will talk to you,' explained the voice.

This just wasn't fair at all – one-way vision. I felt totally disadvantaged and I knew that a disaster was looming. A non-visual breakfast television show replaced the initial voice and I tried to prepare myself for what was to come. Maybe it wouldn't be so bad after all. The sofa sitters sounded in jolly fettle, just ripe for an early morning chat about the Falklands. But blow me, the hour struck and they went over to the news! I relaxed momentarily only to wake up to the fact that yet again someone was talking to me. Double fool that I was, I again admitted my existence and a question came my way. I was talking to this newscaster bloke, not the smiling ones. My only memory of what happened next was that my inner pleas for a hole to open up and swallow me went unheeded. I was flying blind and abruptly adopted a totally defensive frame of mind.

Anyone training you how to handle this type of interview in limbo will advise very strongly that you look at the camera. In fact, you must stare at it in an almost rude way. If you fail to do so in that unnatural manner, an impression of extreme shiftiness is created. The last thing that I wished to convey image-wise on television was shiftiness. Such vibes would not help the Islands at all. I was far keener to project an aura of reliability, intelligence, sound common sense and no nonsense. I remembered the instruction all right, but what did I do? I just kept looking away. The sideways glance was irresistible. It felt so awkward staring into that huge, impersonal camera. How can a rational human being talk in an animated manner to a giant machine in a broom cupboard? I stumbled and defended. I admitted nothing except my name and the voice that was vaguely familiar had to squeeze that out of me. In short, it was a disaster. I must have looked like Dr Crippen when confronted with the famous telegram. I felt that I needed to crawl back to my hotel through the sewers. When I saw the video clip later, it was every bit as bad as I had feared. My colleagues at the Secretariat demanded to see it. I showed it to them as part of the Christmas celebrations one year. It improved morale enormously. They demanded to see it again the next year and the year after that.

The strangely named 'FIBS' – the Falkland Islands Broadcasting Station – was somewhat smaller than the BBC. The corrugated iron finish of their headquarters created the impression of a garage or largish lock-up shed. Inside there existed some fairly sophisticated radio gear and some fairly untidy offices. This rather folksy radio station shared our airwaves with the military blast from the British Forces Broadcasting Service. You might imagine that being interviewed within this cosy and familiar environment would be a doddle. Words like 'country' and 'hick' come to mind. Many visitors to the Islands have begun by feeling the same, among them some notable UK politicians. After all, who could possibly drop the loaded question or bowl the unplayable googly? The answer was Patrick Watts MBE.

Patrick was Mr FIBS. He was a gritty, wiry, probing, warm-hearted man who cared deeply about his Falklands heritage and Preston North End Football Club – the allegiances being just about in that order. His attachment to the Islands is easy to understand. He was born an Islander and was intelligent and fiercely patriotic. He was broadcasting news of the Argentine invasion in 1982 right up to the time they entered Stanley. In fact, they had thugged their way into the studio while he was on the air and ordered him at gunpoint to stop the rather pointedly anti-Argentine music he was playing. Patrick has a penchant for a good confrontation and his argument with his assailants was heard live throughout the Islands. His unique brand of courage in that unusual situation provided inspiration for a myriad of subsequent unco-operative posturings by ordinary folk.

Patrick had been awkward to the Argentines and he managed to retain the ability to be awkward well beyond the war. It was all part of his overwhelming charm. He could spend ten minutes asking straightforward questions and then hit you with a real cruncher just as you were starting to feel smug. He did it with everyone he interviewed, whether they were a visiting minister of state or just a disposable chief executive.

His affection for Preston North End was far more difficult to understand. He didn't just support them by watching for their score on a Saturday. Some innocent in Preston supplied him with a blow-by-blow account of every move and he relayed this information to anyone who pretended to listen. He wrote letters to the manager about the players. He also wrote to the chairman about the manager and believed that he had the answer to all the problems of any particular season. I once asked him why he had chosen to lavish his not inconsiderable support upon Preston. If he had lived there, had relatives there, been there once as a child or even dreamt about it one night, I could have understood. But no, the reason was simply that he had selected them to support in his youth and had been loyal ever since. Towards the end of our time in the Islands he was appointed as the part-time Preston North End scout in the Netherlands – unlikely, you might think, but nevertheless true.

FIBS programming consisted of the *News Magazine*, the ever-popular 'Announcements' and 'Flight Schedules' – a notice as to who would be travelling to where on our FIGAS planes the next day. One's initial reaction to these schedules was that they were as interesting as reading the telephone directory, although if one wanted to travel it was by far the best way of finding out when and how one's journey would take place. As time passed and we began to know the people and understand some of the relationships (it is impossible to understand them all – and if one does, they will be different tomorrow) the flight schedules became far more absorbing. We began to play the Falklands game of guessing why someone might be going somewhere. With doctors and vets it was pretty easy – Mrs so-and-so's back must be playing up, that horse we saw limping last month is now in need of care and attention and so forth. But why on earth should that rather attractive young female student be going to that particular farm? It was a game for the informed. Tourists and visitors could never understand the Islanders' fixation with 'Flight Schedules'.

FIBS was a glorious mixture of amateur and professional. Nobody could doubt Patrick's skill and knowledge of his craft, but to supplement the daily fare all kinds of untrained airwave occupiers were drafted in. Local programmes badly done were generally preferable to a superb offering from the BBC. I couldn't resist – rather than bore Jean with my collection of CDs, a whole community lay at my mercy! My programme was called *Unchained Melody* and I used Peter Sellers' wonderful version of Bluebottle singing as the signature tune. The challenge wasn't so much selecting the music or even chatting about it; the problem was with the equipment.

James T Kirk in his swivel chair had less of a challenge. Buttons, sliders, knobs, coloured lights, microphones, cartridges and a couple of CD players all had to be mastered. I had to boldly go without having a clue as to where I was heading.

The programme lasted an hour, but because of announcements and the lag in the FIBS system the real length had to be no more than fifty-eight minutes. To begin with, I was sensitive about that and recorded each programme with meticulous care. I re-recorded minor errors and perfected the nuances of each comment. Then I speeded up. In fact, I became so blasé that I tended to go straight through, glossing over any mistakes in a cavalier manner. So astonishingly confident had I become that one week, when slightly pushed for time, I elected to go 'live'. I believed that nobody would notice.

In the other non-live studio and in charge that evening was 'Evergreen Tony Burnett'. Tony had become a good friend. He had emigrated from the UK to the Islands as a younger man and for some reason had then stopped ageing. His hair was black, his physique was lean and supple and he moved with remarkable speed. I know all that because he consistently gave me a hiding at the very game I had helped invent – Falklands Tennis. He also had a way with words, a kind of bedside manner on air, and would present music from his youth to his fans. Jean was one, so we listened as the years rolled back to the Everly Brothers, Frankie Vaughan, Neil Diamond, Billy J Kramer and such like. However, even though his body and musical taste were firmly fixed in a bygone age, I was happy that at least Tony was around should anything go wrong that evening.

The introductory bit went OK and then the very first CD I tried to insert wouldn't work properly. I covered up with a bit of useless chatter and tried again – it still refused to kick in with the sound I was anxious to hear. Panic seemed like the best option. Tony, listening in the next room and ever helpful, realized something was wrong and came jogging in, jet black hair falling ever so gently over his smooth and unfevered brow. I continued to chatter garbage as he leant across me to see if he could fix the offending machine. I explained to the listeners (probably no more than a handful) that this was an embarrassing moment and I had had a few of them in my time. In fact, I proceeded to tell them about another embarrassing moment from my past to keep them entertained. Jean, listening at home, was by now shouting abuse at the radio. I was muttering about the farmer who told me (when I was a student on a field course) that if the injection he had just given the sick sheep didn't work, it would be 'meat pies'. And I replied that I didn't know that sheep ate meat pies! At that moment, Tony lost his handhold and literally fell on top of me. He may have been lean, but he wasn't necessarily light. We were both helpless with laughter. Out there on the spacious Falklands ether, the sounds generated by this sequence of bad luck were up front for all to hear. I suspect the folk in Camp, who tend to have the radio on for company, were beginning to take an interest in the programme. It was mayhem, chaos, disaster and incontrovertible proof that one's self-confidence had been misplaced yet again.

Chapter 35

PINOCHET, POACHING AND POLITICS

The relationship between Argentina and the Falklands has dominated the Islands for decades. When Jean and I arrived the war had been over for twelve years but still the dark shadow of the much larger country hung over the Islands. The skua stands waiting for the opportunity to gobble up a penguin chick, a threatening and ever-present reality. It was like that. Folk back in the UK imagined that the strife of 1982 had solved the problem, but Argentina managed to keep up a momentum of propaganda that pervaded Falkland society. Every local news programme and all editions of the *Penguin News* seemed fixated.

Argentina's Foreign Minister, the witty and resourceful Dr Guido Di Tella, had invented the 'charm offensive'. This did not mean that he espoused the principle of self-determination for the Islanders, far from it, but it did mean that he was trying to win us by charm. He set out to convince those who had been unexpectedly invaded in 1982 that the fledgling democracy in Buenos Aires would be a jolly good crowd to get in with.

The offensive itself actually did have a whimsical charm. There was a childish attraction in the Christmas messages and gifts that were showered on the Islands. Books, family photographs and frequent phone calls were among the weapons trained upon us. There was even a tenuous offer to pay individuals huge sums of money to forsake their birthright. One Christmas we all received a video, which had been created to persuade watchers that being Argentine was a great privilege, and there was an almost religious zeal to the thing that was truly misplaced. Watching it, we were treated to the sight of a macho Argentine farmer standing in front of a magnificent farm entrance with beautiful mountains sweeping the skyline and ripening corn swaying in the breeze, telling us in broken English that it was good to be alive and Argentine as well. The inference that all our farms would become like his if we became Argentine was too incredible to be taken seriously.

Di Tella sparked with new ideas. One Sunday evening Jean and I were having a quiet supper when there was a knock on the conservatory door. There in the darkness, was a well-spoken young man who said he was from Mori in London and would I be able to answer some questions. In the UK such an event would be as unexceptional as a daily newspaper. However, eight thousand miles down the RAF umbilical it was fantastically unlikely. I gaped at him. The government was aware of every entrant to the place and what they had come for. They all filled in forms at passport control, which stated the purpose of their visit. My curiosity was aroused, so I invited him in.

He sat uneasily in front of the peat fire. He opened his laptop computer and began to ask questions. Were we Islanders? How long had we been in the Falklands, and so forth. I asked him who had sponsored this poll. He said it had been commissioned as confidential and he was unable to reveal his sponsors. My inquisitive attitude alerted him to the fact that he might be wasting his time, so he asked what I did in the place and I told him. That was when he closed his computer. The stream of questions came to a halt. He remained polite and has subsequently become a friend, but on that first encounter he was guarded and beat an orderly retreat.

It transpired some months later that the poll had been funded from Buenos Aires and I never doubted the hand of Di Tella behind it. But it didn't help him much, as the loaded question about accepting cash came out with a strong 'No deal' answer. Nevertheless, it exemplified the relentless pressure that was being applied. Di Tella's English was superb and he would even phone Islanders for a chat. Occasionally a local would swear at him and slam the receiver down, thus earning a few rounds of drinks the following evening.

In 1997 our councillors were persuaded to take part in some face-to-face talks with Argentines at Chevening (the UK Foreign Secretary's official retreat). For a while there was a hope that both sides might be persuaded to give some ground in order to open up contacts and begin to live in a neighbourly fashion. However, our two representatives had little alternative but to walk out when the Argentines revealed that they wanted to discuss sovereignty. This fundamental issue was at the heart of the problem and the deeply held views of both sides appeared irreconcilable. Various well-meaning peace brokers, both amateur and professional, did their level best to persuade both in Stanley and Buenos Aires, but to no avail.

Di Tella would send unofficial envoys who conveyed ideas to councillors and media alike. The visits were spasmodic, but the pressure was always there. When various islands or farms came up for sale there was the chance that they might be the subjects of an offer from an Argentine. Some of the applicants carried two passports and thus we could find ourselves trying to head off the acquisition of a farm from someone with part-European nationality. This created legal problems and required special legislation. It was also a source of immense temptation to the farmers concerned. To their credit, they put 'Island-cred' and loyalty to the cause ahead of personal gain.

The summer of 1998/99 was a good one. We saw long, sunny days, sparkling waters and lobster-red tourists who had underestimated the power of the southern sun. As far as any links with the 'coast' went (the term much preferred to 'mainland'), the Islands' councillors held firm on their ban on anyone travelling on an Argentine passport. They had also set their face against any semblance of a direct flight between Argentina and the Islands except for the occasional visits of relatives to the Argentine war cemetery. All this had been prominent in most of their election manifestos two years before. As a policy it had served well. It was a strong bargaining position that infuriated the Argentines.

Dr Di Tella said he espoused an 'open skies' policy. To him this meant that flights to the Islands should land in Argentina if that made commercial logic and all passengers could travel freely whatever their nationality. It sounded reasonable and the answer we always gave was that we would like that as well, but only after the claim was dropped and our right to self-determination acknowledged.

Stalemate existed, unless the Argentines could find the nerve to stop the weekly flight from Chile and thus create significant pressure. That was probably too strong a move for them to make. It might be interpreted as trying to meddle in Chilean affairs and Argentina had recently worked hard at improving its relations with its long, thin neighbour. Then two unrelated happenings that Harold Macmillan would have called 'events' transformed the political landscape.

The first was to do with squid. The larger of our two main species, the Illex, collectively move around in the South Atlantic and that year they decided that the Falklands waters were singularly attractive. The Taiwanese had suffered from the collapse of the Far-Eastern economies twelve months previously, so they were short of ready cash and balked at paying fishing licence fees. Their fishing vessels began serious poaching within our two hundred-mile exclusion zone. It may seem harsh to appear critical of the brave men from what was independent Formosa, but they can be a perishing nuisance when they choose to be so.

Catching Illex is a matter of jigging – yes 'jigging'. This method of fishing struck me as particularly bizarre on first acquaintance, but it is phenomenally effective. Fishermen use immensely powerful lights to attract the slippery creatures towards the surface and as they arrive, thousands of little jagged hooks on vertical lines are jigged up and down impaling them. The jigging arms hang over the sides of the vessels, creating an odd enlarged rowboat appearance and ink from the captured squid can give a nasty, rust-like stain to the sides. The vessels are neither quaint nor attractive and conditions on board are reported as being pretty uncomfortable. The power of the lights is quite a feature. It is said that Earth-struck astronauts could see the jigger lights around Japan from the moon. The glow in the sky is a feature of the Falkland night in the fishing season and it makes poachers rather easier to find, as their method forces them to fish in darkness surrounded by self-generated brilliance.

Over fifty of these vessels steamed into our waters without acquiring licences and began catching the accommodating squid, who loved the bright lights just as surely as Dr Johnson loved London. By far the largest proportion of income to the Islands is from the sale of fishing licences and the presence of the piratical Taiwanese was not only damaging all our conservation efforts, it was also infuriating the companies who had paid good money to fish legally.

Our fisheries patrol aircraft spotted the poachers easily enough and took photographs, but encouraging them to stop breaking the law was quite a challenge. They simply ignored any form of contact, whether by radio or a close approach by patrol vessels. They repainted their names, changed their call signs and generally made rude oriental gestures in our direction. Short of boarding them with cutlasses between our teeth or firing at them, there wasn't much we could do. Supporters of diplomatic technique will be delighted to learn that the protests lodged through all the proper channels brought a studied but correct response from Taiwan just as the season was ending.

Some solutions are just too obvious. With the Royal Navy having a couple of surface ships in the area, why didn't they have a go and thus ensure the security of our income? We thought of that too – many times. But it couldn't be done. It was all to do with Rules of Engagement, international treaties, and the fact that the military presence in the Islands was to discourage Argentina from attacking, not to see off poachers. So we decided to mount a gun on our own patrol vessel and train up our volunteer Defence Force to use it.

This energetic attempt to enforce the law was met with a sequence of bureaucratic obfuscation by London. Only a purist in the manifold excuses and delays that are the stock in trade of a professional civil service would be interested in the full story. Suffice it to say that by the time we had the gun delivered, had adapted the ship to take it, had trained our men to use it, had liaised to the utmost with the local military and had agreed terms of engagement with the MOD, the DTI, and the FCO, including the Minister of State, the fishing season was nearly at an end. The UK Civil Service mirrored the Taiwanese in ensuring that the status quo was maintained. Such intuitive stalling transcends continental and cultural boundaries.

However, we did manage to engage one particularly bold poacher. It was a Saturday afternoon when the decision to fire at it was taken. We did so in strict accordance with every rule in the book. We had a brand new governor who made sure of that. Our lads chased it beyond the edge of our zone, pinging bullets off the bow as it ignored our presence completely. Frustrating, but then we weren't allowed to board, nor were we using ammunition that could make a hole in the reinforced section of the hull. We had all sorts of ideas that might improve matters for the following season, but they too would require approval from Her Majesty's government. The income to the Islands had been seriously threatened and councillors were all too aware of the consequences of having to dip into reserves to maintain standards. The obvious thing to do to combat poaching is to have a tight reciprocal deal with one's neighbours – this we clearly did not possess. If only Argentina would co-operate with us it would be to our mutual advantage.

The second set of events initially centred on General Pinochet, who had been detained by the British government and seemed to be spending his time having his picture taken sitting impassively in a large house in Surrey. The news that the Chilean government were 'advising' any airlines flying to the Falklands to stop doing so as some kind of lesson to Britain, filtered through on the evening of Friday, 11 December 1998. It did so via CNN TV news, followed hours later by the FCO. As an unforeseen event, this had to be in a class of its own. At least an earthquake generally has some tremors before it happens. The Pinochet situation had absolutely nothing to do with us, yet we were the softest of targets for this kind of gesture.

The very next day some sixty passengers were due to fly to Chile. Some were outbound on holiday, some were on their way home and some were businessmen accustomed to the odd inconvenience, but not geared to being stranded off the tip of South America for Christmas and well into the New Year. There might be nothing for it but to await the privilege of a RAF flight to the UK in order to get to South America. Possibly a long stay in Stanley over the festive season was to be the hors d'oeuvre followed by an entrée of sixteen thousand miles instead of three hundred and fifty.

There were around twenty coming in – tourists, returning Islanders, family visits and so forth. Then there was the freight. This wasn't just the fruit and fresh vegetables for the Islanders; cruise ships were already en route to Stanley with their cold stores running short. Never mind international diplomacy – get a sense of proportion. Here were ageing Americans that might find their lettuces flaccid. The plea to avoid panic voiced by the Governor on the airwaves made many feel that panic was the most viable option. The situation was becoming serious. This was where government came in. Our sleeves were rolled up for action. Cometh the hour, cometh the committee. We were asked to consider the options. A blank sheet of paper was what we started with, and that was our best moment. We never really progressed beyond that point. A quick spin of the globe in my study showed that our geographical position created a natural isolation that was hard to overcome.

No other Chilean airline would want to fly, and even if it did their government would almost certainly forbid them. Anything remotely connected with Argentina was a non-starter with our politicians. South

Africa was four thousand miles away, so were Rio or Sao Paulo in Brazil. Montevideo in Uruguay at two thousand miles looked possible, but to get from there to the Falklands required flying through Argentine air space and permission to do so was by no means a certainty. In any case, one cannot just find a carrier and persuade them to set up a route. It is a matter for regulators, officials, vested interests, subsidies, airframe availability, training, livery, licences, timings, timetables, diversion options and at least a hundred and one other details.

In desperation I even tried to get Air New Zealand to consider diverting their Auckland-Los Angeles-London flight through the Falklands. While spinning the globe it looked like a good idea. We were on the Great Circle Route. What will remain with me for a long time is the sheer amazement in the voice of their manager in London when I spoke to him on the phone. He explained that they had a huge investment in the Los Angeles route and that there were many millions of people and thus potential customers in Los Angeles. He was exceedingly patient with the weirdo on the line as I tried manfully to get the silk purse of international routing out of the sow's ear of MPA to the UK.

Lan Chile decided after much internal discussion to obey the request of their government, but rather courageously not to do so until 1 April 1999. This at least avoided the immediate problem of dealing with stranded travellers. It also bought time in the sense that the Straw ruling became suspended when the House of Lords judgement was challenged. Another Pinochet decision was to be made. The Islands waited, caught up in judgements far away over which we had no influence whatsoever and that could have had a huge impact on the lifestyle of all of us. To add to the problem, our friends in the military machine decided to take that particular moment to introduce a reduction in the Tristar service. The seven per lunar month were to be slashed to six.

One of the most common afflictions to which Islanders succumb is 'conspiracyitis'. They imagine that the Foreign Office spends millions of man hours per annum planning how best to stitch them up in some way and force them to communicate with Argentina. Who would be man enough to deny that since fears have a foundation in history? Especially if sitting in the Fox Bay Social Club! The twin pressures of no Chile flight and fewer Tristar seats were easily interpreted as proving the existence of just such a scheme. Then the Kosovo crisis struck – Tristars were in even greater demand to shift troops around.

So Lan Chile ceased to fly to the Islands as of 1 April. Then Jack Straw decided once again that Pinochet could be extradited, subject to a lengthy appeal process. Our chances of retrieving the situation became remoter by the day. The Chamber of Commerce in Stanley asked me when the Chile flight would be restored. Without wishing to be pessimistic I estimated ten years, but said it could be as soon as five. They were alarmed.

Argentina realized that these events had dealt them a strong hand. Here was a chance to create a bit of pressure and demonstrate that they were a force to be reckoned with in the South Atlantic. They might even be seen as being helpful. The intransigent 'Kelpers' would at last have to talk or suffer. The wolf sensed that Red Riding Hood might want to co-operate. There was a great deal of talk about the solidarity of Mercosur (the South American Common Market) and a kind of brotherhood in the Southern Cone. Argentina were also assisted by the fact that the Falklands policy of no airlink with them was beginning to look a bit obscure to the rest of the world and even unnecessary to some of the citizens of the Islands. A group of visiting MPs from Westminster confirmed that the lack of a link between the Islands and Argentina not only looked unfriendly, it was tending to get in the way of UK–Argentine relations.

Thus, by May 1999 the two events had created a situation in which councillors decided that it might be a good idea to talk to Argentina, using the good offices of the FCO. Never before had the elected Islanders been so convinced that the traditional isolationist policies might be questioned and never before had they been so willing to run the gauntlet of a public opinion that was polarizing rapidly. Understandably, the Foreign Office was intensely co-operative. The Foreign Secretary, Robin Cook, made no secret of the fact that he detected an opportunity to make progress. Progress, in his terms, was convincing the Islands that they really should allow Argentine passport holders to visit. After all, his job involved looking after Britain's interests and the improving relationship with Argentina held the promise of rapidly increasing trade.

The prize was to be an agreement that guaranteed unrestricted access for Argentines travelling on Argentine passports. The Islands would get the Lan Chile flight restored as soon as possible. (Apparently Chile had already been squared on this, so the principles surrounding Pinochet had vaporized). In addition, the flight would touch down twice a month at Rio Gallegos in Argentina (once out and once back), thus ensuring that not only could the Argentines visit, but that they could also come directly from their homeland. The agreement also said that all parties would agree to co-operate with regard to fishing in the South Atlantic. As this latter undertaking included the discouraging of poachers, it seemed that our councillors had managed to negotiate away the negative impact of the two unfortunate events. However, many Islanders thought that the price was too high.

In the frenetic run-up to the deal, the councillors continued to state that they felt no coercion. Even afterwards, they said in public that no pressure had been applied, but they also stated that the choice was one of 'jumping or being pushed'. An Islander was heard to remark that as far as he was concerned, that 'looked like pressure'. The population seemed split pretty evenly on the issue. Many saw the benefits of the restored links as being fundamental, while others would prefer to retain the ban even if it meant a deteriorating economy. There was a demonstration, a ritual flag burning and several petitions, all with slightly differing emphases.

The Falklands is one of the most democratic places on Earth, with a councillor for every one hundred and seventy people or so, yet the inhabitants exhibit overwhelming apathy on the majority of subjects that politicians hold dear. If one arranged a public meeting to consider complex amendments to the Constitution, then half a dozen folk might turn up if the pubs weren't open or the bingo session had finished. Honourable Members feel aggrieved that their electors show such lack of interest. They seem unaware that if one is a non-politician, an issue has to really get the juices flowing if it is to be more interesting than all the alternative attractions that even Stanley has to offer. However, when something does grip the public awareness, then robust arguments follow, by phone, by radio and in public meetings.

This matter of Argentine access created an ocean of such juice. It became the talking point throughout July. Farmers' Week came and went – the issue was dominant. People met in the shops – it was the first topic of conversation. Turn the radio on and there it was. In my own sphere, the councillors and the governor became so caught up in it that other less pressing matters were shoved on the back burner.

So when the news broke that a public meeting was in the offing, the wave of interest gathered itself like a huge breaker about to crash on to the shore. The silent majority flexed their unused vocal chords. Councillors fresh from making concessions to Argentina were going to be on display. Half of Stanley arrived in the town hall early and the rest kept arriving as the meeting got going.

There was one councillor who had broken ranks with the others on the issue – Mrs Norma Edwards. She had always been anti-Argentine and she was not a lady for turning. Thus, she had suddenly acquired heroine status among a significant section of the audience. Loud cheers welcomed her arrival. Everything she uttered was greeted in a manner that bordered on the sycophantic. Sir Alex Ferguson buying a round in the Old Trafford Arms the night after winning the treble would not have been more popular. She could have talked nonsense and it would have been rapturously received. Some of her colleagues thought she did.

The other six councillors (one was abroad on holiday) drew the sting a bit by taking half an hour to outline the rationale behind their decisions. They made it all seem eminently reasonable. The opposition had promised to score goals, but couldn't get inside the councillors' penalty area. Most of their attacks were long, high balls that were dealt with as surely as the Arsenal defence playing at Highbury. No follow-up questions came when the goalkeeper fumbled the issue. There was a lot of cheering and clapping, but no penetration.

The meeting drifted well past the scheduled time until the councillors knew that they had survived and actually managed to convince some of the waverers. Then the town hall emptied far faster than it had filled. We shuffled down the steps and into the cool night air, mutterers each reappraising their views in the light of what had, or had not, been said. The clever questions were all thought of in the pubs and homes afterwards. Hat tricks were hammered home in the comfortable fantasy world of those who didn't have to shoulder responsibility.

The process itself was cathartic. The combatants felt better for having said their piece. The councillors, however, having taken a courageous decision, began to see the devil in the detail as every word was picked at. All the possible combinations of problems that might arise from having full-blooded Argentines walking the streets of Stanley were debated.

Councillors confirmed that the Argentine link was entirely dependent upon a fishing agreement being in place by 9 October. I doubted whether that could really be achieved even with red-hot civil servants staying up all night. However, before that watershed was reached, the first direct flight from Chile was due on 31 July and there were rumours of the plane being full of Argentine journalists. Then Diego Maradona announced that he would be on the first flight that was to touch down in Argentina on 16 October as a kind of ambassador for peace and football. Certain Islanders stated that if that happened they would 'leave the Islands'. War veterans in Argentina announced that they were implacably opposed to the flight because visitors' passports would be stamped as if they were entering a foreign country. They threatened terrorist action. A new era was rapidly approaching, when tentative and delicate contact between the twenty-six million and the two thousand was crystallizing.

Chapter 36

The Lan Chile flight eventually restarted a week later than originally planned, on 7 August and about thirty Argentine media and business people stepped on to the MPA tarmac as twilight descended. Since the flight did not touch down in Argentina they had taken the trouble to go to Chile first in order to catch it. One, dressed as a gaucho, knelt down and kissed the surface. The symbolism of the act was lost on me, as the tarmac was almost certainly imported from the UK. Others had been tearful and joyous during the flight. We were in for an interesting week, and a week is a long time for a journalist to wait for a return flight, especially as the obvious stories would take only a few hours. So they kicked their heels in Stanley and searched for column inches as they visited the few accessible places they felt held interest. Most of the reporting was fair and balanced. Daily doses of translations from *Clarin* and *La Nacion* became as common and as sought-after as the excellent lunchtime rolls from Leif's delicatessen.

Mr Diego Maradona was not on the flight as had originally been promised. He was suggesting that he might come on 16 October, when the direct link with Argentina was resumed, but a journalist that knew him expressed doubt. She muttered something about the dearth of nightclubs in Stanley.

Those who opposed the new attitude to Argentina remained angry with their elected councillors and physically uneasy at the presence of Argentines. Some of them found difficulty in explaining this emotion rationally, and I knew them well enough to realize that they were not merely resisting progress or change. These were deeply held feelings that stemmed from 1982 and the psychological baggage they carried. The memories were not helped by any hint of Argentine aggression or even slight pushiness.

The week that was a long time for journalists showed that seventeen years is an age. The Islanders had become used to the isolation from Argentina. A visitor from the planet Uranus looking at his map of Earth would find it astonishing that there were no contacts at all between the Falklands and their giant neighbour. Yet that Uranusian's understanding would be based on geography and an incomplete knowledge of the human condition. The Falklands were far too complex for such conclusions to be valid.

So many factors had fuelled the Islanders' perception that the three-hundred-mile gap would remain unbridged for generations. It wasn't just memory of trauma – every indication for every one of the seventeen years had been negative. Di Tella had cast himself as a wooer, but the fact that the claim to the Falklands had only recently been enshrined in the Argentine constitution meant that he had an uphill struggle. It was hardly surprising that in many Falkland eyes the inhabitants of Argentina were bogeymen who were socially and culturally unacceptable.

Yet we awoke on that fateful Sunday morning aware that a number of these very foreign foreigners had moved into our two hotels and most of the guesthouses. They began to walk the streets of Stanley in small clusters, actually asking people questions in understandable English. Doors were closed that might otherwise have been open. Welcoming smiles were not as prolific as usual; where they existed they were sometimes tinged with unease.

The Argentines found the whole thing quite puzzling. There they were, at last on an island that they believed to be part of their own country. They had been taught that in school, alongside more palpable historical facts. Yet the people responded with icy reservation, the language was a bit of a strain and the goods in the shops were far more British than they would have been in many parts of the UK.

The councillors realized that they did not have an overwhelming mandate for their policy and showed it in their posture and evident defensiveness when questioned. The *Penguin News* organized whatever needed doing for the visiting press and it worked reasonably well. The Argentines got a good idea of what made the Islands tick and they even managed to convince a few die-hards that as individual human beings they might not be so bad after all. There were a couple of beer company executives who had made the trip from Argentina to see if we would import their product. In charm offensive terms this had to be given a high score. However, even higher was the score given to the strikingly attractive beer promotion girl who accompanied them. One youthful Islander was heard to remark that the Argentines could 'send a plane load of those any day'.

In spite of the raw edges the visit seemed to be going well. But good news is not often spectacular and it is the job of journalists to cover stories that grab the attention. Just try feeding them good news stories when they ask what is going on – you get absolutely nowhere. It is also the tendency of those who are frustrated by unrequited disagreement to protest. They had demonstrated, they had waved flags, they had argued on the radio, they had signed petitions, some of them had driven vehicles around Stanley all week that were covered in anti-Argentine flags and slogans, but there had been no hint of wavering in the resolve of seven of the councillors. There was a pent-up tension about to be released and rumours of a happening on the final day of the visit were rife. The plan was reported to be something between blocking the MPA road to merely waving flags as the coach containing the journalists passed by.

In the event, around sixty vehicles lined up along the road at a spot some fifteen miles from Stanley. The Royal Falkland Islands Police were determined to ensure that the coach was not hindered by the protest, although the journalists wanted to stop and get newsworthy pictures. In the event, some hot blood spoiled what would have been a robust and trouble-free send off. Islander argued with Islander over the validity of protest and behaviour. Thirty Argentines by their peaceful presence had achieved what thousands of their armed forces had failed to do – divide the population.

August came and went. The 16 October deadline loomed nearer as the calendar ratcheted round. Would there be an agreement? Would the Lan Chile flight actually land at Rio Gallegos in Argentina? The seven councillors believed that agreement had been reached, even though a written agreement had not been produced. 'Enough progress had been made,' they judged. So it happened.

Jean and I had been having a last look at the Chilean Lake District and were returning on that very Saturday. We joined the flight as it flew southwards at Puerto Montt. Our Director of Civil Aviation, Gerald Cheek, had been conferencing in Buenos Aires and was on the plane. Gerald was as meticulous and careful as any Director of Civil Aviation should be. He greeted us by waving a copy of the front page of Thursday's *Buenos Aires Herald*. There was an article about the very flight we had just boarded:

A group naming itself 'April 2 Commando' has sought to heighten tension before the flight by promising to 'destroy the plane with all its passengers'. The group said it would employ FIN 92 Stinger and SA 18 low-altitude Grouse missiles to achieve its goals.

Not exactly the kind of thing to read when easing into one's seat on an aircraft. Personally, I prefer the safety-briefing card. The group certainly achieved its aim as far as Jean was concerned. A bull's-eye on the target of heightening tension had been hit. I looked around at the people I was probably destined to die with. Some were total strangers. What would the UK papers say? 'It is believed there may have been some UK citizens aboard…'

Gerald made his way to the cockpit and chatted with the pilot who confirmed that Lan Chile were taking the threat seriously and would be avoiding any unnecessary flying over Argentine land. Thus we approached

Rio Gallegos from the sea, heading into a consistently vicious seventy-knot wind. There were a few white knuckles in that partly filled cabin. Jean was especially hard to talk to. I wondered if by taking a camcorder sequence out of the window I might capture the missile in its final approach to the aircraft. However, we buffeted our way through the gale to land safely.

Then the real fun began. The pilot ordered us to exit the plane. There were political points to be scored in this manoeuvre. The Argentine authorities would stamp our passports as having entered the country from Chile, but not stamp them again as exiting to the Falklands, as they deemed that to be Argentina already. Many Falkland Islanders would rather die than go through the ignominy of that process. Mutterings emerged from some Islanders on the flight as they squeezed down the aisle.

The day was saved by the fact that Argentina had thoughtfully provided their Consul from Punta Arenas in Chile as a passenger on the flight. He probably outranked the top man on the ground at Rio Gallegos and he made his way to the front of the queue. After a colourful conversation in Spanish on the steps of the aircraft, we were instructed to remain in our seats. It was then that I had time to look at the terminal and the scene beyond and ruminate that at last I was in Argentina.

So this was Mordor. There were men dressed all in black, faces obscured by balaclavas and goggles. They had guns and knives attached to their persons at every available point. They all looked a bit jumpy. Some of them had binoculars and were constantly scanning the horizon beyond the terminal. The land was flat and dull. The day was overcast and the wind gusted to such an extent that one feared the aircraft would move around without the need to start the engines. Some kind of welcoming party was present and stood outside the terminal, gaping at the plane. A few yards away was a group holding placards and flags; they were intermittently excited as one of them started a new chant. One felt rather sorry for them, as there is little to get worked up about simply staring at a stationary plane.

Then the authorities started checking the bags of the passengers who were embarking. I watched as the wind caught hats, coats flapped, bags fell over and raven-haired Argentines went in and out of the terminal seemingly at random. There obviously wasn't another show in town that day. The black-garbed ones continued their detailed surveillance of everything and eventually about thirty people boarded the plane. Most of these were grieving relatives of the Argentine dead in the war. They were remarkably cheerful and yet subdued. One carried a large Madonna that was later to be left among the Argentine graves near Darwin. Surely the April 2 Commando wouldn't fire a missile at these people? They didn't – we arrived safe enough at Mount Pleasant, and drove home through a snowstorm to light the peat fire.

A process had begun. A regular air service between two neighbouring countries that had seen no such contact for seventeen and a half years. Many regarded it as the thin end of a massive wedge, some saw it as an opportunity rather than a threat, and in reality it was probably no more than the beginning of a return to normality. But then, what is normality as far as the Falklands is concerned? Has it ever been, and will it ever be 'normal'?

Chapter 37

TRUMPTON REVISITED

Two factors dominate the Falklands – scale and isolation. Trumpton had a scale problem too, but Camberwick Green was rather cuter than Goose Green, and Chigley provided options for a change of scene that are not available to Islanders. Nevertheless, there is a quaintness about Stanley that is endearing. Is there a fireman named Grub? Possibly one called Dibble? I can offer a chief medical officer called Diggle, so we are getting close.

That police car following – I recognize the officer driving. So does everyone in the Islands, but I actually chaired the panel that appointed him. Nevertheless, I keep a close watch on the speedometer!

That doctor I had just been to see about that ache – he's a personal friend. As for the dental hygienist, she's a great dinner party guest.

The teenager languishing in jail because of something more than a youthful prank – his family background and life history are known by all. The population understands, they know the circumstances, sympathize with the situation yet know that the law must take its course. There is a huge respect for the importance of the rule of law on the Falklands.

Perhaps that person with the characteristic crackly voice is pushing that point of view at the public meeting because of a vested interest? Everyone knows that his income is heavily subsidized by tourist vessels, so understandably he wants more Argentines to visit his Island.

That person could never be made redundant – he's his boss's wife's brother!

Those who live in villages and small communities are familiar with the problems of always meeting the same people and of knowing everyone else's business. But in the Falklands the problem is magnified. There is no other club or society to escape to if your stock declines, there is no anonymity offering retreat. Crime is rare; after all, if you have anything of real worth most people know that it is yours, so the black market is constrained and it would be hard to export it. It is rare to lock one's car or house. It just isn't necessary. Everyone's lifestyle, beliefs, friendships and mannerisms come under public scrutiny. News and gossip become intertwined and people love to play roles and assume postures.

The role-playing is brought about because people have to 'wear so many hats'. An individual may well find himself or herself sitting on a number of committees that have opposing objectives. Such situations are so common that the society gets used to people taking different stances. It is a way of enlarging the population artificially – the same number of people, but they all do more things.

Many have more than one job. Keeping track of them all became quite a problem in government. After all, civil servants are supposed to give their all for their country, not spend the evenings hawking cellular phones or selling Land Rover spares. The private sector complained regularly, as it seemed like unfair competition when this kind of thing took place. It was at that point – competition – that the social and economic aspects of the scale problem converged.

The Falklands economy does not really have recourse to the mechanism of competition to keep prices keen. Nor would it be sensible for the government to introduce cumbersome anti-trust-type legislation. Nevertheless, a perpetual cry came from the Chamber of Commerce: 'Privatize'. So if a service is privatized it becomes a private-sector monopoly with all the risks of profiteering. But would an Islander exploit his fellow Islanders? The answer, as it would be anywhere in the world, is a resounding 'Yes'.

But the lack of competition can lead to absence of innovation and even an acceptance of a traditional way of doing things that becomes decidedly sub-optimal as time passes. This is a constant problem and can only really be overcome – with the present size of the economy – by the businesses taking an enlightened approach.

Some business activities require significant investment and when millions of pounds are involved, those putting up the cash require some kind of stability. They are rightly nervous about competition in such a small economy. A commercial return is a reality in the Falklands just like anywhere else. When the market is only two thousand people or so, there isn't room for two petrol stations, two delicatessens or even one men's clothier. The millions of pounds invested in a fishing vessel may be dependent for a return on the granting of a licence by the authorities. Those 'authorities' are known to be real people and their judgement may be respected or not. Thus, there are anxieties within the business community that relate directly to the scale of the market.

Lip service is given to growth, but there is uncertainty as to what path the growth should take and what speed it might assume. One theory that held credence for a long time was that which envisaged the economy as a cake. The fisheries income controlled the size of that cake, being over £20m per year, and if the population grew then there would be less of that cake for everyone. The model was simplistic, but small and rich seemed preferable to large and poor. On closer examination, the cake argument looked feeble. A growth in population would surely add value within the economy and more than pay for itself. But would that really work, and where should we begin?

Where would new people live? Surely there was a housing shortage due to family restructuring and the migration to Stanley from the camp?

What would new people do? Wasn't there a risk of creating unemployment when in practical terms none existed, and wouldn't that mean a burden on the current inhabitants?

Then there might be a dilution of the political control, which had emerged in recent years to be more democratic. Already the Islands had become home to a significant number of St Helenans who did many of the tasks Islanders found unattractive with good humour and a cheery spirit and there had been murmurings about them! What if someone who had no real empathy with the Island culture were to become a councillor because of a block vote of some kind, (about one hundred and fifty votes could secure it) – wouldn't that change the whole life of the place?

I recalled the googly bowled by my predecessor at my interview for the job. It had taken me nearly five years to appreciate the dynamite packaged within. The answers are not obvious and this debate is critical to the future of the Falklands. If the population remains around the two thousand mark, then there is an inherent instability about the economy. It has built up substantial reserves of over £140m, but the income from the fishery would be hard to sustain if ocean currents shifted and the squid decided to go elsewhere. So why not get the economy moving anyway? Where are the markets? Where are the raw materials? Where are the skills? The answers are not all that encouraging. The largest economic presence nearby is Argentina. Unless oil, gold or diamonds comes up trumps the major resource looks like being squid for many years. Skill levels are improving rapidly, but then they are elsewhere too and the average income per head in the Falklands must be among the highest in the Southern Hemisphere.

How large does Trumpton have to become to join the real world? I suspect that only an economist should answer that, and even then other economists would almost certainly contest the answer. But the hard facts are that unless the population and the economy begin to grow with vigour, the really long-term future must be in doubt, especially as long as the Islands remain isolated. It is bad enough being eight thousand miles from home, but far worse if you have an aggressive neighbour.

Can the e–commerce revolution help? It has already helped communications. Many Island inhabitants enjoy the delights of the Internet, but adding value to the opportunity will surely prove more difficult. Yet the Falklands has a great deal to offer the rest of the world.

The appeal of tourism is obvious and although the capacity of the Islands is small, that is in keeping with the sanctity of the wildlife and the tranquillity that the specialist tourist may seek. The unique ability to provide a truly 'organic' environment is another factor in the Islands' favour. It should be possible to produce food that is totally untainted by any chemical problems, and that should have a niche market that can be tackled. Then the benefits of being a gateway to Antarctica, the last unexploited and under-utilized continent, could well be massive as the twenty-first century progresses.

Living in the Falklands can be a very pleasant experience. In many ways it is like travelling back in time. And that can recapture an era when a society really was an entity, when commuting didn't exist and when one had time to ask the question: 'What shall we do this evening?' Many of the expatriates enjoy it because it represents getting off the helter skelter for a year or two, of having an identity within a community and of living at a pace and dealing with issues that have been forgotten in much of the developed world. The Islander cynics class expatriates as 'Mercenaries, Misfits, or Missionaries'. It is hard to argue with that analysis except that I would add 'Adventurers'.

For the sake of the Islands and the Islanders it is to be hoped that they have the wisdom to deal with the problems of scale and isolation, of growth and engendering workable and neighbourly relations with Argentina. Having lived through the debate for some years and seen the strength of latent ability, I am confident that such wisdom exists.

Chapter 38

The most important inhabitants of the Islands are not those who dwell in Government House (sorry, Sir), nor do they work in the civil service hierarchy. In their most self-effacing moments the eight elected councillors, taking all things into consideration, would have to admit that they are not necessarily the bee's knees. The real stars, the ones that are world class, those that tourists should travel thousands of tortuous miles to see, are the wildlife. They are the essence of the place. They belong to the Falklands in a way that is totally natural. Their heritage can be traced in millennia rather than decades. The tourist board's slogan 'Where Nature is Still in Charge' pays scant respect to the good and great of the community, but it is largely true.

Say 'black browed albatross' ten times quickly. As you lower your voice in order not to disturb the person next to you, allow me to introduce to you this elegant Island inhabitant. Firstly, it is large. It is to a raven as a raven is to a sparrow.

Secondly, the lower part of its body is as white as anything I've ever seen. Here is whiteness that a soap powder marketing manager would die for, and apparent softness of texture that your head has never experienced on any pillow. That whiteness is contrasted by the black eye shadow that enables rapid identification.

Thirdly, it looks massive and quite incapable of graceful flight when sitting on a nest. Think of a huge robust body that Bernard Matthews would engineer into turkeys if he could, and a kind of graceful dumpiness reminiscent of a long-range jumbo jet.

Fourthly, when you watch these huge birds take to the air, you cannot fail to be impressed by their sheer aeronautical aptitude. Stretch the eye of your mind and see this giant cruiser of the southern oceans unfolding and flexing its wings as it checks their enormous span before launching from the edge of a three-hundred-foot cliff to soar above the crashing abyss of waves below. Did you catch sight of those comically large, bright beige, webbed feet?

It is not always easy to see these birds, even in the Falklands. Out at sea they can be spied all over the place, but they are very selective with regard to housing. They nest well away from the few people that inhabit the

Islands. The western extremities provide their favourite haunts. This is where they choose to lay their substantial eggs and nurture their spiteful little chicks. Not all of nature's youngsters are as lovable as they may look, and these fluffy hell-raisers are supreme spitters. If your child behaved like this, I am sure that most of your visitors would complain; indeed, after a while you would have no visitors at all. The chicks, although covered in an appealing light grey down, also have a characteristic black stripe on their face, which makes them look as though they have a false beak attached with elastic. It may be that this is exactly what it is, because I never got close enough to check it out. Fortunately, I was warned about these little blighters, as once hit with this spit, one's clothes become smelly for ever, with a pungent fishy odour.

Yet the archbishop-like winged parents just gaze passively, caught up in the beauty of their feathered vestments. They sit enthroned on substantial mud plinths, a larger version of the mini volcanoes so painstakingly constructed by Gentoo penguins. The light brown cones are clustered together and are generally no more than a couple of feet apart in any direction. On the incredible uninhabited Jason Islands, colonies stretch for several miles along the coast and a few hundred yards inland.

We were able to visit the Jasons by cadging a lift in a rare passing helicopter from Carcass Island one day. It is a wonderful sensation to be transported to one of the most isolated places in the world and feel that you could be about to walk where no human has ever set foot. We landed softly, well away from the wildlife sites. The rotor blades slowed to silence. The small, but eminently distinguished group, a general, the Governor, the Commander and so forth, emerged and began to walk around the ridge to the north-facing coast. There were no paths created by humans or sheep, so we picked our way over rough ground and then through even rougher tussock. I followed the undignified thrashing about in a jungle of grass generated by Bibi (for once not an acronym), wife of CBFFI, as we approached the sound of the sea. A huge clearing opened ahead, and our stumbling ceased. We were at the edge of an enormous community of albatross. The scale of this megalopolis of the species was staggering. Albatross as far as the eye could see. Individual birds merging into a soft, feathery mass against the dirty green slope of the hillside as distance took out the detail. We wandered through that amazing environment, tiptoeing in between the mud plinths while the massive birds simply sat on them and looked at us. Occasionally I was nudged by a probing orange beak to see what my trousers were made of, but when it was clear that as nest-making material denim was non-standard, they just got on with the job of sitting and watching out for the striated caracaras.

If they are around, these remarkable birds will introduce themselves. Known also as 'Johnny Rooks' they are virtually unique to the Islands. Highly photogenic, with shining black feathers and a wonderfully curved orange beak, they pose endlessly for pictures to be taken. But be wary of their friendship: they are the archetypal merciless bird of prey, with a penchant not only for albatross and penguin eggs but also for young lambs.

They begin by selecting one that may seem a bit weaker or has strayed from security and then they swoop at it to try and peck its eyes out. Once the lamb is blinded, they set about the carcass. Unusually, they are also very tame. They approach humans without fear and steal whatever seems attractive. Cameras, sandwiches, rucksacks, hats – all these have been snatched and carried skyward, only to disappear completely or to be dropped in some inconvenient position. On one occasion our son's rucksack, being too heavy for the ambitious bird to carry aloft, was moved down the beach until it rested close to a bull sea lion. Retrieving it was not an easy task.

Striated caracaras can attack humans and, if their claws are extended, give a nasty gash on the head. As we watched the albatrosses watching the caracaras, our helicopter pilot received just such a blow. Yet we never found the caracara to be as implacable an enemy as the skua. The inhabitants of Orkney are well acquainted with their cousins, the 'Bonksies'.

When walking across rough Camp the locals sometimes advised us to take sticks to wave above our heads. In the early days we didn't really take this warning very seriously. Yet we were to learn that one of the most stressful interactions with wildlife on the Falklands is to walk across open ground close to penguin or cormorant colonies during the skua nesting season. It is inevitable that you will be attacked. These dark-eyed, heavily built predators stake out their territory with great precision. They are generally equidistant from each other and so your best route is to bisect the distance between each nest. Once we realized this we found ourselves taking a very erratic course as we tried to avoid upsetting them. Sometimes they simply watched and let us go; on other occasions one of the pair took off and did a careful recce of how threatening our walk really was. As the maximum distance that we could be from a nest was about thirty yards, we were almost always seen as bad news for Mr and Mrs Skua. We became targets for the low-level assault.

They fly directly at you, usually in pairs, arriving simultaneously from different points of the compass. The approach is fast, silent and no more than three feet above the ground. Naturally, we swivelled our heads like cheap puppets, but these birds knew what they were about. They used the natural lie of the land to approach from below the skyline; their dark brown colour made them all but invisible. As they reached us they surged upwards, aiming for our heads in a final thrust. Their speed, weight, determination and general unpleasantness meant that we really couldn't spend time appreciating the scenery. Usually they screeched just as they were about to bop us on the head, but not always. What with watching our footholds, looking out for the next skua territory and scanning three hundred and sixty degrees, it was always a great relief to reach the security of the Lodge. Waving sticks is all very well, but arms become numb with the effort. I suppose it could be fun for the masochists, but it mitigates against enjoyment of a straightforward walk.

Not all birds are good looking. The facial appearance of the turkey vulture must cause many a twitcher to lower their binoculars. Their ugly red faces were all too apparent around Sulivan House. They sat on the roof and chimney all day reminding each other never to look in a mirror. Occasionally they would circle around the house waiting expectantly for the carcass of the Chief Executive to be thrown out. While the scouts hovered in anticipation, others would scramble around the edge of the chimney, presumably enjoying a bit of heat from below. Their weight and movement often dislodged quantities of soot that would then tumble down the flue, gathering more soot as easily as a petition in the Globe Tavern gathers signatures. The result was a small avalanche of very black and very hot particles that would bounce over the fire and challenge ageing reflexes by coming to rest on the mat.

Our natural neighbours at Sulivan House included much that was memorable in wildlife terms. But the most lovable of all was the logger duck. Properly named the Falklands flightless steamer duck, or even *Tachyeres brachypterus*. They nested all around the perimeter of Stanley Harbour and the couple right outside Sulivan were called Laurie and Lanny after notable local personages. We were able to watch them through the seasons, to share in the thrills of nest-building, egg-sitting and chick birth. The chicks were highly vulnerable when small. Gulls and other airborne predators abounded but we believed that the local cats actually gave the family the biggest problem. Seven or eight eggs might hatch, but after nature had had its way there seemed to be an average of only three left.

Loggers look comical. Although the bodies are greyish brown, the male and female heads are quite distinct. The male sports a bright orange beak and the female's is a pleasantly subdued matt turquoise. They have enormous chests and an ungainly waddle. It seems as though their feet are too big to be attached to the same body and they have difficulty placing one in front of the other without tripping up. Yet they are immensely proud and insanely territorial.

There are flightless loggers and flying loggers. The non-aviators, who are in the vast majority, steam instead. This is achieved by a noisy flapping of wings and skimming across the water at some speed without actually taking off. This creates spray and the illusion of steam. The aviating cousin, *T. patachonicus*, looks pretty similar and Ian Strange in his ever-useful pocket book *A Field Guide to the Wildlife of the Falkland Islands* tells us how to identify one cousin from another and admits to the difficulty by saying 'However, unless viewed together, difficult to differentiate'. If you see one in the air, the chances are it is the flying kind.

Laurie and Lanny defended their territory with quite unnecessary vigour and patrolled their fifty yards of coast all day. They didn't get on very well with their neighbours and both families would 'torpedo' each other by lowering their heads in the water and swimming straight for confrontation. Normally discretion would triumph and there would be a final turn away just as convergence seemed likely. Then they gave a shaking of the head, showing that they would have won in any case. However, sometimes a real fight ensued – and what a scrap that could be. The males would beat around and try to force their opponent under the water, biting the neck and aiming for a drown. They were cute to us, but probably looked like warlords to each other. Often, in the first light of dawn, the creaking of the logger was the noise that wafted up from the waterside. Except on Saturdays that is, when for some reason, possibly related to overtime payments, the mechanized road sweeper would patrol needlessly right outside.

I never considered myself a wildlife freak, yet after five years I believe that the pristine nature of the environment and wildlife is the most important feature of the place. The human activity may be fascinating and the ruggedness of the scenery has a unique charm, but it is the seals, the birds and the penguins that get the first prize. The relative lack of humans must be a major factor in preserving something so thoroughly worthwhile. If the economy really does get moving then there is an inevitability about nature's inhabitants becoming scarcer. Sustaining the wildlife is of prime importance. Once again, the microcosm of the Falkland Islands government has a macro problem that would challenge countries with far greater resources.

Chapter 39

FAREWELL AND WELCOME HOME

I hate farewells. Get them over with and go. Yet by 1 December 1999 we had been farewelling for the best part of a month. We had done our last wildlife drooling, been to West Falkland to savour the unique atmosphere of the Fox Bay Social Club and winged our way to the deep south-west, where the Robertsons farm Port Stephens. Peter Robertson is not known for having wimpish views on farming and life, and he has seen a few years of both. He owns some fabulous scenery. The highest cliffs, the most glorious curved mountains, the most interesting geology, all are his. Yet getting a sensible living from it is nigh impossible. But he and his family love it and tackle their problems with style and robust skill.

Our goodbyes had been accompanied by weather that had been as good as we could remember. Places normally perk up just as we are leaving. In November 1999 sunny days followed one another with a certainty that was disconcerting. We expected it to stop. On the occasions that we were able to get out to Camp, the brilliance of the coastal scenery reinforced the indelible impression it had already made on our minds. Everyone was charming. All that renowned hospitality made a late burst to give us a memorable final impression. Even the civil service had become civil. Had I become 'the devil you know'?

The morning was dull and uninspiring as we drove the road to MPA for the last time. By now I was hating everything being 'last time'. Our five and a quarter years of Falkland life were over. The inevitable contract end had arrived. I had ceased to be 'honourable' at midnight. Once again we were embroiled in change, we were retracing our steps to go and make a fresh start back at the previous finishing post. The Shogun bumped and weaved, the stone runs remained enigmatic and the sun burst through the mist to wish us a perverse goodbye.

But the reality was that our perspectives were shifting. Our minds were looking to the future. Would the house be in a reasonable condition? Would our boxes arrive safely? Could the harpsichord, acquired in the Islands, be brought up to mint condition? When could we get a dog? Would Oldham Athletic be worth watching? And what about the next step in my unconventional career?

The RAF Atlantic experience that we had come to know so well passed and we watched the sun rise over Brize Norton as we stood in the now modernized arrivals area. Travelling with our military friends had improved in five years, but neither of us would be missing the experience.

All the roots so carefully pulled up were going to have to be repotted. It was a Thursday and we stopped on the motorway to get a paper. The date at the top was 2 December – the news was current and we luxuriated in its immediacy. The food, yes even in a motorway service area, seemed fresh and the service was snappy. OK, maybe the service wasn't that great, but on that arrival day we were in an optimistic frame of mind.

The house was strangely unfamiliar. We tentatively opened the locked room to view those things we had hidden from the tenants. Did we really feel it had been worth keeping this stuff, never mind secluding it? After unpacking we sat exhausted in the lounge, absorbing the fact that we were really home.

The house wasn't too bad, considering six different families had lived in it. The harpsichord was still on the high seas and we certainly wouldn't be getting a dog for a while. Oldham looked so pathetic on paper that I couldn't bear the prospect of watching them in the flesh.

Our first Sunday back home arrived. I looked at the folded *Sunday Times* as it sat on that same occasional table and reached for the Appointments Section with considerable trepidation.

Acknowledgements

I owe a debt of gratitude to the many friends who said, 'You must write a book about it.'

David and Vivienne Roberts and Malcolm Cooper were a source of great encouragement during the writing, and I am also thankful to Dr Fillipo Galimberti for ensuring that the facts in the Leo chapter are correct.

However my chief acknowledgement must go to all those who live and work in the Falklands. They gave me the opportunity to tackle a fascinating job and I hope that the ever-changing colours of their existence are fairly captured in these pages.

Andrew Gurr, 2001